Language Learning:

A Lifelong Process

Language Learning:

A Lifelong Process

Joseph Foley

and

Linda Thompson

Arnold
A member of the Hodder Headline Group
LONDON

Distributed in the United States of America by
Oxford University Press Inc., New York

First published in Great Britain in 2003 by
Arnold, a member of the Hodder Headline Group,
338 Euston Road, London NW1 3BH

http://www.arnoldpublishers.com

Distributed in the United States of America by
Oxford University Press Inc.
198 Madison Avenue, New York, NY10016

The advice and information in this book are believed to be true
and accurate at the date of going to press, but neither the
author[s] nor the publisher can accept any legal responsibility or
liability for any errors or ommisions.

British Library Cataloguing in Publication Data
A catalogue record of this book is available from the British
Library

Library of Congress Cataloging-in-Publication Data
A catalog record for this book is available from the Library of
Congress

ISBN 0 340 76281 0 (hb)
ISBN 0 340 76282 9 (pb)

1 2 3 4 5 6 7 8 9 10

Typset by Pantek Arts Ltd, Maidstone, Kent
Printed and bound in Great Britain by MPG Books Ltd, Bodmin, Cornwall

What do you think about this book? Or any other Arnold title?
Please send your comments to feedback.arnold@hodder.co.uk

The process of language development is . . . a continuous process, that goes on from birth, through infancy and childhood, and on through adolescence into our adult life.

Joseph Foley and Linda Thompson

Contents

List of figures

List of tables

Transcription conventions

(( ))   Contextual information and comments on utterances

****   Unintelligible utterances

?=   Suggested interpretation of utterances

{ }   Orthographic transcription of the sound(s) made by the speaker

italics   Utterances in languages other than English

[ ]   Approximate equivalent in English of preceding utterances made in other languages

NVR   Non-verbal response

?   Marking the end of an utterance where an interrogative meaning is thought to be intended

!   Marking the end of an utterance where an exclamation is thought to be intended

1

What is language?

Preposition. An enormously versatile part of grammar as in 'What made you pick this book I didn't want to be read to out of up for?'

(Winston Churchill)

We begin our consideration of language development by posing the question 'what is language?' This first chapter outlines a conceptual framework for understanding what language is and how this definition of what it means to learn language has changed over time. It is not possible to discuss language without reference to some of the structural features that comprise a language or linguistic system. For some readers, who have studied language development or linguistics before, this may be familiar territory and some of what we have to say may be similar to other descriptions that you already know about. For other readers, this may all be quite new. This opening chapter is important because it provides an introduction to our particular view of language development and what it means to learn language(s). There are important aspects in which our description which may differ from some other descriptions. This is because we are trying to provide an explanation of how all children learn the language(s) of the homes and communities in which they are being raised. Previous descriptions have tended to focus more on descriptions of how monolingual children learn one language. Our concern is more diverse. We suggest that you use this chapter as a point of reference as you continue to read through the other chapters of the book.

Language is a complex system of signs for communication. It comprises a number of structural features. While it has become somewhat fashionable to disregard structure in language learning and to focus instead, almost exclusively, on communication, we stress that it is important to understand the ways in which language systems are systematically organized because it is with and through these structures that meanings are created. Communication is created through the structures. These structured systems range across language use and include sounds or phonemes in spoken language, words or the lexicon, as well as the grammar. These elements or units of the linguistic system cannot be considered as separate from each other. They are all interrelated and work together to create meaning. Hence we argue that meaning or communicative aspects of interaction are not separate from the structure of the language. Meanings are created with and through the structural features.

We begin our exploration of language with an outline of the hierarchy of linguistic units that individually and collectively distinguish linguistic systems one from the other and combine to create the uniqueness of a particular language or linguistic system. In this way, it will be demonstrated that language is actually a complex composition of interrelated linguistic (structural) features, and that language is first and foremost a highly structured, rule governed, linguistic system. The rules have been derived through use by the users (the speakers, readers and writers) of the language, who through their everyday interactions have arrived at the structure or guiding principles.

There are exceptions to this naturalistic approach, whereby governments or learnt bodies have attempted to prescribe the rules of a particular language. One example is the Académie Française which meets regularly to set the parameters of the French language. The Académie prescribes the number of words and expressions that may be borrowed or loaned from other languages and which are permissible to include in official French language use, for example, radio and television broadcasts.

These formal attempts to prescribe rules of language use have not enjoyed the widespread impact imagined. It is the speakers of the language who through their everyday use of the system bring about change or maintain the stability. It is important to stress that all language and linguistic systems are rule bound and rule governed. An ongoing debate in education circles is the difference between children's spoken and written language. It is often assumed, and sometimes even argued (cf. Honey 1997) that spoken interaction is not only different from spoken text but that it does not have strict rules of use. This is not the case. While spoken texts do differ from written texts in a number of important ways, both are governed by rules. Both are systematic and highly organized.

However, the rules of spoken language differ from the rules of the written language. This is because different channels of language, speech and written text perform different functions of communication. The important point to note is that all languages and all forms, be they spoken, written, electronic, and so on, are governed by rules of use and it is by adhering to these that effective communication is achieved. There are, of course, ways in which individuals can work outside of the existing rules for a variety of communicative effects. This is one way in which changes in language use can occur. Language is dynamic. It changes over time, from context to context and with speakers and the changes that do occur can become systematically regularized as new rules.

So when it is said that one person speaks Hokkien or another speaks Portuguese what in fact is being implied is that the person can use and understand the rules of that particular linguistic system and has a pretty sound grasp of the rules of the system, at each level of linguistic structure. This knowledge about the language system may be intuitive, that is the speakers may be able to apply and use the rules extremely competently but they may not be able to explain to others what the rules are or even explain why they do the things they do with language. Perhaps it is necessary to explain what is meant by the term intuitive knowledge. Intuitive knowledge is deep-seated knowledge of something which has been learnt but which the learner cannot recall having learnt. It should not be confused with innateness, something that people are born with. Most speakers' knowledge of the linguistic system they use remains at the intuitive level of understanding. They can speak the language, and understand others but they cannot necessarily explain the rules that govern what they are doing. Through the processes of education intuitive knowledge may become overt knowledge that the learner can reflect upon and talk about. A distinguishing feature of educational knowledge is that it is overt knowledge and pupils, as part of the education process learn the rules of language, for example, spelling, punctuation, pronunciation, etc.

In 1975 the Department of Education and Science (DES) in the UK published an extremely influential report on the teaching of English in primary schools. Entitled *A Language For Life*, the Bullock report as it is popularly known, outlined a skills based four-part model of the (English) language as reading, writing, speaking and listening. It is a model has dominated language curricula and language teaching. Bullock's model can be illustrated diagrammatically in Figure 1.1.

Speaking	Listening
Writing	Reading

Figure 1.1 A four-part skill based description of language learning

Learning to speak and understand a language has been primarily associated with the early stages of learning, learning that takes place in informal social contexts such as the home, while learning to read and to write have become established as the central feature of primary education. This model will be reconsidered later.

As a starting point for understanding more about language development it is first important to understand something of the structure of the linguistic system. The defining linguistic features of a specific language system form a hierarchy that begins with the sound system and what is generally accepted as the smallest unit of linguistic analysis, the phoneme. For readers who are not familiar with the structure of language the following section outlines in general terms, some structural features that combine to create a language system.

1.1 Phonemes or sounds

Language comprises a number of individual sounds. These are called phonemes. Each language or linguistic system comprises its own unique set of phonemes. The sounds system varies from language to language. Crystal (1995: 426) reminds us that English has 20 or so vowels and 24 or more consonants. How many of these can you list? While these are each important individually, they are of particular significance in the ways in which they combine with each other to create the unique sound system that distinguishes the varieties of English spoken in diverse geographical locations from Australia to Zambia. There are over 300 ways of combining the vowels and consonants of English to produce units of meaning within the English language system.

In addition to these phonemes, languages also comprise patterns of stress and intonation or in the case of some languages, for example, Chinese and Japanese tones. These features are frequently referred to as prosody. Together, they combine to comprise the phonology of the language. There is evidence to suggest that we begin to learn the phonological system of the language in which we are being raised before we reach our first birthday. Halliday (1978a) one of the founders of the school of systemic functional linguistics (SFL) suggests that the phonological contours of language are the genesis of meanings, the genesis of the semantic system. Systemic linguists, in their description of children's language in the first years of life, focus on the phonological contouring that the baby makes as one of the key ways in which the young child is beginning to communicate with others (Halliday 1978b and Painter, 1984 & 1999). These phonological contours are referred to by Halliday as tones and they will be discussed in greater detail in Chapter 4.

Some researchers describe baby sounds in terms of biological needs and functions. However, there are other researchers who support the view that babies, even in the first months of life, are capable of a degree of linguistic sophistication. Recent research by Thomas Lee Hun of the language information sciences research centre at City University in Hong Kong suggests that newborn infants are sensitive to subtle distinctions in the language spoken by their primary caregivers, in this case their mother's language. He suggests that just a few days after birth babies can distinguish between the sounds of the language system spoken by their mother from the sounds of other language systems. Lee Hun's longitudinal eight-year research programme, has listed the language development stages of eight Cantonese speaking children aged between 18 months and 2.5 years. It is the largest child language research to date in Chinese-speaking communities. From his findings he further claims that the babbling of 10-month-old babies reflects the phonetic characteristics of their mother's language. Hence the babbling sounds of 10-month-old babies born to Cantonese-speaking parents are made using some of the basic units of sounds (the phonemes) of the Cantonese language. Similarly, babies cared for by English speakers will at around 10 months begin to formulate English phonemes as spoken by the person who is caring for them. So at the very early age of only 10 months, young language learners have begun to create the sounds of the dominant linguistic system in which they are being raised. At present we do not yet know how babies being raised in bilingual and multilingual contexts and households learn their dual language systems. This will continue to be an exciting area of research and discovery. It is not yet clear whether young babies recognize the sounds they hear as separate linguistic systems, nor do we yet know when they begin to make this distinction. However, the implication of Thomas Lee Hun's research in Hong Kong supports the view that language learning actually begins at a very much earlier stage than previously thought. For comparison, an earlier report by Qui (1985 referred to in Halliday 1992), suggests that during the earliest stage of language development (what Halliday has termed the protolanguage), when the young child is constructing unique signs into a system, it is not possible for the observer-hearer to distinguish the linguistic system in which the child is actually being raised. Or as Halliday prefers, 'what the mother tongue was going to be'. It was thought that the protolanguage stage of early language development continued into the first year of the child's life. However, Lee's work suggests that the transition from protolanguage to the mother-tongue is beginning before this at the age of 10 months. The sound system of a language is in many senses regarded as the building blocks of a language. It is individually, and in combination that phonemes form larger units of meaning.

Our view is that the foundations of language learning actually begin even before birth. By suggesting this we do not support the claim of Pinker (1994: Chapter 4) that babies are born talking but only that at birth babies are already attuned to some sounds within their limited linguistic environment. We draw upon findings from recent neo-natal research to support this view. For instance, we know that the dominant linguistic environment for the baby in the womb are sounds related to the mother, her voice, heartbeat and other body sounds. However, the mother does not circumscribe the baby's linguistic environment. There is evidence of the neonate's awareness of and response to sounds in the wider contextual setting. The neonate responds with body movements to sounds and noise. The way the neonate moves arms and legs in response to the mother's voice is different from the movements made in reaction to extreme, loud sounds or noise such as loud music and unexpected noises such as banging of fireworks. Hence it seems that at 12 weeks the neonate is developing hearing capacity and the development of response to the mother's voice that can be observed as different from the reaction to less familiar sounds and noise. Whether we call this language remains debatable. However, it can be understood as an indication of developing awareness of sounds in the environment and attunement to the distinction between sound and noise.

English is an international language, spoken by an increasing number of people around the world. Current estimates from a survey commissioned by the British Council, *The Future of English* (Graddol 1997) suggest that 100 million people would be learning English as a first, second, foreign or additional language at the start of the twenty-first century. Hence it is worth considering how children learn the phonemes of English in all of the geographical locations where English is spoken and being learnt by children.

1.2 Learning the phonemes of English

Phonemes, the smallest units of a language system, are learnt systematically. They are the distinctive sounds of a language and distinguish one language from another and one variety from another. The number of phonemes varies from one language to language and between varieties of a language.

Children need to learn to recognize and pronounce the set of phonemes that make up their own language. Table 1.1 below lists the order of the phonemes acquired by English speaking children who are growing up in an English speaking environment.

Table 1.1 The acquisition of English phonemes from M. Aldridge (1991:15) 'How language grows up', in *English Today* 25: 14–20

Phonemes	Median age of acquisition in English	
p/b/m/h/n/w	1;6	
k/g/d/t	2;0	
f/y	2;6	
r/l/s	3;0	Vowel system complete
ts/s	3;6	
z/ʤ	4;0	
ө	4;6	
ð	5;0	Consonantal
ʒ	6;0	distinctions are complete

While Aldridge's description is important for those interested in children's developing language, it is important to emphasize a number of points:

1 language learning is highly individualized, hence not all children will necessarily follow precisely the order outlined in Aldridge's description;

2 the order of the acquisition may vary from child to child and be different even for siblings within the same family;

3 there are frequently differences between boys and girls;

4 this description is based on monolingual English speaking children who are growing up in an English speaking environment in England and hence the order and sequence may not necessarily apply to all varieties of English or to children who are also learning other languages in addition to English;

5 there are a number of physical, contextual, emotional and other factors that may influence an individual's actual development, performance and

competence in learning a particular language, so while this outline is useful it should be used with some caution for describing an individual child and particularly so if used as a measure against which linguistic development is being judged or assessed.

Indeed all discussions and general descriptions of how children learn language need to be prefaced with the caveat that all children are unique and individual. Hence their particular pattern of language use may vary, sometimes considerably, from the broad descriptive frameworks you will read about. The models and frameworks are useful as indicative generalizations rather than very precise descriptors of the order in which individual children learn specific features of their language system. Also, it is important to remain cautious in using these generalizations to describe the language development of children who are learning more than one language. Children who are learning English, after having already learnt another system, or who are learning different languages simultaneously may differ in significant ways. It may not be helpful to use models and descriptions derived from monolingual English speakers for understanding bilingual and multilingual children learning English.

While studying children's language development you will, hopefully, be reading a great many different books and journal articles on the topic. It is important to bear in mind while you are reading, that different studies of children's language development focus on different aspects of linguistic development. For example, the seminal study by Roger Brown (1973) of three children, Adam, Eve and Sarah, learning English as their first language identified 14 morphemes that English speaking children learn and the order in which these are learnt. These are to be found in Table 1.2.

It is useful to compare Brown's order of morpheme acquisition with Cook (1994: 15) who reports the findings from a number of studies of both children and adults who are all learning English as a second language and who are from a range of different first language backgrounds as diverse as Korean, French and Vietnamese. The order of morpheme acquisition for these learners, as one might expect, is somewhat different. They appear in Table 1.3.

Consider Tables 1.2 and 1.3.

1 What comments can you make about the order of acquisition for second language learners?
2 Suggest reasons for this order of acquisition. In particular, consider the connection between the items listed.
3 Do a library search to find out if other studies have been carried out in your own language environment.

Table 1.2 Morphemes learnt by English speaking children in order of acquisition suggested by Roger Brown (1973)

Brown's order of morpheme acquisition	Include some samples
1. Present progressive (*ing*)	
2. On	
3. In	
4. Plurals (-*s*)	
5. Past irregular	
6. Possessive (-*s*)	
7. Uncontractible copula	
8. Articles (*a*, *the*)	
9. Past regular (-*ed*)	
10. Third person regular (-*s*)	
11. Third person irregular	
12. Uncontractible auxiliary	
13. Contractible copula	
14. Contractible auxiliary	

Table 1.3 English morphemes learnt by second language learners suggested by Cook (1994)

Cook's order of morpheme acquisition	Include some samples
1. Plural -*s*	
2. Progressive -*ing*	
3. Copula be *is*	
4. Auxiliary be *is going*	
5. Article *the*	
6. Irregular past tense *went*	
7. Third person '*s*'	
8. Possessive '*s*'	

4 Consider the significance of these findings for children who are learning a variety of English that is different from the standard or Received Pronunciation (RP) varieties.

5 Consider the implications for these learners if they are assessed for performance and/or proficiency using tests designed and validated with native English speaking children of the same age who are learning a standard variety.

We now turn attention to other features of language development.

1.3 Learning words – the lexicon

All languages have words, a vocabulary or 'lexicon'. Crystal (1995: 426) suggests that some speakers of English have an active lexicon, that is the words they actually use, comprising as many as 50,000 words and a passive be understanding (i.e. words that are understood but which may not actually be used of a further 25,000 words. While this may represent the upper limits of the learnt lexicon, it gives us an idea of the extent of one person's repertoire of words. Of course, some of the lexicon is highly specialized. For example, some hobbies or leisure pursuits or workplace activities have a highly specialized vocabulary. This is sometimes referred to as 'register'. Professional groups operate with registers that many non-specialists find difficult to understand. For example, lay people frequently find correspondence on legal or medical matters incomprehensible because of the specialist register used. Some companies also develop a register or company-speak as a way of fostering corporate identity for employees. Registers can also be difficult for the outsider to understand because of the ways in which everyday lexical items are given particular, specialist meanings within a particular context. This may also be true of school subjects such as mathematics where common vocabulary or terms take on a specialist subject meaning. Learning the lexicon demonstrates one way in which learning language is a lifelong activity. New social environments and activities invariably require people to learn new lexical items. For example, on entering the world of work and paid employment individuals frequently need to expand their lexicon. Medical pupils for example need to learn 1500 new words for the parts of the body during their first year of medical training. They also need to learn a new language because most of the medical lexicon is derived from Latin. Learning the common, everyday lexicon begins at around the age of 12 months. By the age of seven years children have learnt around 2600 words. This is an impressive vocabulary learnt at the rate of one new word per day from birth. In reality however, the pattern of learning the lexicon is less evenly spread. It may even include periods when children seem to lose or not use words they have learnt. This is quite usual in the early years of learning language.

Point to ponder

- Consider your own experiences of being a pupil of language. List some of the specialist lexicon or register that you have had to learn recently as a pupil.

1.4 Learning the grammar or syntax

The grammatical structure of language is known as syntax. The term syntax comes form the Greek word 'syntaxis' meaning arrangement. It is the way in which words are arranged to create meanings. The grammar or organization is not arbitrary. It is highly rule governed. However, there are elements of choice that individuals can exercise. In spoken language each speaker contributes to the organization through structured interaction or turn-taking. Written texts are somewhat different. The punctuation plays an important function in the creation of meanings (cf. Halliday 1992).

Until the 1970s most linguistic analysis focused on small units of language, for example, phonetic variation (Labov, Trudgill, Milroy) or the structure of the sentence (cf. Chomsky). However, with the growth in interest in naturally occurring language, and authentic texts, defined as the language that people actually use in their everyday lives as opposed to artificial language generated for the purpose of analysis and discussion, the focus of analysis has subsequently changed. Increasingly there is not only interest in the phonemic, phonological and lexical features of language but also in the organization and relationship between speakers, what they say, how they say it and the ways in which the utterances are mutually influential during the course of interactions and exchanges. This has inevitably led to study of longer stretches of language, particularly the structure of conversations and written texts. This is frequently referred to as discourse.

Discourse or text

In considering discourse or text it is important to bear a couple of points in mind. Firstly, people rarely speak in sentences and most spoken language is essentially unplanned. Discourse is the structure of naturally occurring language that frequently extends beyond the sentence. Inherent in the description of language as discourse is the view that language is dynamic, socially oriented and interactive. Analysing discourse therefore involves focusing on the utterances of more than one speaker and trying to understand how these are interrelated and connected. Zellig Harris (1952) is considered to be one of the first linguists to attempt to describe language at a level other than the structure of the sentence. He was interested in structure of text and how sentences relate to each other. His early pioneering work has influenced many more recent descriptions of how language is actually used by people in their everyday lives.

Learning language(s) means learning more than the mere structure of the linguistic system. It also demands that the child learns to be communicatively competent in a range of social situations, interacting with a variety of different people for different (social) purposes. This will be described in more detail in Chapter 4. To continue to answer our question 'what does it mean to learn language,' it is necessary to think beyond oral language, speaking and listening and to consider how children learn to communicate through different channels including written texts. Of course, not all children do learn to read and to write and of those who do they may not necessarily learn to read and write the language(s) they speak.

1.5 Learning to read and write

Phonology, lexis, syntax and discourse are all features of both spoken and written language. Some (but not all) languages also have an alphabet that leads to the creation of written communications. So our description of the component features of language also needs to account for written forms of language. For the purposes of this book we shall refer to both spoken and written language as 'text'. This is common practice among some linguists including discourse analysts and systemic functional linguists who are interested in the creation and organization of discourse in social contexts rather than only the discrete component features of language like the phoneme or sentence structure.

The orthography and written language

Not all languages have written forms but let us consider those that do have a written form. The written text is made up of a series of symbols, letters or characters that can be combined together to form units of meaning. There are frequently differences in the features and structures of spoken and written texts. Written forms of language are more highly organized that the spoken forms, with few if any, deviations accepted. For example, 'color' (without the letter u) is accepted as a standard written form for some varieties of English, including American English, whereas 'colour' (with the letter u) is the standard version for other varieties. The two are not interchangeable, yet they would be regarded as mutually intelligible, i.e. understood by users of each variety. This is a relatively trivial example but it serves to demonstrate that written text, like spoken language, can vary in the detail while remaining intelligible.

Can you think of other examples of spoken and written language that are mutually intelligible but not interchangeable?

Once an orthography exists then written texts can be produced for a range of different functions. In their excellent ethnographic account of young children learning to read in China John E. Ingulsrud and Kate Allen (1999) describe the diglossic reality where pupils arrive at school speaking different dialects. However, achieving literacy in China means learning the standard spoken language, Putonghua, literally the common language of the people. Thus becoming literate requires learning a new language. This begins on the first day of school. Through a range of methods children learn, first the phonemes and then the individual romanized letters of the Pinyin written system. After six weeks in school the Chinese characters are taught. The alphabetic system of Pinyin is then gradually phased out and the children begin the task of building a repertoire of character recognition and production. This example may seem extreme in comparison with the approaches to literacy adopted in other contexts where children may also arrive in school speaking a non-standard variety of the language. However, other situations, while perhaps less stark in contrast, share similarities. For example, children may begin school speaking a variety that differs phonemically from that of their teachers, or from the standard written variety. The learning curve may not be as steep for the young Chinese learners but it may not be as obvious either. Teachers may not necessarily be aware that the transition to literacy requires learning a new linguistic system, the system of written text.

Learning to be literate

Learning to read is a central concern for primary education. Learning to read, becoming functionally literate are important stages in this process. However, these are to be considered interim. Education literacy will frequently require learners to engage in the canon of literature. It is inevitable that once there is a written form of a language then the range and types of texts created will proliferate. It becomes possible to create more texts for an increasing variety of different purposes and functions. With an established orthography in place written texts can be produced for the mass circulation of news and information and services. Hence it becomes possible for one text to interact with a large number of people. It also becomes possible to establish traditions through text that are capable of surviving across time from one generation to the next and across geographical distance. With written text communication becomes less personal and more anonymous. Written texts make it possible to generate a literary history and heritage of enduring texts that transmit language, as well as ideas, culture and social values, through texts across generations. Written texts are as diverse as spoken language. It is in part through written text that communities can build their heritage and historic identity. Written texts can and do influence the thoughts, ideas and language of the present. These texts can establish a literary canon alongside which contemporary ideas and language are compared. The invention of the printing press and subsequent availability of affordable texts is considered to be one of the most significant contributions to social justice and political empowerment. This demonstrates the social significance of written text in our everyday lives. Literary culture, heritage literature, novels, poetry, drama, works of nonfiction as well as dictionaries and biographies and religious tracts (the Bible and the Koran) exemplify what it is possible to create through written texts. All demonstrate the links that exist between language, culture, history and other social activities and experiences shared by people and ascribed with values of varying kinds. There tends to be a distinction between a society's written texts in that not all texts are considered of equal worth and value. Some, including selected literary, poetic and dramatic texts are frequently associated with high culture and hence carry what Bourdieu terms cultural capital. They are considered to be prestigious and carry high cultural value, while other written texts, frequently those that enjoy a wider circulation or greater familiarity are accorded lower cultural status. Low culture texts remain extremely influential probably more than the highly valued mainly because they achieve a wide circulation and readership.

Points to ponder

- Consider your own daily reading. What range of texts do you read?
- How would you describe these texts in terms of their cultural capital and literary function(s)?
- It is probably clear from your own reading that we do not always read demanding texts at the upper limits of our reading ability. Does this matter?

Popular press and mass circulations

At the turn of the century when pundits were reflecting on the human condition and the radical changes in living conditions during the years 1900–99 the invention of the printing press is cited frequently as one of the most significant advances, one that had radically altered life conditions for vast numbers of people. With its invention (and more recently information technologies which will be discussed below) it became possible to produce large quantities of texts, very cheaply and very quickly. Many groups, communities and societies have regular written press circulations. The daily press is the ubiquitous creation of daily, topical publication. Many people routinely expect a choice of quality daily newspapers, offering everything from political analysis and information to entertainment. This is expected to be cheap and easily affordable. As well as mass circulation for news and current affairs, there is also in many societies and communities, a wider range of print, including magazines covering leisure interests, hobbies and special interest groups. Typically the reader is spoilt for choice when it comes to this type of reading material. Cities are highly literate environments, with written information from street names, road signs, advertising hoardings vying for attention with commuter timetables and other immediately written information. More recently, video screen displays have contributed to the information flow in city centres including Tokyo, Singapore and elsewhere around the world. For the individual, learning to be literate becomes an important aspect of learning language. Written texts differ from spoken texts in a number of significant ways and the manner of learning to read and write is quite different from learning to talk. Literacy learning is frequently (but not exclusively) associated with formal learning in institutions. It is considered a cognitive challenge of abstract reasoning and is hence very different in perception and process from the interactions associated with learning to talk. Text messaging has given rise to rapid change in the form and features of written text and it is young people who have acted as catalysts and agents of this significant linguistic development and change.

Points to ponder

- Consider the written texts within your own print environment. List texts that you read that are embedded within your daily life.
- Some people consider being a student in a college or university means being immersed in an environment rich and saturated in written forms of language. How did your linguistic life change when you became a learner in the place where you are currently studying?
- How would you describe your text environment?

Information communication technology

The single most important and influential development of recent times must be the creation and spread of technology for communicating and as an alternative way of conveying information. This has come to be known as ICT (information communication technology). ICT communications use audio and visual channels of communication. ICT has impacted on the ways in which people communicate with each other. Along with the new channels of communication, the new technologies have created new codes for communicating, new ways of interacting and new language for these new ways of being literate. ICT texts combine the standard orthography of the alphabet with a range of codes and symbols. Features of text including font size and colour become features of the text and the channel of the communication. ICT communication, electronic messaging systems, pagers, voice and email facilities, interactive games and television have all contributed to a rapid change in the ways we use language. These recent developments are vivid examples of the ways in which language use does not remain static. Language is dynamic and needs to change over time to fulfil new social functions.

So far we have given consideration to linguistic features of the language system. The ways in which individuals make choices from within the range of permissible options has become an aspect of language use that emphasizes the social dimension.

1.6 Pragmatics

Pragmatics is the study of the factors that govern our choice of language in social interactions. These choices include the appropriate selection of syntax, sounds as well as the choice of lexical items. Developmental pragmatics is concerned with how a child learns the rules of interaction that guide interactions with a range of different interlocutors in a range of differing social contexts. Parameters of pragmatic competence include:

1 The ability to perform and select from a range of different speech acts (Searle 1969).
2 Demonstrating knowledge of the rules that govern conversations including: turn-taking, selection of appropriate discourse topics and the ability to maintain, develop and re-negotiate these topics.
3 Learning politeness strategies and formulae.
4 Creating connected discourse with continued themes across turns and utterances within turns.

5 Maintaining interactions in a sustained way, across utterances and turns.

6 Being able to accommodate to the listener or audience to ensure that the communication is effective.

Cameron points outs that the word 'pragmatic' is derived from the Greek *pragma*, meaning 'deed' and writes, 'Pragmatics is the field of enquiry that deals with how language can be used to do things and mean things in real-world situations' (Cameron 2001: 68).

In summary, pragmatic competence requires learning the art of conversation and of creating meanings in and through interactions with others. Pragmatic development also includes social sensitivity to other speakers and oneself in relation to these interlocutors. Since interaction involves others, success is dependent upon successful negotiation at a number of different levels of the exchange. Learning language therefore requires learning how to interact with others. Discourse analysts suggest that some of these strategies include:

1 Knowing the rules of turn-taking.

2 Handling interruptions from other interlocutors.

3 Back-channelling to maintain the thread of the conversational topic.

4 Signalling intentions such as elaborating and terminating the interaction.

5 Being inclusive by engaging others in the interaction in a meaningful way.

6 Accommodating to interlocutor(s), the listener or audience.

7 Being able to initiate, sustain, develop and re-negotiate and switch the topic of conversation.

8 Using strategies for repairing conversations.

9 Having some degree of control over all of these devices.

Within the field of pragmatics there have been two highly significant contributions, namely Austin's (1911–60) Speech Act Theory and John Searle (1976). Neither address the young child learning language specifically but they are important because they identify non-linguistic dimensions of what is entailed in learning language(s).

In order to understand how people learn language it is necessary to understand the nature of what language actually is and how people use it. Cameron (2001) offers an overview of the nature of language and from this it is clear that a number of disciplines have contributed to our current understanding of the nature of language. Insights have come from a range of unrelated disciplines. These perspectives include:

Anthropology	Dell Hymes (1977) the ethnography of communication
Philosophy, linguistics	Austin, Searle, Grice and descriptions of pragmatic competence that has focused on the structural features of language including the structure of interactions; texts (both spoken and written)
Sociolinguistics	social aspects of interaction, identity, culture and broader issues of context, politics, language planning, etc.
Psycholinguistics	language and cognitive function, brain activity, thinking and learning

Seen in this way it is easier to understand the complexity of what is involved in learning a language. Learning language demands learning constituent aspects of the linguistic system: phonemes, the phonology, lexicon, grammar as well as appropriate use, pragmatics and the social norms of use. These are rarely learnt as discrete aspects, except perhaps in formal language learning situations or in foreign language classrooms including EFL. Most children learn these rules for their first language through the processes of learning the language. Since language is a semiotic activity these rules are learnt in and through social interaction with others.

If we consider all of these aspects, Figure 1.1, our skills based, four-part model of learning language as listening, speaking, reading and writing, now seems rather narrow. This basic model was expanded further in UK publications from the DES in 1984 and 1986 which described a fifth part to this model. This fifth dimension was developed from an idea first explored in the Bullock Report. It became known as 'knowledge about language' (KAL) and suggested that a knowledge of the forms, functions and structure of language was equally important as the skills of reading, writing, speaking and listening. The notion has been elaborated upon since in publications such as the *Language in the National Curriculum* (LINC) materials for teachers (Carter 1990). Hence, the original skills based model can now be extended to include this fifth dimension, as Figure 1.2 illustrates.

Speaking	Listening
Writing	Reading
Knowledge about language KAL	

Figure 1.2 A five-part model of language learning

Like reading and writing, KAL is a feature of language learning associated with formal, school learning. Learning in the classroom also requires talking about texts. In order to do this teachers and students need a language for talking about language. In order to reflect this our model can now be extended to incorporate these additional dimensions:

Speaking	Listening
Writing	Reading
KAL	Metalanguage

Figure 1.3 A six-part model of language learning

Let us attempt if not a definition, then at least a clarification of what it meant by the term 'metalanguage'. Metalanguage is a specialist language (or register) for talking about language. It is means by which learners can make explicit their intuitive knowledge about language. It is a very important feature of school learning and literacy development, particularly beyond the early stages. KAL is very difficult for individuals to access at will partly because it remains at the level of intuitive knowledge. Hence, when considering what it means to know a language it is important to go beyond the four skills of reading, writing, speaking and understanding, to include knowledge about language or KAL, as well as metalanguage (ML) within our conceptual model.

1.7 Summary

In this chapter we have outlined a number of features or units of analysis that combined create a linguistic system. Our description is not exhaustive. We have tried to indicate the realm and richness of the parameters of language use so that in our consideration of how children come to learn language we do not become too narrow or focus only on the form or structure. We have tried to suggest that linguistic systems are complex, hierarchical and highly organized. Early studies of child language development have tended to focus on specific aspects of these features to describe either the learning of grammar, or the lexicon or the development of morphology for example. More recent descriptions of what it means to learn language have focused more on children's socially situated use of language for interactions with others. Descriptions of how children learn language(s) have rarely taken the integrated approach that reflects the system from the child's perspective. The description outlined here suggests that learning language is more than learning to listen, speak, read and write. We are suggesting a description of learning language that also includes learning *through* interaction as well as learning *about* language. Hence our view of learning language has three developmental stages:

learning language → learning through language → learning about language

The next chapter will describe some of the most influential studies on child language development that have informed our understanding of how children learn languages(s).

Points to ponder

- Write a summary statement on what is required to learn a language.
- What are some of the difficulties young children may face in learning their first language?
- Make a list of the big debates and issues in the field of language development and language acquisition. You should continue to add to this list as you read through this book.
- Map your own learning of language(s) along your lifeline indicating approximately the ages when you began aspects of your learning.

2 What we know about language learning

> At first the infant,
> Mewling and puking in the nurse's arms,
> And then the whining schoolboy
>
> (William Shakespeare)

2.1 Introduction

The study of language development and how young children come to learn the language(s) of the community in which they live has been of long-standing interest to different people, with a variety of interests and all for very different reasons. The aim of this chapter is to present an overview of some of the most significant studies and writings about how children learn language. The contributions are drawn from a wide range of interests including philosophers, psychologists, sociologists, as well as linguists and parents. The overview presented will provide a broad framework within which readers can identify particular contributions to the field of language development. This overview should help you to make critical evaluations of the descriptions you read about. Through comparisons, a broad picture of what we already know about language development will emerge.

The study of children's language is not a new field of enquiry, although the very first studies are very different, in significant ways, from those currently taking place. Among the first publicly recorded accounts of child language are the diary studies first reported in the late nineteenth century. These diaries were frequently the accounts written by parents, of their own child's language development. One of the very first recorded studies is that by T. Haine (1876) who reported a study of his daughter's language from when she was born to the end of her second year (24;0). This was published in the learned journal *Mind*. Another of these early diary studies is Charles Darwin's diary record of his son, published in the same journal, *Mind*, as a response to Haine's account. These and other diary accounts remain significant contributions to our understanding of the early features of young children's language. They can be characterized as detailed, meticulous diary records by parents, of their own children. It is perhaps not insignificant that these two reports of one boy and one girl, would stimulate further debate and research into young children learning language. Accounts of these and other diary studies can be found in David Ingram (1989) *First Language Acquisition*. These insightful studies provide rich data sets of individual children learning to communicate and they make engaging reading. At best they are meticulous accounts, undertaken by dedicated and devoted parents. While they are all highly individualized they do offer important general insights into language development. The approach used is not unique to these early diary accounts. Importantly, their approach, of an intense focus on an individual child has become established as a child study, a *bona fide* approach to studying young children particularly in the fields of psychology and linguistics. The tradition of studying one's own child(ren) has been continued by later researchers including the linguist Michael Halliday (1978) and later by Clare Painter (1984 and 1999) amongst others. Both offer in-depth studies of their own children learning English.

Present day studies of children learning language may now seem far removed from the approach adopted by those early pioneers. Of course, it is inevitable that recent studies, carried out with the high-tech electronic equipment including video, audio recording and sophisticated transcribing equipment have made the researcher's task somewhat paradoxically, both easier and more difficult. It is now easier to capture actual utterances, gestures and interactions electronically on audio and video tape. However, the actual amount and diversity of the data so easily collected, can make the researcher's task of analysis and collation far more complicated, time consuming and complex, so researchers have to make choices about their focus of interest. While diary studies of individual children's language marked an important start to the field of research they were also highly individualized, rather ad hoc and unsystematic in their approach to data collection and subsequent analyses. So it remains that while these accounts are interesting and insightful they are limited because they have not always led to general principles or to a unified theory of how children actually learn language. However they do mark an important initiation into the study of children learning language. Not all of them are devoted to monolingual children. Hoffman (1996) provides an overview of some diary studies of children learning languages other than English. Perhaps the most famous and widely known is Leopold's study of his daughter Hildegård. Table 2.1 presents some studies of children which have been compiled through diary observation records.

Table 2.1 Some of the reported baby biography studies

Year	Researcher	Child(ren)	Age range	Publication
1876	H. Taine	daughter	0–end of 2yrs	Issue of *Mind* (journal)
1877	Charles Darwin	son		Response to Taine in *Mind*
1889	William Preyer	son Axel		(1882) *The mind of the child*
1939-49	Leopold	Daughter Hildegård	0–2 years	Slobin (1972) *Leopold's Biography of Child Language*
1933	Bloomfield			Five steps in the acquisition of language

From your readings, add other accounts to this list.

These diary accounts which we can term, baby biographies, are rich, detailed accounts of individuals' language development but they have been criticized more recently by linguists because they lack linguistic sophistication. They focus largely on details such as vocabulary, sentence length and speech sounds. Hence, some claim they portray a partial picture of language use and cannot be considered as data sets in the present day understanding of that term because they present no data for other researchers to consider. All that exists are diary notes and as detailed and meticulous as these are, they cannot be considered reliable data. However, they do make interesting reading and offer many informed insights in to the processes of learning language(s) and the study of young children.

2.2 Baby talk

More recent studies of child language development have aimed at outlining general descriptions or features of developmental stages. One such study is that by Jane Stark (1986) who suggests five stages of vocal development, summarized in the following table.

Table 2.2 Five stages of vocal development from Jane Stark (1986)

Stage	Age	Characteristics
Stage 1 Basic biological noises	Birth–8 weeks	This is the first stage of sound production – babies are born crying.
Stage 2 Cooing and laughter	8–20 weeks	According to Stark (1986) these are sounds produced when babies are in comfortable states and in response to the caregiver(s) smiling and talking.
Stage 3 Vocal play	16–30 weeks	Longer segments of sound are produced. These contain variations in pitch and stress, as well as other aspects of sound control. These are the beginnings of the phonological system.
Stage 4 Reduplicated babbling	25–50 weeks	A series of consonant–vowel syllables in which the consonant is the same in every syllable e.g. dadadada, nahnahnahnah. Not found in interactions with adults. Found in imitation games towards the end of year 1.
Stage 5 Non-reduplicated babbling	12 months +	Combinations of vowel–consonant–vowel and consonant–vowel–consonant. Towards the end of this stage, stress and intonation patterns can be imposed on the babbling. The baby babbling begins to sound like language.

2.3 Longitudinal studies of children learning language

Perhaps the most interesting accounts for those with interests in education emerge from the longer term descriptions. There have also been a number of longitudinal studies of children learning language. Table 2.3 outlines some of the main studies. The children were recorded with their ages at the time of the observations, together with some information about the research method or type of information obtained. You may find it helpful to continue to add to this table as you read about other research and studies of children learning language(s).

Table 2.3 Longitudinal studies of children learning language

Researchers	Children	Ages in months	Methodology/ sampling schedule
Braine (1963)	Andrew Gregory Steven	19–23	Parental diary of all multi-word utterances produced. For Steven, there were tape recordings for 4 hours over a 4 week period (12 sessions)
Miller and Ervin (1964)	Susan Lisa Christy Harlan Carl	21– 24– 24– 24– 24–	Initial weekly 45 minute sessions; later every 2 months/2–3 sessions for 4–5 hours Sampling over a 2 year period
Bloom (1970)	Eric Gia Kathryn	19–26 19–27 21–14	8 hours over 3 or 4 days every 6 weeks
Brown (1973)	Adam Eve Sarah	27–44 18–27 27–44	2 hours every 2 weeks 2 observers present 30 minutes every week

From these studies some general stages of linguistic development emerge. These include early sounds or what Stern calls a pre-linguistic period. Thereafter, Roger Brown's study has prevailed as a developmental framework that begins with a period of single word utterances; two- and three-word strings, then Stage I the emergence of semantic roles with syntactic relationships; Stage II modulation of meanings or phonology,

Stage III modalities of the simple sentences, then Stage IV the embedding of one sentence within another and finally Stage V the coordination of simple sentences and prepositional relations.

Although language is frequently the focus of child study observations, other things are also happening as the child is learning language. Language development does not happen in isolation from physical growth and social development. Figure 2.1 outlines the physical organs of speech that develop throughout early childhood.

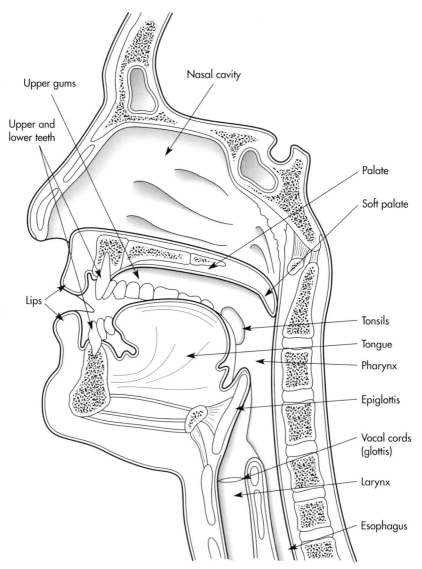

Figure 2.1 The physical organs of speech production

2.4 Language development and physical factors

These physical apparatus for speech production (talking) and reception (listening and hearing), dependant upon the condition and presence of the physical organs illustrated, are particularly vulnerable to damage through illness or injury in the early years of childhood. These can impact on immediate and later language development. In developing a socially situated and socially motivated description of how young children learn language other factors, including seeing what is happening in the environment also become important. Babies and children are learning to talk at the same time as other important growth is also taking place simultaneously. There are some aspects of language development that are directly linked to physiological aspects and psychological growth. For example, read the following article reported in the *The Times* newspaper on 13 May 1999.

Babies who sleep in the dark have better eyesight later

Nigel Hawkes, Science Editor

Millions of parents may be putting their children at risk of becoming short-sighted by leaving the bedroom light on at night. Even a dim nightlight could be enough to triple the risk of short sight in later life, American researchers say. Leaving the lights fully on increases the risks even more, says the team, led by Dr Graham Quinn of the Children's Hospital of Philadelphia. He recommends that infants should be put to bed without any artificial light in the bedroom, at least until they are two. After that, it appears to make no difference. "The earliest years of life appear to represent a critical time in the proper growth and development of the eye," he said.

The scientists asked the parents of 479 children aged between two and 16 whether their children slept with the lights on or off, both now and when they were babies.

They report in *Nature* that of the children who slept in darkness before the age of two, 10 per cent were short-sighted. Of those who slept with a nightlight on 34 per cent were, and of those who slept in full artificial light 55 per cent were.

"Our findings suggest that the absence of a nightly period of full darkness in early childhood may be an important risk factor in the future development of near-sightedness," said Professor Richard Stone, senior author of the paper. The study did not establish a causal link "and there are undoubtedly other risk factors".

Gill Adams, of Moorfields Eye Hospital in London, urged parents not to worry. "The authors themselves have suggested further research. I would not deny any child frightened of the dark the comfort of a low-luminescence nightlight."

The Times 13 May 1999

Consider the implications of these findings for language development.

In addition to eyesight and the organs of speech and hearing there are also other aspects of physical growth and development that can impede and impinge upon language development.

Cruttenden's (1994) table links stages of language development with other aspects of physical dexterity, beginning at just a few weeks after birth and continuing up to the point where may children enter formal edu-

Table 2.4 Language and motor development (after Cruttenden 1994)

Age	Motor development	Language development
0;3	Head self-supported	Babbling begins and continues until at least 1;0
0;6	Can sit with assistance – Bouncing	
0;9	Crawling-sitting without support. Pulls to stand but falls to sit	Babbling and intonation sound more like human language
1;0	Can walk when holding hands	First words
1;3	Can walk unevenly	Lexical overgeneralisations (continues to around 2;6)
1;6	Can walk and crawl downstairs backwards	
1;9		Two word utterances
2;0	Can run well – can walk up and down stairs one foot at a time	Three word utterances
2;6	Can sit on pedal cycle but with feet on the ground	Vowel system complete for many children. Utterances of 4+ words
3;0	Can ride pedal cycle. Can walk upstairs with alternating feet	Nominalizations
3;6		Onsonantal system complete for many children
4;0	Can walk downstairs with alternating feet	Syntax now generally standard within a limited range
5;0	Can run up and down stairs	Some children have difficulties with i) fricatives ii) consonantal clusters iii) /r/

cation at the age of five years. Halliday (1978) has also linked the child's first independent movements, like crawling, with a wider social engagement, as an important stage in language development. (See Table 2.4).

Arrange to visit where you can observe a young child. How much of what you have read about in this chapter can you find evidence for? You will learn about how to observe young language learners and collect relevant data later in the book.

So far, we have established that while young children are learning language other significant developments, for example physical growth, are also taking place. Hence learning language cannot be considered separate from other aspects of the child's life and situation. The next section will describe the work of those who have linked language development with other aspects of learning. We begin with outlining the relationship between language development and more general learning or cognition.

2.5 Language and cognition: Jean Piaget (1896–1980)

The work of the Swiss developmental psychologist Jean Piaget (1896–1980) marked a significant shift in approach and emphasis in the study of children's learning language. His experimental studies with three children Jacqueline, Lucienne and Laurent were essentially concerned with the growth of knowledge. His view (at variance with Vygotsky's whose work will be discussed later in Chapter 3) was that language does not constitute the source of logical thinking. On the contrary, Piaget's position was that language is structured by and dependent upon thought. Piaget's work was more scientific and systematic than the previous diary observations, although his methodology has been criticized (cf. Donaldson 1978). The long term influence of Piaget's work and ideas is still evident in the organization and content of many primary school curricula around the world. The approach, characterized by discovery learning activities and incremental stage descriptors of development is sometimes referred to as the 'constructivist' approach or 'constructivism'. It has influenced the ways in which primary and pre-school teachers teach and assess children, and how they are trained to differentiate learning tasks to meet and challenge each child's differing stages of development. Although Piaget's ideas are based on his data from just three children, his more systematic approach to observations and data gathering allowed him to go beyond mere description to propose a theory of child development that linked development in cognition to language. Piaget proposed a five stage theory of how children learn in early, middle childhood through to adolescence. This can be summarized as follows:

Stage I: the sensory motor stage: birth–2years

Random and reflex actions	0–1 month
Primary circular reactions	1–4 months
Secondary circular reactions	4–8 months
Coordination of secondary schemata	8–12 months

The chief characteristics of the sensory motor stage are:

- The child's intelligence is demonstrated through motor activity (movement, gestures) without the use of symbols.
- Knowledge of the world is limited but developing and based largely on physical interactions.
- Object permanence (the memory of an object even when it is not longer in sight) begins early at around seven months.
- The physical development that allows for greater mobility allows for the child to experience new and different things that lead to cognitive development.

Stage II: the pre-operational stage: 2–7 years

(toddler and early childhood)

- Intelligence is increasingly demonstrated through the use and manipulation of symbols.
- Language matures while imagination or fantasy develops.
- Thinking or cognitive processing is said to be non-logical and non-reversible.
- Egocentricism dominates.

Stage III: stages of concrete operations: 7–11/12 years

(approximates to the years of primary education in many societies)

- Intelligence is demonstrated through logical and systematic manipulation of symbols related to concrete objects.
- Conservation of seven conceptual domains related to the learning of mathematics and science is demonstrated in: number, length, liquid, mass, weight, area and volume.
- Operational thinking develops.
- Egocentric thought including private language or speech for oneself diminishes.

Stage IV: formal operations: 11–16 years

(approximates to the years of secondary education in many societies)

- At this stage the learner can deal with abstractions without reliance on concrete operations and aids.
- Is capable of abstract reasoning and of internal reflection.
- Two additional skills develop: hypothetico-deductive reasoning, the ability to speculate on possible outcomes and deduce what might happen, and prepositional thought, the ability to evaluate the logic of propositions without reference to real world examples or circumstances.

While the ages should only be used for guidance and not taken as absolute points of transition, many education systems have been founded to coincide with these broad stages of development. Classroom activities and practices in a variety of contexts around the world can also be said to have originated in part from Piaget's ideas about learners and their need to engage with concrete objects during learning activities (Ko Peng Sim and HoWah Kam 1992). Discovery learning methods and play based activities are characteristic features of nursery, kindergarten and pre-school settings as well as of early primary school education in many places.

Criticisms of Piaget's work focus on the methodology of his study, the small size of his sample and the lack of agreement over the age related stages of development. Attempts to apply Piaget's ideas in formal education settings have met with little success. Case (1985) and Flavell (1985) are among those who have replicated and extended Piaget's work. Both argue that Piaget overlooked or under emphasized important cognitive achievements of some pre-school children. Margaret Donaldson (1987) also replicated the Piaget experiments and obtained very different results by using contexts and situations more familiar to the young learners she was assessing. She found that when the experiments were repeated with the context and detail changed to reflect the child's first hand experiences, the child's ability to perform the cognitive tasks required was greatly enhanced. Her findings have led to criticisms of Piaget's work. However, Piaget's contribution is of particular importance to those interested in language development specifically because of his descriptions of what he terms 'egocentric speech' and 'social speech' and also because many are also interested in the relationship between language and thought, language and learning, language and socialization and the role of language in enculturation.

Consider an education system with which you are familiar. Can you detect any aspects of curriculum content and/or organization that you can link with Piagetian theories of how children learn?

2.6 Language inside the head

We have seen in our descriptions so far that the numerous descriptions of early language that currently exist rely on a developmental sequence that goes from crying (in all its many forms with all its variety of functions) through to the stage of babbling, after which descriptions focus on one word utterance, followed by two word utterances. While these serve as a useful broad description of the early stage of language development they become problematic for two reasons. On the one hand they do not fully account for the range of uses and purposes that young children are performing with this seemingly limited range of utterances, while, on the other hand, it is not possible to continue adequate descriptions of child language development by simply increasing the number of words or even morphemes in the utterances they make. This is because more words per utterance are not necessarily an indication of development, nor do more words or morphemes necessarily reflect an enhanced linguistic repertoire. Secondly, by focusing attention solely on the number of words and morphemes in children's utterance it is possible to overlook the actual complexity of their developing linguistic competence. As the child's repertoire develops it becomes necessary to look beyond the actual utterance for explanations of the processes in which the child is engaged. Language learning links with cognition as well as social behaviour. Figure 2.2 illustrates language as a versatile resource for thinking and for social interaction.

Figure 2.2 Language as a versatile resource: for thinking and for social interaction

It is as this point that research interests and the direction of the investigations and descriptions of language development diverge. One set of descriptions verges towards the internal or cognitive aspects of language development, i.e. what is happening inside the child's head when language is being processed and produced, while the parallel set of descriptions focus on the external or social impact of the child's utterances (including pre-linguistic or protolanguage which includes behaviour such as crying). Those who subscribe to the latter interests also suggest that the child's environment can and does exert influence on their immediate language productions and processing as well as having longer term impact and influence. These two fields of enquiry that emerge are each concerned with different aspects of the child's development: the social, as described by sociolinguists and the psychological, as described by psycholinguists. These fields are more familiarly known to us as 'psycholinguistics' and 'sociolinguistics'. Perhaps the most influential linguist working in the field of internal or psychological descriptions of language and the mind is Noam Chomsky.

2.7 Noam Chomsky

The focus of Chomsky's (1957) work is the generic syntactic structures of different languages. The explicitly stated goal of his theory of universal grammar was to define the logic of language acquisition. He defines this linguistic competence as the 'deep-seated mental state that exists below the level of conscious language use by which even young children are allowed to generate a large set of utterances' in their talk. He describes the emergence of grammatical structures 'as innately determined by the biological function of a Language Acquisition Device' (LAD) which is intuitive and unique to human beings. Chomsky (1957) demonstrates mathematically that there exists 'well defined classes of morpheme sequences' that cannot be generated by any constituency grammar, no matter how complex. It should however, be borne in mind, that Chomsky originally used language to demonstrate an individual's knowledge of systems and rules, the parameters and principles of language. His real interest lay in understanding the configurations of the mind for which the structure of language (or grammar) simply serves as evidence. Too frequently this has been misunderstood or misrepresented as knowledge of the grammar system being a prerequisite for language learning. This was not Chomsky's point. Chomsky's description focuses on the grammatical structures of the language as a means of demonstrating the ways in which young children learn one aspect of the 'rules of language'. Chomsky generated the now famous sentence 'Colourless green ideas sleep furiously' to demonstrate his view that 'the notion of grammatical cannot be identified with meaningful' (Chomsky, 1957: 15). Unlike other linguists (for example, Christie; Halliday; Hasan and Painter) Chomsky makes no attempt to link the structure of form of the language to the meaning.

Discuss Chomsky's sentence with a friend or classmate. Do you think that it does demonstrate his point that grammar can be separated from meaning?

Chomsky's seminal description of child language is highly significant. However, it is not without critics. Romaine (1984) presents an account of child language acquisition that stands in contrast to Chomsky's. By focusing on the sociolinguistic skills that young children must learn, Romaine (1984) describes the acquisition of communicative competence in child language development. Her approach emphasizes the sociological aspects of language use, while Chomsky's focuses on psychological aspects. Romaine criticizes Chomsky because:

> he idealises the actual processes of language acquisition. He assumes that it takes place instantaneously. This allows him to ignore the intermediate states attained between the initial and steady state, the role of these intermediate states in determining what constitutes linguistic experience and other kinds of interactions that may be essential for the growth of language in the mind.
>
> (Romaine 1984: 258)

Romaine (1984: Chapter 9) further criticizes Chomsky's LAD because it views child language acquisition in terms of a progression through a series of more or less discrete stages, becoming increasingly closer to adult grammar until mature (adult) language use is achieved. This conceptualization of child language acquisition has reinforced the Piagetian view of the child as a 'lone scientist' or 'mini-grammarian'. From the Chomskyan viewpoint, children's utterances are regarded as merely lesser, under-developed and simple versions of adult grammars. However, perhaps the most cogent support for an alternative to the existing Chomskyan descriptions can be found in Romaine (1989: Chapter 8) where she suggests that what is required is a comprehensive theory of language use. Ideally, this would be an approach which would integrate the social, communicative competence aspects of language use, with the Chomskyan, performance dimension.

When it comes to the choice of descriptive framework for describing language development it is not always a clear-cut one between a right way or a wrong way. Descriptive frameworks have to be matched to the specific aspects of the intended description. Chomsky's framework may be considered appropriate for *some* psychological aspects of language behaviour, while other descriptions from sociolinguistics or systemic linguists, for example, offer an approach more compatible with social aspects of language use. Perhaps the most serious shortcoming of the descriptions of language learning that come from Chomsky and his followers (for example, Pinker) is that it does not attempt to deal with authentic texts, i.e. what children actually say in everyday situations. Most of the examples of language are constructed examples that focus only on single, short utterances, sentences at best, rather connected utterances or discourse. It ignores completely the ways in which children learn to interact with others. Margaret Berry (1975: 23) in her introduction to *Systemic Theory* makes a quite different point. She writes, 'while Chomskyan linguistics appeals to the psychologist, systemic linguistics is more relevant for the sociologist'. Perhaps another way of reconciling seemingly contradictory approaches is to broaden the focus to consider in a more comprehensive way, what each contributes to our current understanding of how children learn language(s).

Points to ponder

- Consider the descriptions. To what extent is there overlap in these stages and categories?
- Draw up a list of the areas where these experts (a) agree on features of development and (b) where they differ significantly.

Make an audio tape recording of a young baby less than one year old. It can be quite short, less that one minute. Try to collect three or four different one minute episodes. *It is important that you seek the permission of the child's parents or guardian before you do this.* Play your recordings to a classmate or someone who does not know the baby. Ask them to consider the following. Record their responses either on tape or make your own field notes:

1 Can you describe the sounds that you hear. How would you describe them?
2 Are these sounds are made by the same baby? Give reasons for your answer.
3 What can you say about the baby on the basis of what you hear? Again, give your reasons.
4 Is this a boy or a girl? Give reasons.
5 Can you identify what language(s) are spoken in the home?
6 Can you match or link the sounds you hear on the tape with any of the definitions or descriptions of language development that you have read about? How would you categorize/describe the stage of language development based on the sounds that you hear?
7 Can you transcribe the tape? What features of utterance would you need to focus on in order to describe what you hear? Think back to Chapter 1 where an outline of language is presented. What feature(s) of the utterance do you focus on to describe/transcribe these tapes?
8 Can we consider this as talk?
9 Write down a number of words or phrases that describe/categorize the sounds that you hear?

Can you say anything about the baby's physical environment or context from what you hear on the tape? Again, give your reasons.

- List six main features of Chomsky's theory.
- Compare your notes with those of a classmate.
- Together compare a brief summary (no more than a paragraph) of Chomsky's contribution to our understanding of language development.
- There have been a number of critics of Chomsky's work, including other linguists who subscribe to the theory of generative linguistics such as Stephen Pinker (1994) and Foster (1999). List some of their main criticisms. Again, compare your own list with that of a classmate or study buddy. When you are reading studies and reports of child language development try to decide if they are researched from a socially or psychologically orientated perspective.
- Now read the following article by Margalit Fox that appeared in *The New York Times*. It is based on her interview with Noam Chomsky. How have Chomsky's ideas about language evolved?

2.8 Chomsky on Chomsky

A changed Noam Chomsky simplifies
By Margalit Fox, *The New York Times*

Cambridge, Mass. – Noam Chomsky is spinning a fable. Mr Chomsky linguist, teacher, author and social critic, is sitting in a pose so customary that has been captured in scores of photographs; taken since he upended the study of language 40 years ago. He leans slightly back in his chair, one foot propped on the pulled-out bottom drawer of, his desk, hands aloft.

His office at the Massachusetts Institute of Technology exudes both a Spartan asceticism and a pleasant disorderliness: the primary décor consists of piles of paper on the floor.

Imagine, Mr Chomsky says, that some living superengineer, in a single efficient stroke endowed humans with the power of language where formerly they had none.

This simple idea is the cornerstone of Mr Chomsky's newest – and most unconventional – approach to the discipline he founded in 1957. Mr Chomsky, who was 72 on Dec. 7, 2002, is the father of modern linguistics and remains the field's most influential practitioner. Although he has revised his theoretical framework over the years, no modification is as dramatic as the present one, called the Minimalist Programme, in which he largely breaks with the last four decades of his own work. The

Minimalist Programme, said the linguist Morris Halle, Mr Chomsky's long-time colleague at MIT, 'is the most radical thing I've ever heard anybody say in linguistics.'

Though Mr Chomsky's method has changed, his fundamental mission has remained the same: to construct a symbolic representation of the 'language faculty' the inborn mental endowment that allows human beings to acquire, use and understand language. But unlike its predecessors, the Minimalist Programme (or Minimalism for short) seeks to do this in the most streamlined way possible, dispensing with concepts like 'deep structure' and 'surface structure', which were more or less canonical in Mr Chomsky's earlier work.

'All the properties which were explained in terms of deep and surface structure were really mistakenly described,' Mr Chomsky said. 'And they ought to be explained, and maybe can be explained better, without postulating these systems.' Linguists hope his new approach constitutes a major breakthrough in the field.

A slender, sharp-featured man with greying wavy hair and wire-rimmed glasses, Mr Chomsky was dressed casually this morning in a sweater, running shoes and corduroy trousers. His voice is soft and measured, and he speaks as he writes, in perfectly formed sentences that spin out into page-long, reasoned paragraphs. To be in Mr Chomsky's presence, a colleague once said, is to see 'the overwhelming picture of Rational Man standing before you.'

Mr Chomsky's introduction of his theory of language in 1957, often called the Chomsky revolution, has been equated with Darwin's theory of evolution and Freud's theory of the unconscious in terms of its, importance in the history of ideas: it was the first concerted approach to investigating the human mind through a systematic study of how people produce and understand sentences. For the first half of this century, structural linguistics reigned as the field's dominant methodology. Structuralism viewed language as a purely social phenomenon, like tool making or table manners. Deeper questions of language and mind, including how young children can dope out their native language from the wash of adult talk surrounding them, were never considered.

But Mr Chomsky was deeply troubled by this account. In the mid 1950's he began wrestling with questions he felt the structuralists could not answer: if language was simply learned behaviour, what gave people the ability to produce and understand an infinite number of sentences, including those that had never before been uttered? How did children acquire language seemingly spontaneously, without being overtly taught?

Mr Chomsky was by nature a questioner – and, where he deemed necessary, an explorer – of received truths. Over the years, this trait became evident in his political work, including his early opposition to the Vietnam War, his outspoken condemnation of United States policy in Central America, East Timor and elsewhere, and his castigation of the mainstream news media in general (and *The New York Times* in particular) for what he describes as complicity with governmental and business interests.

When it came to taking on 50 years of structural linguistics, Mr Chomsky was singularly well suited for the task. Growing up in Philadelphia, he was exposed firsthand through the work of his father, William, an eminent Hebraist. As an undergraduate at the University of Pennsylvania, Mr Chomsky studied linguistics, mathematics and philosophy, setting the foundation for his novel perspective.

Language, Mr Chomsky came to believe, was rooted not in behaviour but in biology, in an inborn set of principles that speakers unconsciously draw on whenever they produce or understand sentences. The goal of linguistics, he argued, should be to reproduce these principles. Since one couldn't go mucking around in people's brains, the linguist would attempt instead to mirror the workings of those inborn principles with a set of abstract, quasi-mathematical rules intended to generate the range of possible sentences in a given language – in other words, a generative grammar.

Ultimately, he said, the aim of linguistics is not so much to formulate the grammars of specific languages as to describe a 'universal grammar', a model of the shared properties that underpin all human language. It is these universal principles, Mr Chomsky argued, that all people are 'born knowing' and that allow children to acquire whatever native language they're exposed to.

In the late 1950's, Mr Chomsky ushered in modern linguistics with the publication of the monograph 'Syntactic Structures' (1957), which set forth the theory of generative grammar. Early generative grammar was a rococo device. It posited an unconscious level of linguistic knowledge (the deep structure), which was distinct from what people – actually say (the surface structure). It also contained a vast set of grammatical operations, called transformations, used to produce the range of constructions found in actual speech: questions, relative clauses and the like.

But this thicket of rules presented a major obstacle (?) to the development of universal grammar. A true universal grammar, Mr Chomsky argued, must satisfy two conditions. The first requires it to be detailed enough to describe any possible construction in any human language: questions in Navajo, passive sentences in Japanese, relative clauses in Urdu. This is called the condition of 'descriptive adequacy'.

By contrast, the second condition, known as 'explanatory adequacy', required the grammar to be simple enough to reflect the small set of inborn principles that allow humans to acquire and use language.

For years, linguistic research was snagged between these two competing demands. 'The entire development of Chomskyan generative grammar is a history of tension between descriptive and explanatory adequacy,' said Howard Lasnik, a professor of linguistics at the University of Connecticut and a frequent collaborator of Mr Chomsky's. 'In order to have a descriptively adequate theory of language, you need to have a rich variety of descriptive devices available. But here's the kicker: The more devices available, the harder the child's task in sorting through the maze of possibilities.'

This impasse persisted, until the early 1980's, when Mr Chomsky partly resolved it with a more streamlined framework called *Principles and Parameters*. 'People were discovering completely new and unexpected properties of languages,' he said. 'It was beginning to become possible to find what at some level we know must be true: that they're all cast in the same mould, otherwise you couldn't learn any of them. And though they look extremely different, you began to see how they really were variations on the same theme.'

Out of this work, the Minimalist Programme emerged in the early 1990's. Minimalism takes as it point of departure an essential fact about language: it is a system of communication connecting sound and meaning. Now comes the unorthodox part: Minimalism speculates that this system has been optimally designed, that the connection of sound to meaning was forged as simply as possible, as by the divine superengineer of Mr Chomsky's fable.

Any theory of language, therefore, should reflect this simple design. To that end, Minimalism jettisons most of the baggage of early Chomskian grammar. What remains is a single, multipurpose mechanism used to generate the same rich array of sentences that transformations did.

Ideally, the Minimalist Programme will do what earlier models could not: be both simple and complex enough to fulfil the competing demands of a true universal grammar. Some linguists say it holds out at least a tentative promise.

Others, however, find Mr Chomsky's new programme difficult to work in, and they continue to use alternative models that have sprung up over the years. 'There have been a whole lot of linguists who have adopted it and seem for reasons that are incomprehensible to me to find it attractive,' James D. McCawley, a professor of linguistics at the University of Chicago, said. 'There are others, like me, who find it completely unintelligible.'

As Mr Chomsky is quick to point out, Minimalism is years away from being a full-fledged theory (hence the term programme). 'It's difficult, and it's also a shot in the dark,' he said. 'You don't have any particular reason to 'believe that it's going to work'.

Should it succeed, however, he will be that much closer to realizing the goal he set for his field 40 years ago.

'The subject,' Mr Chomsky said, 'is trying to find out how humans really work.'

2.9 Summary

This chapter has outlined the development of child language studies from the highly individualized early diary accounts written by dedicated parents, to the more systematic studies carried out by social and cognitive scientists, including Piaget, as well as the groundbreaking longitudinal study of three children undertaken by Roger Brown.

Points to ponder

- Consider your own experience of primary and secondary education. Can you find examples of Piaget's influence on aspects of your own education, for example, in the organization of the curriculum, the school organization, and so on.

- If you are a teacher, consider a teaching environment that you know well, for example, a teaching practice classroom. Can you identify aspects of Piaget's influence?

- Make a list of the big debates and issues in the field of language development and language acquisition. You should continue to add to this list as you read through this book.

- As a revision of this chapter you may like to list the main features of early baby biographies.

- Compare the stages of language development proposed from the early studies with those suggested by later studies. In what ways do they differ?

- Look again at the overview of the structure of language development presented in Chapter 1. Can you match any of these longitudinal studies with specific features of language development e.g. phonemic, grammatical, lexical, and so on?

- What are the implications of the findings/models proposed?

- Spend some time doing a library search. Can you find any studies of children learning other language, for example, Chinese, Malay, Tamil or any other languages that you may know, are interested in or are learnt within your own community? Prepare an annotated bibliography of your search to share as a group activity.

2.10 Further reading

Berry, M. 1975: *An introduction to systematic linguistics 1: structure and systems.* London: Batsford.

Bloom, L. 1970: Language development: form and function in emerging grammars. *MIT Research Monographs 59.* Cambridge, MA: MIT Press.

Brown, R. 1973: *A first language.* London: George Allen & Unwin.

Chomsky, N. 1957: *Syntactic structures.* The Hague: Mouton.

Cruttenden, A. 1994: *Gimson's pronunciation of English.* London: Edward Arnold.

Dene, P. and Pinson, E. 1993: *The speech chain: the physics and biology of spoken language*, New York: Freeman and Co.

Flavell, J. 1985: *The development of the psychology of Jean Piaget.* New York: Van Norstand.

Fox, M. 2000: Chomsky on Chomsky – a changed Noam Chomsky simplified. *The New York Times.*

Hawkes, N. 1999: Babies who sleep in the dark have better eyesight later. *The Times*, 13 May.

Ko Peng Sim and Ho Wah Kam 1992: *Growing up in Singapore: the pre-school years*. Singapore: Longman.

Romaine, S. 1984: *The language of children and adolescents*. Oxford: Basil Blackwell.

Stark, R.1986: Pre-speech segmental feature development. In Fletcher, P. and Garman, M. (eds) *Language acquisition: studies in first language development*. Cambridge: Cambridge University Press.

3 Learning to communicate

For many expressions . . . to know their use is to know their meaning
(Wittgenstein, *Philosophical Investigations* 1953)

3.1 Introduction

Many descriptions of language learning, particularly the earliest years of learning, focus primarily on the linguistic components or the structural features that constitute the child's utterances and use of language. Hence, an increase in the number of words uttered and the development from one word, to two word utterances is marked as an important stage in development. However, there is increasing recognition from linguists, psychologists and educators that this is only one part of the complex nature of language learning. With particular regard to socially orientated approaches to language description and specifically within functional linguistics, attention is turning away from discrete aspects of a child's individual utterances to focus on the organization of the interaction and thus on the effectiveness of the conversation and how children get their messages and ideas across to others. These are features of interaction that have been of central concern particularly to researchers interested in children's 'communicative competence'. There is some debate amongst researchers about whether clear boundaries do or should exist between structural features of language and the communicative functions. Some linguists regard pragmatic development as integral aspect of 'communicative competence' while others claim the two to be distinct. The chapter will explore from within a socially orientated description of language what is meant by the term communicative competence. We shall identify the specific features of pragmatic competence that contribute towards developing communicative competence and continue to suggest that this is a feature of language that can be observed developing beyond childhood and throughout the lifespan. We continue our description of what it means to learn language(s) and outline some of the social and contextual factors that influence the processes. We shall expand our existing definition of what it means to learn language to focus specifically on the development of communicative competence and how children learn to interact with others.

3.2 The development of pragmatic and communicative competence

In linguistics there is a longstanding distinction made between what a person can say and what they actually do say. People do not always operate at their maximal in any aspect of their abilities. Language is just one amongst many examples of this elected underperformance or pragmatic choice. Hence in everyday interactions people do not demonstrate their maximal linguistic ability; they merely do what is necessary to get their message across efficiently and effectively. This distinction has been variously termed *langue vs parole* (Saussure 1974) or performance vs competence (Chomsky 1965). Extending and elaborating on the notion of competence the American sociolinguist, Dell Hymes (1964) was the first to begin to focus specifically on the competence aspect of learning language and to build a picture of the communicatively competent person. He identified a number of features that contributed to communicative competence. His description contrasts with existing descriptions in that he does not focus solely on the grammatical structure of what people say. Hence with Hymes's description came a shift in focus from grammatical competence to a broader communicative competence. For Hymes, being communicatively competent requires being able to communicate effectively and appropriately in a range of different social circumstances, for a variety of different social purposes. In this sense, a communicatively competent individual is one who is able to achieve a wide range of social functions with and through language. Becoming communicatively competent is a central aspect of learning language. It requires learning the rules that govern language at all levels, the grammatical, the lexicon, the phonology, and so on.

However, significantly it requires more. Becoming communicatively competent also means learning the socio-cultural rules of appropriate behaviour that constrain what is possible between interlocutors in given interactions and in given contexts. For the child and the competent interlocutor, this includes an understanding of the semantic implications of the utterances of others. The notion of communicative competence suggests that just as the overt structure of language at every level from the phoneme to the grammatical is governed by rules, so too is our *use* of language. Gumperz and Hymes (1964) and Slobin (1967) were the first to characterize the nature of communicative competence and to suggest specific features that constitute communicative competence. In hindsight it can now be explained as the knowledge and integration of a number structures at social, cultural and linguistic levels. Communicative competence in an individual is the ability to integrate the knowledge of social, cultural and linguistic structures in order to produce and contribute to the ongoing interaction and hence that are meaningful to others. This expands our view of what it means to learn language(s). It suggests that while structural features are important aspects of learning language(s) they create other parameters that are also important. Key terms associated with the notion of leaning to communicate are 'appropriateness' or 'appropriacy'. Hymes in his original description of context of situation suggested that communicative competence is:

> The knowledge of sentences, not only as grammatical but also as appropriate. [The child] acquires the competence as to when to speak, when not, and as to what to talk about with whom, when, where and in what manner. In short, a child becomes able to accomplish a repertoire of speech acts, to take part in speech events, and to evaluate their accomplishment by others.
>
> (Hymes 1974: 277)

Appropriateness applies at a number of levels. Hymes's definition stresses the significance of the social context(s) in which language learning takes place. Hymes, like Halliday, suggests that language serves a range of social functions. Dell Hymes (1967: 8–28) in the *Ethnography of Speaking*, outlines the component parts of learning appropriate language use within a speech community as an embedded structure comprising of: the Speech Community, Speech Situation, Speech Event, Speech Act and Speech Style. His description of learning language is centred around learning how to use language in specific social situations. Central to his description are five strata of embedded contexts that influence and even determine what is appropriate language use. These are, in order of hierarchy: Speech Community, Speech Situation, Speech Event, Speech Act and Speech Style. Figure 3.1 combines these five strata in the same diagrammatic form that systemic linguists use to illustrate the ways in which contexts and language structure metaredound, that is, they are mutually influential and creating.

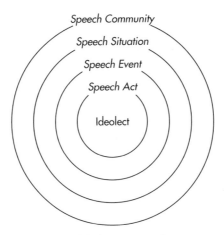

Figure 3.1 Five strata of embedded contexts of situation

These five levels form a nested hierarchy of *context of situation*. Each stratum plays a role in influencing what is appropriate language use and social behaviour. However, this is not to suggest that individuals have no scope for individuality, for they can and do make personal choices that differentiate one speaker from another. All however, remain within the broad contextual parameters of what is considered to be appropriate. Even within the structural influences, individuals make individualistic choices and use language in unique and individualized ways. Hymes did not present his contexts of situation as this nested hierarchy. However, it is implicit in his description that interactions take place between individuals in given contexts. Some of these contexts are physical places, like a home, places of religious significance, public places, and so on. Some *contexts are created* through the interpersonal interactions between the interlocutors within these situations.

Hymes (1968) details, in the mnemonic 'SPEAKING' specific aspects of what it means to be communicatively competent.

> Setting and the scene – the setting is the physical place where the interaction is situated, while the scene refers to the psycho-

logical or mental frames that each of the participants bring to the interaction. Each person will bring different mental frames to bear on the interaction because each person will have different previous linguistic and social experiences. Mentally, in terms of the scenes, each discourse brings some remnant of these previous experiences and encounters to the new interaction by means of a psychological expectation of what can and may happen.

Participants – the participants are those people present, the interlocutors creating the social setting. While some participants may actually participate in and contribute to the creation of the discourse, this is not necessarily true of all. Even non-participants contribute to the ongoing interaction, if only by their mere presence. For example, two people engaged in a conversation may say different things, or the same thing but in different ways, if they know that someone could hear what they were saying. Hence the participants are all of those people present. In some situations, for example, during a concert or theatre performance, the audience while present have but limited and selective opportunities to contribute to the event. Being present, in attendance but silent is part of the requirement of being a member of the audience. Being silent, clapping applause at appropriate places is demonstration of appropriate behaviour and communicative competence for members of an audience.

Ends (goals and outcomes) – the ends or goals are what each of the participants aims to achieve through participation in the interaction.

Act – sequence is the order of the message, the form that it takes and the communicative content. Some acts have highly structured sequences that need to be observed in order for the communication to be effective. For example, in some cultures, politeness strategies are two parts exchanges:

Speaker A: makes a request
Speaker B: replies politely, thanks/thank you or some other appropriate form
Speaker A: is then communicatively obliged to conclude the exchange with the politeness formulae 'you're welcome' or something similarly appropriate.

Key – the key is the tone, or manner in which an utterance is made for example, mocking

Instrumentalities – these are the range of potential channels available for the interaction. For many years this was simply a choice between speech or the written channel. More recently new channels have emerged. Our choice of channel has been expanded and now includes electronic channels such as using voicemail, phonemail, email in addition to face-to-face encounters and other styles of written communication. These developments required some people to learn new ways of achieving familiar ends. For example, the choice of channels for contacting friends, sending greeting and messages have now expanded to include electronic greetings, as well as recorded voice messages in a range of different channels. For some, particularly adults, this has meant learning new language and new ways of using language to achieve these communicative ends.

Norms of interaction require knowing the rules that govern different types of discourse. While these are linguistically specific and the structure of the utterance can be described there is also in addition information that the interlocutors need for communicative competence. Norms are determined by the social and cultural contexts of the interactions. They may vary from context-to-context even in the same language.

Genres or types of texts that exist within a speech community. Genre will be discussed in more detail in later chapters.

Hymes's definition of communicative competence brings in the cultural dimension to our definition of what it is to learn a language. He stresses the importance of language learning and silence (when not to) as part of the child's socialization into a given social and cultural context. The uses of the language(s) that the child learns are determined (not pre-determined) by the functions which that language serves in the specific speech community in which the child is being raised. Hymes, in his definition, stresses that each language does not always and everywhere play the same role. So for example, one utterance, can have a variety of roles and perform a range of functions. We shall see examples of this in Halliday's description of Nigel's language which will be presented in detail in the next chapter.

Hymes's definition carries implications for our understanding of children's communications in different cultures where a range of child rearing practices, and expected norms of behaviour will be taught and assumed. Expected linguistic behaviour in one culture will not necessarily be the same in other cultural contexts. This will be the case even within the same language community. For example, although French is spoken in Paris,

Montreal and Mauritius, effective communication will take place in each of these French-speaking contexts. Hence, what it means to learn French, the same language, may differ from context to context. These varying patterns of socialization and enculturation will become particularly significant if comparisons are made across and between children. For example, it is not unusual for tests (particularly of reading or language) that have been designed in and for one context, for example the UK or USA, to be used, without amendments or modification in quite a different context. This transfer may not always be appropriate and can lead to erroneous judgements about a particular child's actual competence.

Hymes's notion of communicative competence and Halliday's description of child language learning allow for the possibility whereby each discourse participant (including children) can play an instrumental role in the negotiated construction of the social context in which they are participating and creating. Each individual speaker is potentially empowered to contribute to the social context through participation in the discourse through their interaction(s). This approach to understanding language learning extends our description to include social features such as power relation and negotiating strategies. These are to be regarded as important dimensions to children's developing competence and learning language(s).

The descriptive frameworks that aim to take account of this broader understanding of learning language for example, Halliday and Hymes, contrast with Chomsky's (1969) description of child language development as the emergence of a finite number of grammatical rules, innately determined as part of what he termed a Language Acquisition Device (LAD) and from which a infinite number of sentences can be generated. However, an increasing number of researchers have sought to reconcile child language learning with other aspects of learning including social and cognitive development, in the belief that a more integrated approach can lead to deeper understanding of what it means to learn language(s). Suzanne Romaine's (1986) book *The language of children and adolescents: the acquisition of communicative competence*, sets out a description of language development that contrasts sharply with the Chomskyan description. Romaine (1986: xi) describes children's developing communicative competence as 'the range of sociolinguistic skills that children need to learn in order to be able to interpret and produce utterances, which are not only grammatical but also appropriate within particular contexts'. In her conclusion she notes that neither innate universals nor social environment can alone account for how children learn to communicate. Her view is that children's developing communicative competence emerges as a continuing interaction between the social and the grammatical, as an ongoing and continuous process which begins before the child starts to speak, and which is never actually complete. However, Romaine (1986: 03) warns that some aspects of competence are more purely linguistic than others. She suggests that it is important not to conflate a sociolinguistic theory of communicative competence and a more general socio-psychological theory of action or human behaviour.

This view contrasts with attempts by others, for example Wells (1999) to develop a socio-cultural theory of education that combines language with social and cognitive aspects of learning and Halliday's conceptualization of a language based theory of learning (outlined in Chapter 4). Both attempt to integrate language learning with a more general theory of learning that embraces wider social and cognitive aspects of human experience. These descriptions are entirely compatible with our own of language learning as a lifelong process that begins but which is never actually finished or completed. Romaine emphasizes that communicative competence continues to develop well into adulthood as one learns how to do new things with language. By contrast Foster's (1999) description of communicative competence as including both innate and acquired knowledge can actually reach what she terms the adult stage when the innate component of the grammar is no longer refined by new input, and when the strategies no longer result in new generalizations and rules. There are some limitations to this view because it suggests a point when an individual's language is no longer open to new influences. It is difficult to conceive of any individual, irrespective of age, living a totally static life devoid of any new experiences. It is suggested that life experiences bring their own influence to an individual's linguistic repertoire, irrespective of the person's age.

Saville-Troike (1982: 6) is among those who offer a broader definition of what it means to be able to communicate. She includes both social and cultural knowledge in addition to linguistic knowledge in her description and outlines a wide range of linguistic, interactional and cultural phenomena that contribute to being communicatively competent. These include linguistic knowledge, interactional skills as well as cultural knowledge. Each comprises a number of component elements. These are as follows:

1 Linguistic knowledge
   (a) verbal elements
   (b) non-verbal elements
   (c) patterns or elements in particular speech events
   (d) range of possible variants (in all elements and their organization)
   (e) meaning of variants in particular situations

2 Interactional skills

    (a) perception of salient features in communicative situations

    (b) selection and interpretation of forms appropriate to specific situations, (roles and relationships – rules for the use of speech)

    (c) norms of interaction and interpretation

    (d) strategies for achieving goals

3 Cultural knowledge

    (a) social structures

    (b) values and attitudes

    (c) cognitive maps and schemas

    (d) enculturation processes (transmission of knowledge and skills)

These parameters are compatible with our model of language learning presented in Figure 3.2 the domains of language learning as an integration of social, cultural and cognitive facets that combine to allow for the creation of each person's ideolect, or highly individuated way of speaking.

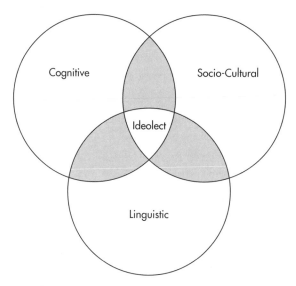

Figure 3.2 Interrelated domains of language development

    Ninio and Snow (1999) address the development of pragmatics in learning to use language appropriately which they define as:

> The study of the use of language in context for the purpose of communication. Thus, developmental pragmatics is concerned with how a child acquires the competencies underlying the rule-

governed employment of speech in interpersonal situations. The criteria applied in assessing the pragmatic success of an utterance have to do not with grammaticality (the criterion applied within the domain of syntax) or truthfulness and interpretability (the semantic criteria), but with appropriateness and communicative effectiveness.

Ninio and Snow (1999: 347)

Thus they support a distinction between pragmatics, semantics and syntax and hence concur with the central tenet of formal linguistics in their definition. This view stands in contrast to the description of Halliday and other functional linguists (cf. Christie Martin, Hasan) who do not maintain any distinction between the pragmatic, semantic and syntax aspects of linguistic description. Indeed they go further and suggest the language system is inherently contextual and therefore cannot comprise autonomous components. They suggest that pragmatics is the study of language in context and that all language is *per se* contextualized. If we understand language in this way it changes how we study young children learning language(s) and how we describe what they say.

Saville-Troike (1982: 213) further stresses the central role which language plays in the enculturation of children. She notes that language is:

1 part of the cultural body of the knowledge, the attitudes and the skills which are transmitted from one generation to the next;
2 a primary (though not the only) medium through which other aspects of culture are transmitted;
3 a tool which children use to explore and manipulate the social environment and establish their status and role relationships within it.

Fluency is one aspect of conversational competence described by Fillmore (1979) who identifies the need to distinguish between how people speak their language(s) and how *well* they speak it (authors' emphasis). He uses the term 'maximally gifted speaker' to describe a person who can fulfil all of the following four abilities that he considers emphasize the maximally gifted speaker. These are:

1 the ability to talk at length, fill time with talk (he cites the professional example of a disc jockey but maybe there are other professionals, for example, teachers who also seem able to do this);
2 the ability to talk in coherent, reasoned and semantically dense sentences, mastering the syntactic/semantic resources of the language;

3 the ability to have appropriate things to say in a wide range of contexts;

4 the ability to be creative and imaginative in language use including telling jokes, punning, varying styles and creating metaphors.

Fluency is an important aspect of learning language(s). Indeed Fillmore's criteria were intended to describe adults' use of language.

Descriptions of learning languages that take the broader perspective and focus on wider issues are frequently derived from fields of study other than linguistics. Ochs and Schieffellin (1983) combined their research backgrounds and interests in anthropology and linguistics to write *Acquiring Conversational Competence*. The volume presents a number of empirical studies that focus on specific features of learning communicative aspects of language development through children's participation in conversational exchanges. Their description includes specific aspects of conversational competence including repetition and non-verbal features of interactions such as eye direction and gaze. Although the volume concentrates on aspects of socialization, in particular interactions between adult care-givers and children, the methodological frameworks presented lay significant foundations for subsequent descriptive studies of the social and pragmatic aspects of children learning language. Their findings (Ochs and Schieffellin 1986: 183) that two children aged 2;6 and 3;6 were able to sustain interaction over twenty-five turns, paying detailed attention to each other's utterances are an important contribution to understanding child–child interactions. They suggest that even very young children demonstrate an emerging sense of metalinguistic awareness and pragmatic phenomena. Their work is significant because it is based on descriptions of children's naturally occurring language rather than structured laboratory based elicitation language tasks. McTear (1985) also gathered natural everyday interactions between his daughter, Siobhan (aged 3;8) and her friend, Heather (aged 4;0).

All of these descriptions of language development place language within a social context and link it with cognitive understanding of how the world works. Others, for example, Bernstein (1975), Halliday (1975) and Mercer (2000) have all used the term 'commonsense knowledge' to describe this combination. The next section will link with some of the frameworks that help to explain how people build their commonsense knowledge with and through the medium of language.

3.3 Schema Theory

The term schema was originally used by Bartlett as early as 1932 to describe organizational or contextual structures. Schema are important because they describe how people anticipate social and events, situations in terms of their previous experience(s) of similar contexts, events and situations. For example, on the basis of the experience of the first day at school, children begin to construct expectations about subsequent experience of life at school and in some cases may even decide that they do not like it and may prefer not to go back to extend their schema of the experience. Early experiences form long lasting and influential impressions. As individuals we construct schema for all aspects of our daily lives. Some constructs are highly individualized while others are more general semantic maps of common events and contexts. These schemata are what Tannen (1979) terms 'structures of expectation'. They are the mental schema through which we anticipate what to expect of unknown future events. Our structures of expectations serve to nurture individual expectations of likelihood, based on previous experiences of similar or dissimilar events. We build up schema and structure our expectations of future events on the basis of our past experiences but we continue to develop, expand, and refine these schema as we go through life in the light of our new experiences. Our developing schema or frames of expectation do not only prepare us in what to say and how to behave but they also influence our assumptions and expectations about a whole variety of things including the people we might meet, the places we might visit, the roles and responsibilities we may be expected to assume, as well as what to say and how to behave appropriately when we get there.

We know for example that after only a short time in school, children become aware of the specific behaviour expected of children at school. They quickly learn to become pupils (Willes 1983). People very quickly become socialized into all sorts of social contexts. Schema play an important role in that socialization process. They also help to guide individual's behaviour in situations that require highly regulated and ritualized patterns of behaviour, for example, doctor–patient encounters, pupil–teacher interactions, telephone conversations, and service encounters like sales–customer interactions. These social encounters are bound by the norms of behaviour specific to the culture and society in which they take place. Using the telephone in an English-speaking context may be very different discourse from using the telephone in other language contexts for example, even when the language of the interaction is English. The second theory to influence linguistic understanding is Frame Theory.

3.4 Frame Theory

Framing is an established feature of discourse. The notion of interactive frames was first explored by Bateson (1972) in his book *Ecology of the Mind*. The term has also been used by discourse analysts (Sinclair and Coulthard 1975; Tannen and Wallat 1982) to show the ways in which people signal significant developments in the discourse, during their interactions. Some frames are highly individualized, others serve as markers of specific speech communities. Some are used to show agreement, disagreement, to reinforce solidarity between the speakers. It is also claimed by some researchers that frames are also gender markers. There are some texts (or forms of language) in which framing is more significant and necessary than others. For example, framing in written texts is an important signalling of the development of the discourse and the cohesive structure of the text. We shall be returning to this when we consider how young children learn to write. In spoken texts frames are important ways of signalling what is to come later in the discourse. This leaves the third and final influence, Script Theory.

3.5 Script Theory

The concept of scripts emerged from the field of computer science and artificial intelligence (AI). Both fields have influenced our understanding of how language works, and the attempts made by computer scientists to create programs that were capable of understanding human language. Scripts account for the cognitive connections made by individuals to construct a semantic map, or personal understanding of things, including particular words or social events or personal experiences.

In our everyday conversations, personal encounters and experiences, we try to make connections between our previous experiences and the present one. We try to connect what we already know (or think we know) with any new information that we receive. So for example, if we have a speaker with English and say, Chinese in their linguistic repertoire, that person will try to fit any utterance they hear within their existing language repertoire. Young children learning a language do not at the very early stages of learning, distinguish one language from another. They do not perceive the two as separate or different. They continue to try to make sense of all utterances within the linguistic repertoire they have. Of course, these connections are made at the intuitive level of language operation and as individuals we remain completely unaware of the processes in which they are engaged. This is true even for adults. These mental representations or connections are referred to as scripts. Schank and Abelson (1977) defined scripts as 'a predetermined, stereotyped sequence of actions that defines a well-known situation'. This would account for why we go through very familiar routines, for example, driving a car or reading a book without thinking about the component parts or sub-skills that are required of us in performing these activities.

When we are driving, for example, we do not need to consciously remind ourselves to check the clutch, hand-brake, rear mirror or carry out other routines that have to be so overt and conscious when, for example, we are just learning to drive, or when we are actually taking the driving test. There comes a point in our learning when these sub-skills are almost second nature to us and we do not even realize that we are remembering to perform them. It is at this stage that these once learnt routines become intuitive knowledge, so deeply embedded in what Chomsky terms our deep seated competence (mentalese), that we do not need to think about them overtly, in order to perform them competently. It is as this stage that they become our scripts. Scripts, just like other aspects of our linguistic repertoire, are highly personalized and in some ways perhaps unique to individuals. However, just as with language, there are common elements in the scripts that individuals construct for themselves and it is these common elements, or shared facets, that enable us to communicate and share meanings with each other. We construct an individualized understanding and meaning of our world through the scripts that we build. These then become worlds shared with others through our personal contact and communications with others and importantly, language is the means by which scripts are shared. Raskin (1985: 81) defines a script as 'a large chunk of semantic information surrounding the word or evoked by it'.

Frame, Script and Schema are all theories of learning that link learning about the world or the development of commonsense knowledge with language development. They hence emphasize the social dimensions of learning language. These are aspects of language description referred to in the literature as 'pragmatic competence', 'sociolinguistic strategies' and 'socio-cultural competence'. They are descriptions of language use that complement the psycholinguistic descriptions by linguists such as Chomsky who focus on the internal aspects of language development, or what is going on inside the head.

The findings from the ethnographic study *Becoming bilingual in the nursery school* by one of the authors (Thompson 1999) can be summarized as follows:

- Children create their understanding of the world through their exploration of the space available in settings.
- Children create their understanding of the world through the time they spend doing particular things.
- Children create their understanding of the world through their social encounters with other people.
- Children create individual histories from common experiences.
- Children create different scenes (Hymes) from a common setting.
- A child's experience is highly individualistic even in a shared setting.

The study suggests that there are three features that contribute to the child's internal cognitive construction of scenes. There are: the linguistic, the social and the cultural. It was suggested that these three elements combine to contribute to the children's experience within the kindergarten. These are the time that they spend doing particular tasks, the people they interact with and the language(s) of those interactions. Hence it is suggested that the creation of schema or scenes is multi-dimensional and multi-layered, comprising the social, the linguistic and the cultural dimensions that combine to create the cognitive. What is not clear and

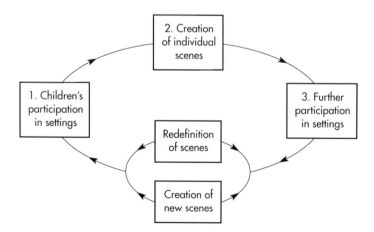

Figure 3.3 Stages in children's creation of scenes

where there is ongoing debate is how these three dimensions actually contribute to the construction of the intra-psychological reality for each child. This suggestion raises important questions. Do children refine or re-define their existing scenes and schema on the basis of new encounters and experiences? Or do they create new scenes and schema to compensate and complement their existing constructions?

There are others, for example the Russian psychologist Vygotsky who offers a more socially orientated explanation of learning language. The next section outlines his views.

3.6 Lev Vygotsky (1896–1934)

Lev Vygotsky is a highly influential Russian psychologist whose books (1962, 1966 and 1978) have been recommended reading for psychology undergraduates and students training to be primary school teachers, since the 1970s. It has often been set alongside the descriptions outlined by Piaget for purposes of comparison and contrast. Vygotsky was working in Russia in the 1930s, his career developing in parallel to Piaget who was working in Switzerland at the same time. However, it was not until 1962, when edited translation of Vygotsky's work were translated into English, that his views became accessible to a wider audience. Vygotsky's view is the idea of the child as a social being, as one involved in the social order of things from the very early stages of life. He links the person with the environment in which they are living and learning. His view is that language is inextricably tied to cognitive and behavioural systems, to the way people think and their social behaviour. He describes languages as interacting with the individual's cognitive and social development and as serving their continuous development. The three aspects of the person the cognitive, the social and the linguistic are interdependent and continue to develop in an inter-related way throughout the lifespan. Vygotsky (1962, 1966 and 1978) regards human activity as a tool and suggests that people use tools as a means of achieving, changing and transforming themselves and their lives. He developed this view to include the use of sign systems that include spoken language(s), written language(s) and number systems, all of which are created by societies to serve their unique needs. He suggests that these systems are not fixed but that they are dynamic and amenable to change. This can be the case at an individual level. People can change the language they speak and/or aspects of how they speak, as too can nations. For example, after some debate in 1998 it was decided to introduce some changes to the spelling and writing system of the German language. Other nations have also reconsidered their national language policy and some, such as South Africa, Malaysia and Singapore have decided to change their national languages for a variety of reasons. These changes in Nation Language Policy impact upon individuals and their daily lives, requiring them to change and transform themselves.

Vygotsky parallels the child's development in spoken and written language with cultural changes in the use of these sign systems. His theory rests on the fundamental premise that development occurs on a social level within a cultural context. He suggests that the child learns by internalizing processes witnessed in the social activity of the environment. The young child moves from a social plane to an individual plane, or in the terms of Vygotsky's theory, from the inter-psychological functioning to intra-psychological functioning. Vygotsky's view of the child learning can be summarized as determined by social functioning. In his view the structure of an individual child's mental processes mirrors the social milieu from which they are derived. Vygotsky's (1981: 163) summarizes his socio-cultural theory as:

> Any theory in the child's cultural development appears twice, or on two planes. First, it appears on the social plane, and then on the psychological plane. First it appears between people as an interpsychological category, and then within the child as an intrapsychological category. This is equally true with regard to voluntary attention, logical memory, the formation of concepts, and the development of volition.

The connection between these two planes is to be found in the mediating function of signs, and in particular speech. Experienced first through interactions with others, the functions of speech are gradually internalized until they become the means for self-directed mental activity. Hence, central to Vygotsky's theory is the view that intellectual growth is contingent upon learning language which he regards as the social means of thought. His view of thought and intellectual development as dependent upon language have been developed and expanded by others including Luria (1978). The Vygotskyan perspective has a number of key concepts that help to explain how this ontogenesis takes place. Speech which begins as a shared social activity and which is created by the child through interaction with others becomes a principal means of the mental regulation and refinement of their individual behaviour. Vygotsky and his followers describe three types of regulations inherent in communication activities. These are:

Object-regulation: a person can be said to be object-regulated when directly controlled by the environment. This can happen in a number of ways. Prabhu (1989) outlines one example of object-regulation within the educational context. He suggests that when a school or classroom syllabus is dominated by text books and other materials these assume intrinsic power because of the ways in which they are used by teachers, administrators, inspectors and others as controlling mechanisms. Equally, it is possible for any national curriculum, for example the one introduced in the UK in 1988, to be regarded in this way. Object-regulation is not confined to the specific learning materials. The actual space and organization of the learning environment can also be viewed in this way. The organization of the furniture and the degree of flexibility inherent in the organization is a further example. In classrooms and corridors where there are displays, questions about who decides the topic and content of these and whose work is displayed also illustrates ways in which the organization of a learning environment convey value systems and hence regulate.

Other-regulation: when a person is controlled by another person. The teacher in the classroom for example can use this form of regulation as both a positive and negative influence. It can either be used by the teacher or by any adult, as a means of imposing control over the child or as a way of supporting the child through to understanding in a structured environment.

Self-regulation: where speech or spoken language is used to control oneself through self-directed utterances. Vygotsky (1962) suggests that this is denoted mature linguistic ability.

A central idea to Vygotsky's descriptions of language learning in young children is that of inner or private speech. This is sometimes referred to as speech-for-oneself. He suggests that children find it helpful to speak aloud about what they are doing. This talk can take many forms: as a dialogue or multi-person interaction or as a monologue. Adults who know a young child very well may be familiar with the young child engaged in private speech. The abbreviated structures of such private talk may mean that it is not readily meaningful to the listener. This is partly because the overhearer is not able to share what is going on inside the child's thoughts. Private speech is now held as an important and necessary part of language development. Vygotsky was not alone in observing this kind of speech behaviour in young children. It was also noted by Piaget. However, their views on its function and significance vary. Piaget termed it egocentric speech and explained it as part of the child's development from self-absorbed egocentric behaviour that disappears and merely withers away as the child develops towards more rational thought and becomes more socially aware. In other words, for Piaget, it was merely a developmental stage. Vygotsky however, attaches greater significance to the child's private speech. He suggests that 'speech-for-oneself' is an important tool for helping the child. His view was that private speech becomes internalized as verbal thinking. For Vygotsky speech-for-oneself assumes a much greater significance in the development of the child's language and thoughts. He made two important observations about private speech. Firstly, he noted that when a task became more cognitively challenging the amount of private speech increased. Secondly, Vygotsky (1987: 70) suggested that 'operations carried out by the pre-schooler as overt speech are carried out by the (older) school-aged child in soundless, inner speech'.

3.7 Vygotsky's zone of proximal development

Vygotsky makes a distinction between learning and development. He suggests that learning is related to formal educational situations and contexts while development happens in a more naturalistic or less contrived way. This distinction in his theory leads Vygotsky to describe a central notion of his theory, the 'zone of proximal development', which he uses to explain the distinction between a child's actual development, as measured for example, by IQ tests, and the child's potential development. Vygotsky suggests that in order to assess the potential development level, it is necessary to present the child with a problem, the solution to which is just beyond present mental capacities, and then to allow the child to interact with another (more experienced) person while working out the solution. Vygotsky suggests that the processes by which the child arrives at the solution provides a more accurate assessment of the intellectual capacity than traditional IQ tests. Vygotsky's theoretical construct of a zone of proximal development concurs with the social nature of learning. Vygotsky (1962: 104) suggests that 'what a child can do in collaboration today, he can do alone tomorrow'. This is a view of learning reinforcing the social nature of the activity. It stands in contrast to the Piagetian, constructivist view of the egocentric child trying to work out a view of the world independently and alone, a view that has been criticized by Donaldson (1987) because it underestimates the true capabilities of the young learner. Vygotsky's theory of a zone of proximal development is not a stage confined to childhood. He suggests that it is evident at every stage of human development when a person is moving from not knowing through a learning phase with the support of external agencies, people or other learning supports. This idea has been developed and extended by Bruner (1986) who describes the critical function of the support given to the learner through the zone of proximal development as 'scaffolding', or 'appropriate social interactional frameworks'.

Vygotsky's view emphasizes the role played by adults, competent peers and experienced others in early learning. They each play a crucial supporting role in helping the learner towards the time when they have a degree of control over a new function or conceptual system. When the child has arrived at the stage of independence, learning has taken place and the child is then in a position to achieve a degree of control over what has been learnt. At this point the new learning can be used as a tool and the external agent or scaffolding is no longer required.

Vygotsky's theories of child learning are compatible with Halliday's and other systemic functional linguists. Indeed Wells's (1999) book *Dialogic Enquiry* provides a detailed comparative analysis of the theories of Vygotsky and Halliday and draws them together in to a sociocultural theory of how young children learn. Figure 4.4 illustrates the domains that contribute to an individual's linguistic repertoire. These domains, or intersecting spheres of influence can be considered instrumental in defining and creating an individual's ideolect. It is suggested that the social, cognitive, cultural and life experiences interrelate to create a unique ideolect. In this sense ideolect can be understood on two levels. On the one hand, it is the *id*, the sub-conscious level individual self. Linguistically, this can be understood as a unique way of using language, a person's ideolect. Trask (1993) defines ideolect as 'the speech of a particular individual,' while Barthes suggests that a person's ideolect denotes an interpersonal use of language. There are a number of factors that influence and combine to create a person's unique ideolect. In Chapter 5 we explore this concept further.

3.8 Summary

In this chapter we have presented a view of learning language that goes beyond merely learning the structural elements of a linguistic system. We have suggested that learning language is essentially a socially oriented process and that language is learnt in the company of others. Further, we have suggested that learning language is also linked with wider cultural and cognitive processes and that the young child uses language as a tool for social and cognitive functions. So far we have built up a picture of learning language(s) as activity that is embedded within a range of contexts and situations with the individual inextricably linked to their immediate and wider environment. The next chapter explores some of the origins that have influenced these ideas.

Points to ponder

- Describe a person you know whom you consider to be a maximally gifted speaker.
- Consider what it is that contributes to this.
- Would you or your family or friends consider you to be a maximally gifted speaker?
- If not, what would you need to learn to change this perception?
- Draw a diagram of the embedded contexts of situation in which you are currently living.
- Consider groups to which you currently belong. How appropriate are these descriptions of speech community in these groupings?
- Consider Figure 3.1. What elements of influence would you include in each of these intersecting spheres as contributory factors in the creation of your own ideolect. If possible compare your own list with that of a member of your family or a friend or peer. Discuss the areas of overlap and difference.

3.9 Further reading

Bates, E. 1976: *Language and context: the acquisition of pragmatics*. Orlando, FL: Academic Press.

Daniels, H. (ed.) 1996: *An introduction to Vygotsky*. London: Routledge.

Hymes, D. 1995: *Ethnography, linguistics, narrative inequality: toward an understanding of voice*. London; Washington, DC: Taylor and Francis.

In this book Dell Hymes has revisited, enlarged and re-contextualized some of his leading essays, written over the last two decades, into a volume which addresses the contribution that ethnography and linguistics make to education, and the contribution that research in education makes to anthropology and linguistics. The first section presents a historically grounded view of the role of ethnography in education, and pinpoints those characteristics of anthropology that make most difference to research in education. The second section provides a view of the engagement of language in social life in relation to recognizing and overcoming inequality, with a corresponding critique of the limitations of linguistics and anthropology in this regard. The third section takes up discoveries about narrative, where ethnography and linguistics converge, and shows that young people's narratives may have a depth of form and skill that has gone largely unrecognized. This important volume illuminates Hymes's research as a whole; gives insights into current agendas and issues; and points to new areas for further research. You may want to browse through this volume when considering ideas for your own research project.

Ninio, A. and Snow, C.E. 1996: *Pragmatic development*. Boulder, CO: Westview.

Ochs, E. and Scheiffelin, B. 1979: (eds). *Developmental pragmatics*. New York: Academic Press.

4

A social view of language learning

Question: Mr González, can you read and write and understand the English language?
Answer: Sí

(Richard Lederer)

In the previous chapters we have discussed different descriptions of learning language. The aim of this chapter is to outline in more detail one particular view of language learning in the tradition of systemic functional linguistics (SFL). In order to understand how SFL has developed it is important to consider the origins of these ideas on which it is based In Chapter 3 we outlined the various academic fields including, anthropology, sociology, psychology and philosophy that have influenced current understanding of how children learn language(s). The socially motivated SFL description of language development has its origins in the eclectic multidisciplinary approach. It has grown from the ideas of the ethnographic anthropologist, Malinowski and the linguist J. R. Firth both of whom viewed language as action. They view language as realizing social acts in the context of situations and cultures. Malinowski's view (1923/55: 310) is that in society, language performs certain functions in the everyday lives of the people who live within that society. He explains these language functions in the following three ways:

1 Language realizes action for example, one social action that he describes is handing someone a utensil or instrument and then instructing a person how to use it.

2 Language expresses social and emotional functions. It expresses how people act and how they feel;

3 Language realizes phatic communion. Members of a society create 'ties of union' through small talk, exchanging greetings, gossip and other ways for the purpose of social lubrication, getting along together, being a group or community.

Consider your own daily use of language and provide examples of each of these three functions that Malinowski describes.

Malinowski's distinctions can be regarded as the first classifications of social activities grouped according to their function. He identified three broad functions:

1 service encounters

2 social/emotional genres

3 casual conversations.

For Malinowski (1923/66: 307) 'a statement spoken in real life, is never detached from the situation in which it has been uttered . . . the utterance has no meaning except in the context of situation'. He first expressed these ideas through a description (1923/66: 310–11) of a fishing activity, describing how it unfolds contextually as a social process, with each stage expressing symbolic value and expressing meaning. This description was extremely influential and is now established as a cornerstone of sociolinguistic thought and description. In this description Malinowski regards fishing as a text. Within the text he describes an ordered sequence of events that are generic to the structure of other fishing texts. So from a particular description of one fishing activity he abstracts a general description of all fishing activities. This he does in two ways. Firstly, by showing how fishing, a social activity, unfolds as a generic structure and secondly, by outlining how register (language) choices are made in each structural element of this social activity. This description is the foundation of what we now know as genre and which shall describe fully in Chapter 7. As a framework it has been applied to language use in other specific contexts, for example the classroom (Sinclair and Coulthard 1975); the courtroom (Berk-Seligson 1990) and more recently to describe telephone interactions that take place in a particular type of workplace, call centres (Cameron 2000).

Malinowski's description of generic patterning or genre can be used as a framework for describing other social events in given contexts. For example, it can be used to show how language as social activity unfolds as a generic structure as a text. This it does in a number of ways: by showing the participants' orientations to the relevant institutions and objects with which and in which they are participating. SFL (Systemic Functional Linguistics) now terms this the 'field'. Also, within that text, by revealing the relations between the participants (what SFL terms the 'tenor') and by demonstrating how communications channels (what SFL terms the 'mode' or register/language choices) are selected in each structural element or stage of the evolving genre. At each stage in the unfolding of the social action there are changes which are recognized as having 'linguistic consequences'. Malinowski (1923/66: 311) suggests that 'linguistic material is . . . dependent upon the course of activity'. The activities unfold in contexts and thereby organize the linguistic materials within the text. The activities also determine the register choices or modes that can be made at each stage in the unfolding of the genre. Register choice or language choice, therefore plays an integral role in the construct of social situations. Although Malinowski's origin description was of monolingual speakers, it is possible to extend his description. In making choices from the linguistic repertoire, each individual makes a series of selections or judgements about what is appropriate. The degree of overt control, or conscious selection that we have over this selection is uncertain. The choices have for most people become embedded in their intuitive knowledge, as described in Chapter 1. Those who know more than one linguistic system, bilinguals or multilinguals, select their mode, tenor and register from their personal linguistic repertoire, which comprises all of the languages they know and even combinations of these systems. This practice is established within the literature as codeswitching and will be discussed in feature detail in Chapter 5. The expanded linguistic repertoire of those who know more than one language provides a wider linguistic range from which they can make their choices. The same principle applies to monolinguals who have different styles of speaking within their repertoire. It is probably true to suggest that all people have a broad linguistic repertoire from within which they make choices about what they say, how they say it and indeed, whether they participate at all in certain interactions.

You should reflect on your own linguistic repertoire. What styles of speaking can you identify for your range of interactions?

4.1 A socially situated view of language

Malinowski's original concept of context of situation was developed and elaborated by J. R. Firth. Central to the Firthian view is the actual language text (1968: 173). This has two central tenets. The first is that text should be considered as a constituent part of the context of its situation and the second is that a text 'should be related to an observable and justifiable grouped set of events in the run of experience' (1968: 175). In an expanded description of the first tenet, Firth describes meaning as being created at two complementary levels, the contextual and the linguistic. Therefore, the initial step in the study of a text is to establish situational relations. Firth describes how a text is a constituent feature of the context in which it occurs. His description comprises categories that function in the context of a given situation. For example he establishes the situational relations as:

1 who the participants are in the interaction;
2 what the relevant objects and events are and;
3 what effect the verbal interaction has.

For those interested in describing language use, once these contextual questions have been addressed, then the analysis of a specific text can begin. Firth (1968: 27) suggests that step-by-step analyses are essential because the meanings of texts, utterances and words 'cannot be achieved at one fell swoop by one analysis at one level'. It is important to note that the study of the relations between contextual categories and language is regarded by Firth as the study of semantics (1968: 27). These have been interpreted by linguists in diverse ways. However, there is consensus regarding at least one aspect, namely that the order of the analyses matters less than the agreement that all levels will be included in the analysis. Firth maintains that focus on discrete features will not lead to full understanding of the situation, the interlocutors nor the language used. Firth (1968: 174) likens the meanings derived from the various levels of analysis to the 'light of mixed wavelengths in the spectrum' and only multiple analyses of texts can capture this dispersion. To continue with Firth's metaphor, each level of analysis is seen as shedding light on the meaning of the text; hence descriptions of language development that focus on only one aspect of language for example, the MLU, morphemes, or the grammatical structure, while interesting and important, can only be partial.

   Firth's (1968: 200) linguistic analysis recognizes two general theoretical relations, syntagmatic and paradigmatic. The syntagmatic relations specify how meanings in texts are composed by language forms or structures. They are realized at various linguistic levels within the text, for example, the phonological, the syntactic, the lexical, and so on. However, the paradigmatic relations are established between features of the systems such as the, 'as much', 'this . . . car'. They specify the values of the elements within the structures. Firth's second central tenet is the concept of renewal. His view is that when individuals are involved in a social event they are realizing a social process linguistically. They are behaving as members of their speech community. They are able to relate the ongoing text in which they are participants to previous texts which they have already experienced, either as observers or as active participants. Any current text under negotiation, renews the connection with the linguistic events of similar situational contexts, within a given speech community. This notion has been expanded and developed as 'intertextuality'.

This concept of typeness or genre has implications for understanding children's early language learning, particularly since while learning language the child is simultaneously being socialized into a specific cultural context. Social encounters are therefore viewed as social processes, which unfold as generic structures, step-by-step, each element contributing to the nature and function of the social process, which it is creating. Once a text renews connection with other texts, it can be linguistically stated as a text of a similar or dissimilar type. In this way individuals can learn to behave linguistically appropriately in a range of contexts. The ways in which individuals anticipate social events (or indeed other people and their behaviour) in terms of previous experiences of similar contexts, events and situations, has been described by Bartlett (1932) as 'schema' and by Tannen (1979) as 'structures of expectation'. These have been described more fully in Chapter 3. These features provide the background for SFL descriptions of language use and development. Halliday built on these ideas in specific and important ways.

4.2 The Hallidayan description of language as socio-semiotic

The Malinowskian-Firthian tradition establishes the study of language as social interaction and communication within heterogeneous speech communities. Continuing in this tradition Halliday (1973,1975), proposed discourse as semantic choice in social contexts. His view of language extends beyond an individual's language production, to a description of language as social fact (Halliday, 1977). In 1978 Halliday proposed the formulation of language as socio-semiotic. Rooted in the linguistics of

Malinowski and Firth, language as socio-semiotic presents language as functioning as an expression of and metaphor for, the social processes which it creates and the social contexts in which it occurs. Inherent in the socio-semiotic approach to language description is the notion of language as a dynamic process. Hence, a whole range of modes of meaning are possible (from the concrete to the creative) because language not only facilitates everyday social encounters and supports social action, but it actually creates those contexts.

A socio-semiotic description accounts for the fact that people talk to each other and that language is not sentences but is connected utterances between interlocutors known as discourse. That is naturally occurring and interactive. It allows for an exchange of meaning in interpersonal contexts and between contacts. The contexts where meanings are exchanged cannot therefore be devoid of social or personal values. Contexts cannot be value free. Language cannot be context free. Therefore, language cannot be value free. The context of speech becomes a semiotic structure, taking its form from the culture (or sub-culture) in which it occurs, embracing its mores, traditions and values. This form enables the participants to predict prevailing features of the register. Each society and its sub groups, has its own underlying rules, which govern acts of communication within its speech community. These rules, for appropriate linguistic behaviour, are learnt. Learning a new language is learning how to behave linguistically in a new culture. Learning a first (or subsequent) language requires understanding how everyday social encounters are organized linguistically within that speech community. Thus, individuals who have successfully learnt the rules are able to present themselves as *bona fide* members of that (speech) community. These rules and language behaviours have to be learnt. It is through the processes of socialization, education and enculturation that young children learn to be commicatively competent within the speech community of their family, friends and neighbourhood.

The linguistic tradition as established by Malinowski and Firth and developed by Halliday later became known as British Contextualism and more recently the Hallidayan tradition of Systemic Functional Linguistics or SFL. This approach to language description holds meaning as a socially constructed activity. It supports the view that a descriptive account of context is integral to linguistic descriptions, and that language as social semiotic describes discourse as the semantic choices made by speakers (or discourse participants) to create social contexts in and through their interactions. SFL descriptions of language emphasize the central importance and symbiosis of language and social action and has been concerned with describing how the organization of language is related to its social use. Martin and others suggest that language and social context are semiotic systems in realization with one another. Social context comprises patterns of language patterns.

Halliday is widely regarded by many as the founder of the systemic functional linguistics (SFL) school of linguistic description. Central to the Hallidayan linguistic description of language as socio-semiotic is the notion of language as a dynamic process which not only facilitates social encounters and supports social action but which actually creates those social contexts. Semiotically speaking all social contexts consist of a construct of potential meanings. A socio-semiotic description of a social context needs to account for the social fact that people speak to each other, not in sentences but in naturally occurring, interactive, connected exchanges (discourse). Discourse allows for an exchange of meanings in interpersonal contacts in social contexts. Discourse creates the social context and thus creates the potential for individuals to exchange meanings and create personal encounters. The socio-semiotic description of language use therefore allows for language to create social contexts and personal encounters. To accept both Halliday's description of language as socio-semiotic allows for the possibility that each individual can play an instrumental role in constructing a social context and construing meaning therein. Halliday suggests that language develops to serve needs 'which exist independently of language as features of human life at all times and in all cultures' (Halliday 1975: 32). Halliday's description of language learning is therefore founded in his work developing and extending the systemic functional grammar. His description of language development is based on the detailed observations of his son, to whom he gives the pseudonym, Nigel, learning the English language. Halliday's description has come to be known as language as socio-semiotic.

Some systemic linguists go beyond this. SFL is centrally concerned with demonstrating the ways in which the organization of language is related to the use of language. Martin (1997a: 04) suggests that SFL is concerned with modelling language and social context as semiotics systems that co-exist in a relationship of mutual influence. This he terms, 'realization'. Lemke (1995) suggests that the social context comprises 'patterns of language patterns' and he uses the term 'metaredound' for this complex relationship of realization, whereby language construes the social context, is construed by the social context, and over time reconstrues the social context. Figure 4.1 is frequently used to demonstrate this view of language as creating the context.

SFL treats the organization of language (as social context) as functionally diverse. Martin (1997) models this diversification through three types of linguistic resources which he terms 'metafunctions': These are:

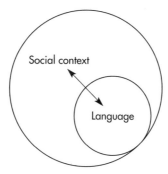

Figure 4.1 Language as the realization of social context (Christie & Martin 1997: 04)

1 the ideational linguistic resources that are concerned with the representation;
2 the interpersonal linguistic resources concerned with interaction and
3 the textual linguistic resources concerned with the flow of information.

SFL takes the view that this intrinsic functional organization is projected onto the context of the interaction, redounding with three variables:

1 the field which focuses in institutional practices;
2 the tenor which focuses on social relationships and
3 the mode which focuses on the channel of communication.

Martin frequently presents this interrelationship as in the following diagram.

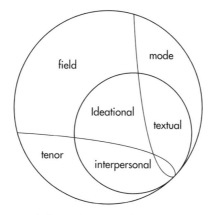

Figure 4.2 The functional diversification of language and social context (Christie & Martine 1997: 05)

The inner circle of language in Figures 4.2 and 4.3 present a stratified model of discourse, with semantics (meanings) metaredounding with lexico-grammar (the lexis or words and the grammar combined), metaredounding in turn with phonology and graphology. Again this complex interrelationship is frequently presented as a diagram:

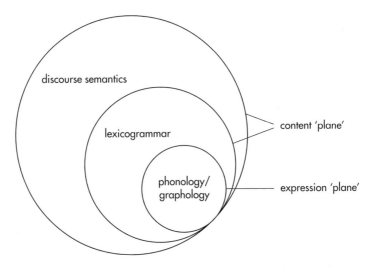

Figure 4.3 Stratification within language as metaredundancy (Christie & Martin 1997: 06)

The theoretical framework of linguistic thinking as described here briefly (and probably over simplified) is important to grasp because it has several implications for the descriptions of how children learn language and how language development continues over time. SFL places context as integral to language use, for function and hence description. This poses interesting challenges for the researcher. For example, Painter (1985) in her description of her son Hal's language development, abandoned tape-recordings as a viable means of data collection for the first 12 months of Hal's language learning because she considered the actual sounds that Hal was making to be less significant that the contextual factors in which these sounds were made. Further, the SFL description suggests that meaning is being created through four planes of interaction. These are:

1 the organization and structure of the utterance;
2 each utterance in relation to previous utterances (including significance silences);
3 the wider social cultural context and
4 the structure of the genre.

It is clearly not possible to capture and record all of these planes of interactions through audio-taped recordings. In order to understand what a child is actually learning and how the child is learning language, it therefore becomes necessary to include more than just the child's utterances in any analytical description if it is to be useful. In trying to come to a deeper understanding of a child's learning language it is necessary to take into account aspects of the context(s) in which the child is being raised, as well as the immediate context of situation as well as the utterance(s) the child is creating. This of course includes the sounds that the child actually makes but it also requires a focus on less tangible features as well. These will include features such as an implicit understanding of the linguistic and social expectations associated with a particular genre, the child's understanding, implicit and explicit recognition of fellow interlocutors, and then the organization and structure of the utterances which the child is creating with others. All of these factors are important in understanding how the young child comes to learn language. Yet these factors, when combined, make the study of language development a highly complex activity. However, to approach the study of language development in this way suggests that accounts of children's learning language can make an important contribution to current understanding of the nature of language. Two of the most important studies into individual children's spoken language development from within the SFL perspective to date are of Halliday's own son, Nigel and Painter's son, Hal. Other descriptions within the framework include Hasan and Cloran's (1990) description of mother–child interactions and Derewianka (1995) *Language development in the transition from childhood to adolescence: the role of grammatical metaphor*. There are also studies of children learning to read and these include Thompson's (1996) description of parent–child book sharing activities.

4.3 Halliday's description of Nigel learning how to mean

Halliday's analytic description of language development is based on the study of one child, his son, 'Nigel'. It is based on Nigel's language from when he was aged nine months (0;9) until he was two-and-a-half years old. The description is essentially socially orientated and differs from cognitive descriptions in that it stresses the fact that language develops because the child is driven by the social need to interact with other people. Halliday suggests that language develops to serve needs 'which exist independently of language as features of human life at all times and in all cultures' (Halliday 1975: 32). Halliday's description is a sociolinguistic description 'in which the learning of the mother tongue is interpreted as a process of interaction between the child and other human beings' (Halliday 1975: 5–6).

In his description of learning the English language, Halliday reports three phases of development. Central to all phases is the link between the sounds of the language (the tones or pitch contours that are defined within the phonology), the structure or form of the language and the subsequent meanings that are created through these forms. This, Halliday argues, is evident in the very first utterances of baby talk. This view can be summarized as sounds that take increasingly systematic structures or forms to create meaning(s):

Sound → form → meaning(s)

Phase 1 the child language phase

Phase I is a two-level or bi-stratal system monologue, comprising sounds and meanings but without words and structures. The meanings are derived from the social function of interaction with others. These functions include satisfying basic needs. Halliday describes Phase 1 of his framework as the child language/protolanguage phase which he suggests typically extends between 0;8 to 1;4, although Thomas Lee's study of children in Hong Kong (discussed in Chapter 1) may necessitate reconsideration of this age range. The transition from child language to protolanguage combines language learning closely with other aspects of the child's physical development. It is associated with a greater freedom of movement that the child enjoys on becoming a little more independent, crawling and moving around alone with some degree of autonomy from others. It is the stage when the child is beginning to construe their own personal signs that they have developed and used to convey meanings into a more general sign system representing that of the family and community in which the child is being raised. These meanings develop around seven recognizable functions that help the child to get things done. Halliday describes them as 'microfunctions'.

Phase I: seven microfunctions of the protolanguage/ child language

1 Instrumental
General demand
Specific demand

2 Regulatory
General command
Specific or intensified command

3 Interactional
General Greeting
Personalized Greeting

4 Personal
Learning
Expression of feelings

5 Heuristic
Initiation
Response   acknowledgement
imitation

6 Imagination   Pretend play
Jingle
Rhyme

7 Informative (In later studies Halliday expressed the opinion that this feature of protolanguage came later than the others).

Phase II

Pragmatic
Mathetic

Phase III

Interpersonal
Ideational
Textual

Characteristics of Phase I systems

At this stage the small child can do quite a lot with language in relation to his or her total behaviour potential. The child can use language to satisfy their material needs, to obtain goods or services (instrumental), to exert control over the behaviour of others (regulatory), to establish and maintain his own individuality and self-awareness (personal).

Phase II the transition to the adult system – uses of language

Phase II 6–9 months marks the transition from monologue into dialogue or into the tri-stratal adult system of language. This is the lexico-grammatical level of sounds and meanings. It is accompanied by the mastery of the principle of dialogue, the adoption and assignment of speech roles. Phase II is further marked by Nigel's set of social functions, language as learning and learning as doing. This description concurs with Leopold's earlier studies. Halliday suggests that at this stage vocabulary and grammar are in principle the same thing. What emerges at this point is the grammar, in the traditional sense of the term, as a level of linguistic form (the lexico-grammar stratum) that combines the structure (grammatical system) with the lexicon (vocabulary). At this phase the child has options and choices in the use of the grammatical system. These choices can be realized as structure and lexis, with lexis expressing the more specific choices. At this stage Nigel is reported to have between 80–100 meanings in his linguistic repertoire.

Phase II 6–9 months or into to the adult system is characterized by two main advances towards the adult linguistic system. It marks the transition from monologue into dialogue. On the one hand the child adds a grammar, a level of linguistic form (syntax and vocabulary) as an intermediate between content and expression, and in doing so is developing towards the tri-stratal (3-level) organization of adult language. These developments in Phase II are also accompanied by the child's mastery of the principle of dialogue, the adoption and assignment of speech roles between the interlocutors. Phase II is further marked by Nigel's initial set of social functions, language as learning and learning as doing. For the child the grammar is a system of potential, a network of options that is capable of receiving from the content level and transmitting to the level of expression. The child is also learning through dialogue, how to interact with others. The child learns to adopt, accept and assign linguistic roles and then to measure linguistic success in linguistic terms. From now on, success no longer consists of obtaining the desired object, for example, but but becomes playing one's part in the dialogue. Phase II can be considered complete when the child has successfully learnt the principles of the grammar of dialogue, that is learning the rules to interact with others. When this happens the child is ready to pass to Phase III and into the adult language system.

Phase III: into the language functions of the adult system

When Nigel entered Phase III the adult system, he is beginning to build up the meaning potential of the adult language. Once begun this continues throughout life. Central to this description of language development is the concept of function. The original social functions survive in the concrete sense as types of situation and setting. These are the settings and contexts in which language serves in the transmission of the culture to the child. There are a number of key features of a SFL description of learning language that differ from the nativist, innate theorists. These are:

1 the emphasis on language learning in relation to all other learning tasks
2 a stress on environmental conditions
3 a focus on the child and
4 the inter-relatedness of social, emotional and intellectual learning with language learning.

It is possible to summarize the ways in which SFL differs from other descriptions. SFL models of language describe language in functional terms to explain types of language use. SFL incorporates a basic distinction between an ideational (representational, reverential, cognitive, denotative) and an interpersonal (expressive-cognitive, evocative, connotation) function of language. In Phase III the adult phase, the learner can build up the meaning potential of the adult language repertoire, and will continue to do so throughout life. Adult language is structured around the two-way distinction of ideational and interpersonal. The grammar of adult language is a tripartite network of options, deriving from two basic functions the ideational and the interpersonal, together with a third, which is that of creating a text or textual function.

Halliday's claim is that children progress from the functional pattern of Phase I linguistic system, to the ideational-interpersonal system of adult language through the systematic use of intonation or pitch contours. The important point to note is that at this phase of development, the child is not using the intonation as it is used by adult English speakers. This full range of adult meaning potential is still outside the child's functional potential but the child is adapting the elementary opposition between rising and falling tones which he or she knows to be significant. So the child, operating within a functional system bounded by the limitations of his/her own (very limited) experiences is described by Halliday as using a rising tone (↑) for pragmatic functions, or for language as doing, and using a falling tone (↓) for language as learning. These two together do not describe the full linguistic repertoire of the young child. There is a further function, described by Halliday as the imaginative function. This includes pretend play and language play. Language such as singing, reciting nursery rhymes or well known jingles and slogans are examples of the imaginative function of language. These have very specific intonation patterns of their own and may be recognized by their intonation pattern alone.

By the end of Phase II, the child has entered the adult language by building up a system that is tri-stratal comprising content, form, expression and which is multi-functional functioning as ideational, inter-personal and textual. In short, the child has begun to learn how to mean. This is the core foundation of language development and it is interesting to note the relatively young age at which the monolingual child has learnt to do this in one linguistic system. Phonological contours or tones are central to the creation of meaning potential. The five tones of the English language that Halliday describes are listed below. Each tone can be tran-scribed using a very simple system. You may want note the symbols for transcribing each of the tones for use in the transcription and analysis of the data for your project.

Halliday's symbols for tones

Tone 1	falling	↓
Tone 2	rising	↑
Tone 3	level	——
Tone 4	fall–rise	∨↗
Tone 5	rise–fall	∧↘

In summary it can be said that the Hallidayan view of learning language involves:

1 learning how to mean
2 creating meanings
3 learning vocal sounds that perform linguistic and communicative functions
4 learning to produce and understand intonation (or tones) as these perform linguistic functions and are central to meaning.

Halliday's model of language development as a process of developing meaning potential and learning to mean emphasizes the social dimension of language learning. Halliday's description of Nigel learning language was the first within the SFL framework. Since that pioneering study other descriptions have emerged. Amongst the most detailed is that by Painter of her son Hal.

4.4 Painter's description of language as a resource for learning

A later study by Painter (1999) of her second son Stephen extends and complements the functional, social aspects of learning language described in the Halliday model by focusing particular attention on language as a resource for learning. From analyses of her son's use of language she suggests eighteen psychological categories of learning language. These are as follows:

1 Meaning as a system and a resource for learning
2 Naming
3 Categorizing
4 Classifying categories
5 Relational process
6 Causal links
7 Embedding
8 Overt discussion of meanings of language
9 Learning technical classifications
10 Learning from definitions
11 Learning abstract categories
12 Recalling specific incidents as generalizations

13 Over-generalizing in dialogues

14 Supporting a generalization

15 Challenging a generalization

16 Graded queries

17 Constructing a problem monologically

18 Reflective reasoning

In this summary Painter (1999) suggests an approach to understanding language learning that elaborates the SFL view described by Halliday. She suggests that what the child learns linguistically in terms of learning language(s) and that this language learning then becomes embedded as learning the actual linguistic structures. The child learns these structures without being explicitly taught the rules. Further, in her study, Painter describes the ways in which Stephen's utterances demonstrate his use of language as a tool for cognition or a resource for learning. Both Halliday and Painter suggest that language is a tool. The notion of language as a tool or resource is important because it reinforces the complementary roles of language. Language is needed for getting things done, for making things happen. Painter confirms the Hallidayan view of language as the medium of socialization and enculturation, and the means of cultural transmission. Her view is that it is with and through language that the child builds an internalized, interpersonal framework for making sense and meaning-making that creates a view of the world in which they are growing up. This internal cognitive schema is built with and through language.

Painter suggests that the child begins learning language through inter-action with others and them moves towards a more private use of language. In this way both Painter and Halliday share the Vygotskian view of language as a cognitive resource that helps the child with think-ing and understanding. Painter suggests that the child develops on from learning with others towards a greater degree of autonomy and self-suffi-ciency. This can be expressed using Vygotsky's terms, as a move from object and other-regulation towards self-regulation. It can be illustrated as a move away from the dialogic interaction towards independent monologue, as illustrated in the following figure:

DIALOGIC---MONOLOGIC

Our description of what does it mean to learn language(s) gives equal emphasis to language as a functional resource for getting things done in social contexts with language as a cognitive resource, for thinking and understanding. We emphasize language as a social and as an internalized cognitive resource for building a view of the world. We stress languages as the channel and resource, with which and through which the child learns to create and build taxonomies. In this sense language includes a number of complementary dimensions that can be summarized in the following diagram.

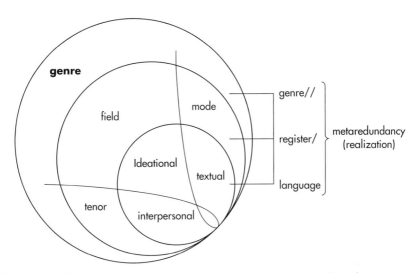

Figure 4.4 Language metaredounding with register, metaredounding with genre (Christie & Martin 1997: 08)

This description of learning language places social contexts as central to learning language. Others, including the sociologist Basil Bernstein (1971 and 1990), have shown that certain types of social context are critical to the process of cultural transmission. The language of these contexts plays a crucial role in the child's socialization and enculturation into the appropriate social and cultural behaviours of the community where the child is being raised. Halliday's description, which places all language behaviour mediated through the basic functions of language, is linked to what Malinowski termed 'context of situation'. These language functions are part of human behaviour. They lie at the heart of the linguistic system and hence can be interpreted as the 'context of culture' (to use another of Malinowski's concepts). The significance of this description is that it explains the way in which language comes to occupy a central role in the process of social and learning, as well as cognition. This may account for the fact that many critics choose to forget when they refer to Halliday's description of learning a language, and perhaps surprisingly is, the fact that intonation, a complex feature of language use, much neglected by descriptive linguistics, lies at the heart of the Hallidayan description of learning language(s).

Central to this description of language development is the concept of the social functions that are achieved with and through language. The original social functions survive in the concrete sense as types of situation and setting, the social contexts in which language serves in the transmission of culture to the child. We can now expand the list of key features unique to a systemic description of learning language presented earlier to include:

1 an emphasis on language learning in relation to all other learning tasks;
2 the stress on environmental conditions;
3 a focus on the child;
4 the importance of the meanings that the child creates;
5 language as a social activity learnt in collaboration with others.

In short, the systemic description views language as an essentially social act concerned with communication with others. Thus contexts, where the child learns how to do this and the others with whom the child learns to do this, become central to our understanding of how children learn language(s).

Halliday's systemic functional framework of how children learn language is highly significant because it attempts to go beyond a description of learning language and to link with other learning. He suggests that (1992: 01) 'when children learn language, they are not simply engaging in one kind of learning among many – rather, they are learning the foundation of learning itself'. He goes on to present his argument for accepting the ontogenesis of language as a general theory of all learning. In his 1992 paper, *Towards a language-based theory of learning*, Halliday outlines 21 features of language development to support his view and which carry implications for accepting a description of language as evidence for a more general theory of all learning as essentially the same human act of learning. These features are:

1 Symbolic acts or acts of meaning starting to construct signs.
2 Iconic (natural) symbols: constructing signs that resemble what they mean.
3 Systems of symbolic acts: organizing signs into paradigms. The stage he refers to as protolanguage.
4 The lexico-grammatical stratum constructing a three-level semiotic system that we call language.

5 Non-iconic (conventional symbols) signs that do not resemble their meanings.

6 Trailer strategy-anticipating the developmental step that is to come.

7 Magic gateway strategy finding a way into a new activity or to a new understanding.

8 Generalization → classifying → taxonomy naming classes, common terms or classes of classes.

9 The metafunctional principle-experiential and interpersonal meanings (from single function utterance, either pragmatic (doing) or mathetic (learning), to multifunctional ones, both experiential and interpersonal.

10 Semogenic strategies: expanding the meaning potential (refining distinctions) moving into new domains, deconstructing linked variables.

11 Construal of information: from rehearsing experiences that we shared to imparting experience that was not shared.

12 The interpersonal gateway: developing new meanings first in interpersonal contexts

13 Dialectic of system and process: constructing language from instances (instances of) text, constructing text from language.

14 Filtering and the challenge zone: rejecting what is out of range and working on what is accessible.

15 Probability: the quantitative foundation-construing relative frequencies.

16 Discourse: the third metafunction-construing a parallel world of semiosis.

17 Complementarities: construing experience from different angles of vision.

18 Abstraction and literacy: understanding abstract meanings and moving into the written mode.

19 Reconstruction and regression: backing off to an earlier semiotic moment while reconstructing both the content and expression.

20 Grammatical metaphor (nominalizing, technologizing); from common-sense grammar to the grammar of objects and technical hierarchies.

21 Synoptic/dynamic complementarity: reconciling two semiotic models of human experience.

This view of learning, language and other things, is important because it suggests that learning language is a lifelong activity, that begins before birth and which continues throughout childhood, adolescence into adult life and throughout the lifespan. Halliday believed that learning should be regarded as a semiotic process, as learning to mean and as expanding one's meaning potential. Having evolved the power of semiosis, humans encode all experience in semiotic terms. In chapter 5 we shall explore some examples of children's interactions and discuss them within the SFL framework of language learning outlined in this chapter.

Points to ponder

- Consider the other languages that you know. To what extent does the Halliday's descriptive framework presented here help you to understand your own processes of learning?
- To what extent do you agree with Halliday's view that understanding how children learn language will lead to a more general understanding of how people learn? Can you think of examples from your own experiences to support your views?
- Do you recognise any of Halliday's features of language development in your own linguistic repertoire?

4.5 Halliday's description of learning how to mean

At the heart of Halliday's description of learning a language is phonological contouring, a complex feature of language use that is much neglected by descriptive linguistics. Practise creating meanings using only one lexical item combined with Halliday's five tones.

Activity 1

In the box below suggest symbols or codes for each of Halliday's tones. They should be simple enough to reproduce so as to be suitable for use in analysing or coding transcripts.

Halliday (1967) tones	Direction of movement
Tone 1	
Tone 2	
Tone 3	
Tone 4	
Tone 5	

Activity 2

In pairs, practise Halliday's five tones saying the following words. Ask your partner to interpret your utterance. Begin with Tone 1

Word	Tone	Meaning
Well	1	
	2	
	3	
	4	
	5	

Word	Tone	Meaning
Hello	1	
	2	
	3	
	4	
	5	

Which do you find the most difficult:

1 to produce the tones?
2 to hear the tones?
3 to interpret the meaning(s) created?

Can you suggest reasons for this.

Activity 3

In pairs, practise Halliday's tones saying only the following words:

Yes
No
Look

Ask your response partner to interpret the meanings of your utterances.

When you have mastered this you are now ready to progress to a two word string!

Can you think of some more one or two word strings where the meanings are completely altered by the change of tones?

Activity 4

Consider the other languages that you know. Can Halliday's description be applied to them. What is an equivalent for the Chinese language and its varieties, for example? Think of examples where:

1 The application works.
2 The application is less obvious.

4.6 Summary

This chapter has considered the question what does it mean to know a language with particular reference to the work of Michael Halliday and the systemic functional linguistic descriptions of language that stress language as a tool for cognitive and social functions and as the means of social semiosis. The next chapter will present some examples of children's utterances that have been used to illustrate in more concrete ways how these ideas are evident in children's talk.

5

Learning how to 'get things done' in the first two years of life

Learning is what I'm doing when I don't know what I'm doing.

(Werner von Braun)

5.1 The beginnings

A great deal of research has been done on how infants learn to speak. Observational studies of young children learning their first words have revealed that they do not simply copy the language they hear around them. Instead, they seem to have a very specific ability to use what they hear to work out how their mother tongue(s)works, despite the fact that much of what they hear may be grammatically incomplete or incorrect. This remarkable ability enables most children to become creative language users with astonishing rapidity, producing sequences of words, which they may never have heard spoken but which conform to the basic rules of grammar. Many linguists, and psychologists use this evidence to argue that language is not simply a means of communication invented by our ancestors, but a biological product of natural selection. That is, they suggest that our capacity for learning and using language must be innate, an instinctive ability which is 'hard-wired' into the human brain (Pinker

1994). While these kinds of questions about human origins are profoundly intriguing, other linguists such as Halliday (1975, 1979), Painter (1984, 1992, 1999), Qiu, (1985), Oldenburg (1990) have investigated the living relationships between language, society and the individual. This, they would argue is no less interesting and important for understanding the human mind. Our brains may be designed for acquiring language, and language may mirror some neurological features of the brain; but, in order to become effective communicators, children have to learn a particular language and understand how it is used 'to get thing done'. Each living language is a cultural creation, which has emerged from the history of generations of a community of users. Children will only learn how to use the mother tongue, the local, specific version of the natural human communication system, by interacting with the people around them in the context of social events. We are essentially social, communicative creatures who gain much of what we know from others and whose actions are shaped by our need to deal with the practical level or everyday life, individual thinking and interpersonal communication. We use language to transform individual thought into collective thought and action (Vygotsky 1978). Indeed some of the most crucial things that ever happen to us, or that we make happen, are achieved by employing language as a tool. One of the key ideas that Vygotsky suggested we should investigate is the relationships between thought, action, communication and culture. This was why Vygotsky stressed the development of tools for the beginnings of human society and he saw language as the tool that enabled human thinking and social behaviour to become distinct from that of other creatures. This image of language as a tool is helpful because it emphasizes that language is used for practical purposes and can be adapted into many functional varieties to suit our cultural needs. So although children may have an innate ability to acquire language, there is no doubt they have a lot of learning to do about how language is used within their society (Mercer 2000).

The studies of child language we will be looking at in this chapter focus on understanding the interpersonal motives underlying the earliest stages of human engagement, when a child picks up and returns understanding, uses it to perform negotiations and dialogue-like exchanges, and learns to control and share the forms of knowledge on which parental culture depends. Trevarthen's (1979, 1980, 1983) research indicated that neonatal behaviour is significant in showing the interpersonal motives as the primary organizers of mental growth. What we mean by mental growth at this stage would be for example, focusing attention, learning to understand and the use of gestures as a means of communicating. Such activities in the development of the cognitive system and advances in its organization are therefore seen not as being independent organizing principles (as Chomsky proposes), but as open from the start to selective influences from the feelings, preferences and abilities of the infant's caregivers. Consequently, it is not the baby alone but the mother–infant dyad which needs to be closely observed, or the caregiver–infant interaction. Detailed examination of the changes in play between these two show that an affectionately reinforced trust forms a bridge, where practised refined engagements of movement are continually being carried forward to increasing subtlety and effectiveness (Trevarthen 1974, 1980, 1987). There is evidence which shows that within the first weeks or months of life, infants display a preference for attending to people over other stimuli (Field and Fox 1985; Messer 1994). For example both the facial gestures and the vocalization of infants vary depending on the interaction. The child constructs a meaningful world with the aid of persons who 'construe' things; they 'act on them, value them and interpret them' (Halliday 1978b: 92). In this construction of meanings, Trevarthen has suggested a two-stage process, primary intersubjectivity and secondary intersubjectivity. These will be detailed in the following sections.

5.2 Trevarthen's primary intersubjectivity

Psychologists have noted that within hours of birth, infants can choose to look at some things and not at others and can track a moving target with their eyes. At this stage the child is particularly interested in persons, using the sounds and /or odours of their mother to target and direct their looking (Trevarthen *et al.* 1981; Field and Fox 1985). Movements of newborns accommodate to maternal holding, respond to caresses and gentle vocalizations, and can mirror some face expressions. The movement of the hands in response to a mother's voice and facial expressions are an important feature of understanding communication and early attempts to respond, in dialogue to others.

The vocalization of newborns, too, are far from just cries demanding unspecified attention or 'pleasure' sounds, called 'coos', represent repetitions of a well-formed 'core' of controlled resonances and duration that can be related to the basic foundations for a syllable of speech (Oller 1986). Hence by six weeks after a full term birth, infants have typically, become well-consolidated in phases of consciousness alternating between alert interest in the world and self-regulating or self-nurturing withdrawal into sleep. Interactions assume a well-regulated 'protoconversational' form, both mother and infant taking, or being granted a lead in the development of exchanges (Trevarthen 1986a, 1986b).

At three months the quality of intersubjectivity steadily transforms with an alertness to the wider world, with the infant observing events increasingly remote from the body (Trevarthen, *et al.* 1981). Gradually the caregiver is no longer the only attractive event but one of several attractions, some of which are simply observed while others become potential physical substance, to be taken in hand by the infant and explored with manipulation and mouthing. This is evident in the ways in which the young infant responds to objects in their environment, such as a toy, a rattle, or the caregiver's hair. What is already important even at this early stage is that children possess an intrinsic and growing motivation to gain knowledge from others (Trevarthen and Hubley 1978). This primary intersubjectivity soon develops and extends to the infant's interest beyond the other person to take in the wider environment of the two, or secondary intersubjectivity.

5.3 Secondary intersubjectivity

The impressive change that takes place in an infant's behaviour around nine months gives the infant a capacity to combine interest in what the mother is expressing interpersonally with interest in an object to which she is referring (Trevarthan and Hubley 1978). The infant has become prepared to withdraw a private, exclusive concentration on what is happening or what this thing is and to admit that another person may be able to convey an idea for a new interest, a new thing to do, with the object. This important step allows the infant to take a gesture and a spoken message as an instruction (Bates *et al.* 1975). Before this change, the infant has no interest, no comprehension of what is wanted.

Psychoanalysts (Klein 1963; Mahler 1963) note a separation of the infant's more individuated self from the mother. In play the infant deliberately imitates, points for others' attention, pretends, takes initiatives in the game (Piaget 1962; Bruner 1981). The infant's awareness of their own actions as being of interest to others, of objects and actions on them being sharable with others, of vocalizations and gestures as messages to be addressed to others and requiring specific and intended responses from them, now makes the world a different place. As was indicated in an earlier chapter, Vygotsky (1966: 44) a general genetic law of cultural development comes into play here:

> any function in the child's cultural development appears on the stage twice, on two planes, first on the social plane and then on the psychological, first among people as an intermental category and then within the child as a instrumental category.

Vygotsky does not simply argue here that social interaction is important for development but rather that there is an inherent link between forms of social interaction and the forms of higher mental functioning. This link is inherent because of the specific mediational role of language. For Vygotsky, the reason for the key theoretical status of interaction is that it makes intellectual resources available to the child through the 'signing' in interaction. Language is an example of the most developed form of signing but not the only one. Others are hand movements such as those used in sign language or the signalling done through semaphore. Thus practices in sign usage become of critical importance to the infant's learning outcomes. Lock (1984) gives an example of Paul a nine-month-old baby whose actions were recorded on video.

Paul is in his baby-walker. His mother comes into the room holding a pair of scissors and stands 'absent minded' in front of him. She looks at Paul and raises his arms. Their interaction proceeds:

> *Mother*: OK, just a minute.
> She puts the scissors down and comes back to him. Paul has not been watching her, but is scooting across the room. She stops in front of him, and before she starts to bend down and move her arms out towards him, he raises his arms. She looks at Paul and he raises his arms.
>
> (Lock 1984: 41)

Infants are not endowed with an innate ability to raise their arms to assist another in lifting them up: an activity that infants are often partners to. It must be supposed then, in the early occurrences of this activity, the child's arms only get raised by the physical consequences of the mother pushing her arms under his armpits: Paul, himself shows no active adjustment to her behaviour. Fairly quickly the child becomes familiar with being picked up, and he begins to recognize his mother's actions towards him. This is evidenced (as indicated in the example given above) by the fact that Paul now shows anticipation of her reactions: he raises his arms himself, and does not rely passively on her efforts. He is learning to expect certain patterns of behaviour.

The final development of this communicative 'gesture' can be seen in the next example. Here arm-raising is used by Paul, not in anticipation of being picked up, but in pursuit of that goal. He makes a request:

Paul aged 10 months (six days): Paul crawls to his mother and scratches her leg while she is ironing.

> *Mother*: What do you want?
> Paul raises his arms.
> *Mother*: No, I can't pick you up now.
>
> (Lock 1984: 42–3)

Some semiotic signallings such as crying to attract attention are notoriously inefficient, mainly because too much of the message is left unsaid. Apparently in response to this problem the developing infant begins to modify his or her crying, complementing it with other, more specific, communicative actions.

Paul, aged 14 months 23 days: mother enters the room holding a cup of tea. Paul turns from his play in her direction and obviously sees this cup of tea. He cries vestigially and so attracts mother's attention; immediately he points towards her and smacks his lips concurrently.

Mother: No you can't have this one, it's Andy's.

(Lock 1984: 44)

Here crying functions both to attract attention and convey the message of the child wanting something. Pointing directs that attracted attention and informs the mother what that something is. Lip-smacking has resulted from a stylization of actually eating or drinking, and its use here leaves the mother in little doubt as to why the child wants the cup.

If we look at the developmental history of the child's ability to combine gestures we find three phases:

1 the ability to use single gestures is developed;
2 single gestures occur in sequences – the child cries and then points or raises his or her arms;
3 a period in which two or more gestures occur together – the child cries and points simultaneously.

A similar sequence is found in language development, the period of single word utterances, the occurrence to two words in sequence, and then multiword utterances. This combination of different actions is evidence of the child beginning to learn one of the fundamental skills of language but this is still not language. It is however, communication. While the child can communicate intentions in a structured manner, the messages conveyed are not objective in nature, nor are they propositional. Language is only implicit in these early communicative activities, and will remain so until the development of what Halliday (1975) and others have termed the protolanguage, a stage of language developed discussed in the previous chapter.

5.4 Protolanguage

As we have seen, from the moment of birth, the child communicates in the form of vocal gestural acts such as cries of hunger or reaching for an object. Such an act is only invested with meaning, however, when it is non-random and symbolic (Halliday 1978b). Around the age of six to nine months the child starts to use sounds as meanings in a consistent and systematic way. At this stage, the infant may employ recognizable words from the adult language or may invent his/her own expressions in order to satisfy material and emotional needs. The semantic functions served by these protolinguistic signs have been identified as 'instrumental' (to obtain material needs), 'regulatory' (to control the behaviour of others), 'interactional' (to interact with those around), 'personal' (to express interests and emotions), 'heuristic' (to find out about the world), and 'imaginative' (for pretend play).

Within each of these functions, the child develops a network of options. These can be represented in terms of a system, that is, a range of alternative choices such as the following:

Figure 5.1 Partial representation in the system of choices (after Halliday 1975: 148)

These networks of meaning are expressed directly by the soundings created by the infant. This primitive two level linguistic system may be presented as follows:

Semantic	*Phonological*
Stratum	Stratum
meanings	soundings

Figure 5.2 Two level or bi-stratal system

The two dimensional elastic space created by this process is described by Halliday as being 'rich in semogenic potential', that is to say having a considerable semiotic range but with distinct limitations. Because of the idiosyncratic nature of many of the signs, the significance of (in this case) the oral sign can often only be understood by those primary caregivers who have shared the contexts in which it has developed and are able therefore to approximate the child's semantic system. The signs themselves are context specific each sign having a single meaning. We can see this examplified in the following extract quoted by McTear from Scollon (1979).

Context	Brenda is looking straight into an electric fan with her hair blowing back.
Interaction	*Brenda:* [fẽi]
	[fœ]
Mother:	hm?
Brenda:	[fœ]
Mother:	bathroom?
Brenda:	[fanĩ]
	[faĩ]
Mother:	fan yeah
Brenda:	[kʰu]
Mother:	cool, yeah. Fan makes you cool

(McTear (1985: 11))

5.5 Into the mother tongue

From around seventeen months, the child's protolanguage undergoes a dramatic transformation. In this period, the child begins to dispense with the protolanguage and to take on the language or languages of the environment. This phase is characterized by a rapid increase in vocabulary and a differentiation between two generalized modes of meaning.

In the transition, invented expressions begin to be discarded in favour of adult-like vocabulary. The child starts to use the mother tongue or first language lexis in exploring various aspects of experience. These frequently include for example, objects, other people, qualities, actions and locations. This development enables the child to go beyond the private circle of immediate intimates, what Halliday refers to as 'the coterie of significant others', and engage with the world as construed by the wider community. In using adult-like lexical items such as 'cat', 'dog', 'bird', the child is now beginning to organize a view of the world and is beginning to create generalizations and to classify things. At this stage, the standard mother tongue lexical item is not tied to any single function or context as in the protolinguistic sign, for example when the child is wanting something (instrumental function). At the same time as this expansion of lexical resources, Painter and Halliday observed the emergence of two rudimentary speech roles: that of commenting and demanding. The difference between the two is typically achieved by the use of different intonation or phonological contours. These two changes have significant implications for the child's developing linguistic system and meaning potential. The experiential and interpersonal elements now have an independent existence and can be continuously and creatively combined and recombined in innumerable ways. The combination of a lexical item with a falling tone is interpreted as having a 'learning' function. (Halliday calls this the mathetic macrofunction, while the combination of a lexical item with a level or rising tone is interpreted as having a 'social' function (Halliday's pragmatic macrofunction).

This development of an explicit opposition between the mathetic and pragmatic modes of meaning brings with it both a continuity and discontinuity with respect to the protolanguage. The self-oriented functions (the interactional and personal) come together in the mathetic macrofunction because it is mainly concerned with using language as an instrument of learning to gain experience about the world. The other oriented functions (the instrumental and regulatory) coalesce into the pragmatic macrofunction, which is concerned with satisfaction of fundamental needs and desires through social interaction. The child's language thus becomes a resource organized around 'language for reflecting on the world' and 'language for acting upon the world'. An abstract level of wording – lexicogrammar – makes up the three level system of adult language, interpolated between the semantic and phonological levels of the two level protolinguistic system described earlier.

5.6 Moving towards an adult linguistic system

At the same time as the lexicogrammatical level is becoming consolidated as an integral part of the linguistic system, the macrofunctions are evolving into the metafunctions of the adult language. In the adult system, the mathetic and pragmatic distinction becomes the organizing principle of the abstract metafunctions – the ideational and the interpersonal.

For example in the data from Wells and Gutfreund's (1987) study, Gerald at 18 months is already naming things which reflects his growing experience of the world.

> *Gerald*: Teddy
> *Mother*: That's Teddy's bed isn't it?
>   Where's Teddy?
>   I think Teddy's downstairs
>   I don't know I think we took him with us
> > (Wells and Gutfreund 1987: 221)

The development of this linguistic system takes place within the intimate relationship of context and language. Context is seen in terms of 'context of situation' and 'context of culture'. Both these contextual perspectives are implicated in the language learning process in terms of placing demands on the learner and in terms of facilitating the learning process. The immediate contexts in which the child participates are constantly providing linguistic challenges for the developing child. The child needs to gain control over an ever expanding range of domains. In each new domain, the child is confronted with new phenomena, which need to be named in order for the experience to be shared. With this, new connections are made between phenomena, which extend and modify the child's developing taxonomies. It is in this way that the child learns. Taking into account the enriched understanding of how phenomena work, the new social roles learnt, and increasing range of roles and relationships, the child learns language and extends the meaning group. A further example from the Wells and Gutfreund study illustrates this.

> Context   Mark at 27 months is standing by a central heating
>   radiator and can feel the heat.
> Interaction *Mark*:   'Ot Mummy?
>   *Mother*: Hot? (Checking)
>   *Mark*:   Been (?= burn)
>   *Mother*: Burn? (Checking)
>   *Mark*:   Yeh
>   *Mother*: Yes you know it'll burn don't you?
> > (Wells and Gutfreund 1987: 218)

So while the child is learning language, other learning, about the world and the way things are in the world, are also developing. While the context outlined above is challenging the child, it is also supporting the child's efforts. The caregivers provide models of richly structured and highly grammatical language use. Moreover the meanings that surround the child are highly contextualized. 'The situation is the medium in which text lives and breathes' (Halliday 1975: 125). We see this happening in the following extract.

Context	Anna aged 25 months, with her older sister, Clara: mother and father are talking about dinner, and mention pizzas.
Interaction	*Clara*:
	Mother:
	Father:
	Anna:

Context   Anna aged 25 months, with her older sister, Clara: mother
             and father are talking about dinner, and mention pizzas.
Interaction *Clara*:   What are pizzas?
             Mother: They're sort of like big round pieces of bread
                        with tomatoes and bacon . . .
             Father: Do you think you'd like those?
             Anna: What pizzas?
             (Mother repeats explanation)
             Anna: Sausage, sausage . . .
             Mother: No, its not really like a sausage, no . . .
             Father: But it has sausage on it, cabanossi.
             Mother: Oh, yes that sort of sausage.
                                            (Oldenberg 1987: 375–6)

Much of our argumentation has so far indicated that language is the primary medium of socialization (Halliday 1978a). In the process of learning language, one is by implication learning systems of meanings – a semantic system together with its realizations. Each instance of text will reveal something of the underlying social system of communication. As children engage in these instances, they will be recreating the social system of their culture. In internalizing the structure of language, the child is also internalizing a particular reality as part of the same process (Halliday 1975; Oldenberg 1987; Hasan and Perrett 1994; Painter 1992). Oldenberg in her longitudinal study of her second daughter, Anna, identified a number of strategies in the process of learning systems of meaning. These are:

1. Modelling: (Anna at 26;4)

Modelling is an important aspect in the learning of language. Bloom (1991) is of the opinion that modelling or imitation as she calls it does not imply that the child is a passive learner of language but that having a model to follow is an essential part of child development. In fact that indications are according to Bloom that children are discriminatory in when they imitate, as they imitate 'only words and structures in the speech they [hear] which they [appear] to be in the process of learning' (Bloom 1991: 430).

Clara: I've got more peanut butter than you, see?
Anna: I more peanut than you.

2. Analogy (Anna at 25;21)

(Anna falls off the chair, and draws a comparison between her action and a character in a book.)

> *Anna*: Fell down wall like Tom Kitten.

3. Generalization (Anna at 27;27)

> *Anna*: (after seeing two clowns in a play knock a hole in a wall) People . . . people . . . people not allowed knock down walls. People should (accompanied by head shaking to signify negative) knock down walls.

4. Inference (Anna at 25;15)

Anna (watching mother chop vegetables) knife sharp. Let me (said with head shaking).

> Mummy (= Mummy won't let me use sharp knife).
> (Oldenberg 1987: 376)

So far our discussion has centred around children who are learning one language, English. However, monolingualism is the exception. The majority of children in the world today, grow up learning more than one language.

5.7 Bilingualism and multilingualism

Increasingly, in the modern world we can no longer talk simply about an environment with one culture but rather about cultures which reflect the heterogeneous linguistic environment of the child. Multilingual environments increase the options available to the child for new ways of thinking and learning. The actual terminology used when discussing bilingualism or multilingualism can be very misleading. Such terms as mother tongue, home language, first language, community language, and heritage language all have some element of ambiguity. Thompson (2000) in the Routledge *Encyclopedia of Language Teaching and Learning* offers the following consideration of the term mother-tongue.

> The term 'mother tongue' has a number of different meanings. Historically the term was used to refer to the first language one

acquired as a child. The origin of the term was based on the assumption that this first language would be the one spoken by the primary caregiver and this was assumed to be the mother. However, with changes and cultural differences in child-rearing practices it is not safe to assume that the primary carer will always be the mother and there have been recent objections to this definition.

As a refinement of the original meaning the following is suggested: the term *mother tongue* is the first language that the child learns and inherent in this description is the assumption that the learning takes place in a naturalistic way, that is, not through formal teaching. Synonyms for mother tongue include:

- first language, the first language the child learns to speak and understand;
- home language, the language used within the home for everyday interactions;
- family language, the language most frequently used within the family or the language used as a lingua franca between family members;
- heritage language, the language which is frequently a means of establishing and reaffirming consolidation with one's origins, though linguistic proficiency is not a prerequisite;
- community language, the language spoken by the immediate community which may be identified as the mother tongue if the mother tongue is a vernacular and less widely used or perceived as of lower status.

These synonyms illustrate the range of meanings given to the term. It is important to emphasize that the mother tongue may not necessarily be a speaker's dominant language or the one most frequently used in everyday life. The mother tongue is the language on which the speaker relies for intuitive knowledge of language, its form, structure and meaning. In the case of bilinguals and multilinguals, the mother tongue is the language chosen for complex cognitive reasoning.

Even the term bilingual can have various meanings. However, putting aside the various nomenclatures, what is of import is the realization that the balance between a child's actual and potential for the use of two (or more) language systems in their daily interaction, is not constant. The balance between the use and competence is continuously changing throughout life. The so-called first language may not remain the dominant language throughout life and may not be the preferred language of use in a wider range of contexts. The ability to code-switch (to use both systems within a communicative event becomes a dimension in the language development of bilinguals). Every conversational interaction between the child and others, whether they be the caregiver, a sibling or peer, reveals to the child not only information about language (its structures and uses, which enables the child to construe its systems), but also information about the world in which this 'languaging' is occurring.

The imposition of one language on the exchange, limits the range of communicative options that young children with multiple languages in their repertoire can demonstrate. A unique feature of the bilingual speaker's linguistic repertoire is the ability to draw on these linguistic systems in their interaction with others. It is possible to outline (see Figure 5.3) a generic pattern of language discourse based on a sequential analysis of codeswitching at the level of turn-taking.

Discourse

Option 1	Silence	(S)
Option 2	Non-verbal response	(NVR)
Option 3	Language 1	(L1)
Option 4	Language 2	(L2)
Option 5	L1 with code-switch into L2	(L1➡L2)
Option 6	L1 with two code-switches	(L1➡L2➡L1)
Option 7	L2 with code-switch into L1	(L2➡L1)

Figure 5.3 Discourse options available to the bilingual child (Thompson 1995: 11)

When discourse participants speak more than one language there is a richer range of discourse options available. Codeswitching (CS) can be regarded as a diverse linguistic resource from which an individual speaker can choose to draw in order to communicate effectively. Figure 5.4 illustrates the generic pattern of codeswitching strategies in much of the data used in this book.

Speaker 1 sets the scene with their choice of language and this will be termed the frame language (FL).

For the bilingual discourse participant (caregiver and child, child and child), the frame of language (FL) of an interaction is important as this can determine the generic pattern of discourse options which are to be made available. If we accept the argument that what has been put

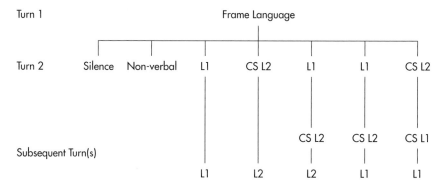

Figure 5.4 Codeswitching strategies (Thompson 1995: 15)

together by the learner are systems of meaning, then it is axiomatic that our most important learning resource is language. Using this resource for learning is to create or participate in the creation of discourse, where meaning becomes observable in its realization in both its lexical and grammatical structures. This means that the processes of learning develops higher mental functions such as the 18 psychological categories identified by Painter (1999) including naming, classifying, comparing, generalizing, making cause–effect links, hypothesizing, inferring and so on, all are most usefully seen as strategies for meaning, or reflections of our thinking processes. Access to a child's developing language is achieved through access to the child's discourse (oral or written texts). What this means is that the view of language which we are outlining in this book is a study of a child's language in use which will lead us to an understanding of a child's potential for thinking and learning.

Studies of the language of very young bilingual children are difficult to interpret for the obvious reason that meaning is still quite closely related to the immediate circumstances and a detailed knowledge of all of the language system used within the child's environment becomes crucial. In the following examples of language use Francesca was 23 months at the beginning of the study. She lived in Singapore environment which has a wide variety of languages and dialectal variations within the community. We can summarize the linguistic context of Singaporean in Figure 5.5 overleaf:

As with the monolingual, the bilingual child's language is difficult to interpret for the obvious reason that meaning is still quite closely related to the immediate circumstances and what the child is trying to say either in terms of pronunciation or semantics may not necessarily be adult-like. Nevertheless, from the earliest stages of the one word, two word utterance, indicators of the developing meaning potential of the child normally first appear, in the process of naming.

Societal level

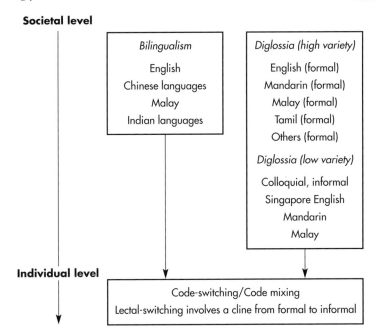

Figure 5.5 Societal and individual linguistic diversity found in Singapore

In a study undertaken by Samboo (1998) her own child, Francesca was exposed to English from birth and only later, at nine months to Malay/Bahasa Indonesian as a Indonesian maid was employed to look after her. Although both her parents were conscious of using an informal or colloquial variety of Singapore English (CSE) with the child, they did try at times to use a more standard form of Singapore English (SSE). This latter form varies little from a standard form of British or American English in its grammatical structures. However, there are some differences in lexis and more noticeably, as one would expect, in pronunciation (see Foley *et al.* 1998a). The playschool environment which Francesca attended three times a week used SSE as the predominant variety of English spoken by the teacher, but the children used CSE among themselves.

According to Painter (1984) and Oldenberg (1987), because of the close relationship between language and learning, it is possible to approximate children's growing cognitive development through the language they use. At times, Francesca uses both English and Malay, but the child is probably not separating out the languages at this stage (see Baker 1993), or understanding them as separate systems of meaning potential.

In the transcripts that follow the main interacts are Francesca and her mother. Francesca's linguistic environment includes Malay/Bahasa

Indonesia and Singapore colloquial English (SCE). There are times when the child's pronunciation is only understandable to the mother (who made the transcription). These have been rendered in standard orthographic transcription except on a few occasions where it is contextually obvious what is meant.

Extract 1: Naming

(Francesca at 23 months; 20 days)

Mother:	What colour is the elephant? What colour is this? What colour?
Francesca:	*Pupu Pupu* [meaning *kupu*: butterfly] ((pointing to a butterfly mould))
Mother:	Make pupu? Butterfly say!
Francesca:	{fi:.}

Extract 2: Francesca at 28;9

Mother:	What is this ((pointing to the picture of a plate of rice))
Francesca:	{waɪs}
Mother:	What's that?
Francesca:	Aye! Oh! What's this?
Mother:	What's that?
Francesca:	{aɪs kwɪm}

Categorizing

Francesca begins to display a limited ability to categorize according to functions, attributes, situations, associations and her experiences. In the following extract, the colour yellow reminds her of bananas; consequently she categorizes bananas as something yellow. When the mother mentions another colour, the child's focus is still on the 'bananas' and what they are for, eating.

Extract 3: Francesca at 23;20

Francesca:	((Holding yellow play-dough)) Banana
Mother:	Banana is yellow. Correct Clever girl! This is blue.
Francesca:	Banana. Eating banana.

Next, Francesca shows her growing knowledge of what birthdays are and consequently she makes a number of the logical connections. If there is a candle, it must be for a cake and if there is a cake, it must be for a birthday and therefore a birthday song must be sung!

Extract 4: Francesca at 23;20

Mother:	Do you want to make anything? ((Still using with her play-dough))
Francesca:	Candle.
Mother:	Candle? We make a candle OK?
Francesca:	OK
Mother:	OK?
Francesca:	Cake. Cook a cake.
Mother:	Make cake. There! I'm making, cooking now.
Francesca:	{Wan} cake! {Wan} cake!
Mother:	There cake! Watch mummy make a cake. See? A cake! Two cakes. See? OK make cake, make candle, come. ((Francesca had been grumbling because she wanted to make it)) Candle! There! Nice? Wait! Don't take out. Make another candle. ((F pulling candles out from the cake))
Francesca:	'Happy Birthday' (F starts to sing)).

This last extract is an example of the child using terms associated with the category of cooking. She uses terms related to the ingredients for making curry, the everyday family food. She is able to name pepper, salt, chicken, and 'pig'. Her choice of the word 'pig' gives an insight into her conceptualization of the world. She has not yet learnt to differentiate between the name given to the animal, and the name given to the animal as food. She is however, familiar with these standard lexical items. She is also aware of the activities involved in the process of preparing the food, such as 'stir'. It is clear that these terms have been learnt by the child perhaps through listening to adult conversations. It is certain that there has been no attempt to formally teach these words to the child.

Extract 5: Francesca at 28;9

Francesca:	Must cooking
Mother:	Must cooking, OK. Must cook, not cooking.
Francesca:	Must stir it.
Mother:	OK, you stir it ((F stirs the curry)).
Francesca:	Mummy stir it?
Mother:	OK. I stir it. What else do you put in curry?

Francesca:	{Chick}. . . ((chicken))
Mother:	What?
Francesca:	Put {pe} ((pepper))
Mother:	OK, put pepper?
Francesca:	You put {sot}
Mother:	You put the salt?
Francesca:	And {stI} ((stir)) cooking
Mother:	And stir it. OK, you stir it? Do you put any fish or meat into the curry?
Francesca:	Any {pI?} ((pig?))

Exophoric reference

In the following the Francesca displays her ability to refer to things and events outside of the present context. This involves a certain ability to draw analogies from her common-sense knowledge of the world around her. Sometimes this means relating to past events in order to make (the parent in this case) understand. In this first extract Francesca classifies trees as producing flowers, fruit and for climbing. She makes reference to the 'Barney' a children's television show broadcast in Singapore.

Extract 6: Francesca at 27;18

Mother:	Trees cry? No. What do trees give you?
Francesca:	{f ws}
Mother:	Flowers and ?
Francesca:	{Fru} ((Fruit))
Mother:	Fruit! Yes!
Francesca:	children {kaIm} on tree
Mother:	The children climb on the tree. Which tree?
Francesca:	Um Barney {kaIm} tree ((referring to an episode in 'Barney' where the children climbed up to the tree-house.))

Questioning

In these extracts the child questions the logic of her mother's warning or threats.

Extract 7: Francesca at 27;18

Mother:	I said don't climb on the table. Where is my cane?
Francesca:	Where mummy {can}? ((cane)) ((after having run away, knowing full well that mummy does not have a cane.))

In this next example, the child is jumping on her mother's bed and her mother is trying to stop her. The mother tries to 'reason' with the child.

Extract 8: Francesca at 25;24

Mother: Sleeping time
Francesca: {d'uwan}
Mother: Why don't want?
Francesca: {wa n} jump
Mother: I don't want you to jump. Mummy's bed will spoil.
               After got hole.
Francesca: Where hole?
Mother: After got hole. sweetie.

In this extract the Mother is using colloquial Singapore English in such expressions as 'bed will spoil. After got hole'. The child clearly understands the communicative intent and indeed asks for evidence of the 'hole' if she is to stop jumping!

Modelling

In these early stages of language development in a bilingual setting like Singapore, it is common place for the child to form language systems. We are deliberately using the term 'mix' here because there is insufficient evidence from research to date to demonstrate that the young learner is actually able to differentiate between the linguistic systems they are combining. However, they do seem to be already conscious that you speak to one person in this way and another person in that way. This corresponds to the one-person-one-language description of children becoming bilingual (Leopold 1949; Ianco-Worrall 1972; Hamers and Blanc 2000; Deucher and Quay 2000; Nicol 2001; Belcher and Conner 2001). It also follows Thompson's generic patterns of bilingual discourse outlined earlier.

In the following extract, Francesca imitates her mother speaking Malay/Bahasa Indonesia to the maid.

Extract 9: Francesca at 25;24

Mother: *Aye, dia punya* pampers *apa 'tu basah. Sangat basah*
               ((M telling the maid [Elfie] that the child's pampers are
               very wet.))
Francesca: *Sangan bas . . .*
Mother: *Sangat basah* [very wet]

Francesca:	*Basah.* dirty. Auntie Elfie!
Mother:	*Aiyoo . . .*
Francesca:	*Aiyoh!*
Mother:	*Sangat basah*, say
Francesca:	*Sangat basah*
Mother:	Means very wet

Thus there seems to be some understanding on Francesca's part of a different kind of communication taking place between her mother and Elfie, the maid.

In the following example Francesca's mother has just returned from work. Francesca is jumping on the bed and after a while the maid is called in to make her take a nap.

Extract 10: Francesca at 25;24

Mother:	Auntie Elfie make you sleep. Mummy also want to sleep. Then evening Papa come, Mummy play with you in the evening, OK?
Francesca:	Jump, jump, jump, jump
Elfie:	Hello *Main* ball *tadi ya, sama* Elfie? [you play ball with Elfie just now, ya?]
Mother:	Aiyoh, sangat keringat [You're so sweaty]
Elfie:	*Ya*
Mother:	*Busuk! Awak busuk* Armpit all *busuk* [Smelly! You're very smelly. You're armpits are smelly] ((Mother starts tickling Francesca))
Mother:	*Busuklah*, you
Francesca:	*Suklah* you
Mother:	*Busuklah*
Elfie:	*Sobayo* ((Elfie misunderstands Francesca)) ((Mother asks Elfie if the towel she is using to wipe F is a fresh one))
Francesca:	*Kaki* [leg] ((when Elfie wipes her feet)).
Elfie:	*Kaki*
Mother:	*Hitam. Hitam* [black. black] ((referring to F's feet))
Francesca:	*Hitam*
Mother:	Eh, you *makan banyak* [You eat a lot?]
Francesca:	***
Mother:	*Makan banyak?*
Francesca:	*Makan man. . .*
Mother:	*Sudah banyak?* [Too much?]
Francesca:	*Sudah manyak* ((M laughs at Francesca's mistaken pronunciation)).

However, it is not yet clear at what stage the young learner is actually able to make conscious or considered options in their choice of language. Children frequently use chunks of language or formulaic expression that they have learnt but which they do not fully understand, either literally or the implicature.

Formulaic expressions

Young children frequently use abstract categories such as numbers, time and so on, but these are frequently formulaic, learnt through exposure to the language and other people's usage, rather than explicitly taught. However, this formulaic learning is an important stage in language development. Examples of learning formulaic language include the rote learning of numbers. Children also learn songs, nursery rhymes and other rhythmic jingles in this way. Once learnt by heart they are frequently recited. In the case of numbers or days of the week, they can provide a useful first step in learning abstract concepts. The following exchange between Francesca and her mother suggests evidence of this formulaic stage of language development.

Extract 11: Francesca at 23;20

((Francesca is breaking up the various bits of play-dough))

Mother:	You're pinching them into bits, is it? OK, how many do you have there? Four?
Francesca:	Four
Mother:	Five now five
Francesca:	Six
Mother:	Give me that please. Six
Francesca:	Seven.
Mother:	Seven
Francesca:	Eight
Mother:	Eight. Clever girl.
Francesca:	Nine
Mother:	Nine
Francesca:	Ten
Mother:	Ten. No still ten. Then else . . .?
Francesca:	{.'.ven}, too
Mother:	Eleven
Francesca:	Twelve.
Mother:	Twelve
Francesca:	Fourteen
Mother:	Fourteen? Twelve. Thirteen, say? After twelve is thirteen
Francesca:	Fourteen

Mother:	Thirteen
Francesca:	One (F starts pinching from the yellow play- dough ball)
Mother:	Now the yellow one. OK one.
Francesca:	{twooooo}
Mother:	Two
Francesca:	Three
Mother:	You're mixing the colours already.

The above extracts demonstrate Francesca's language development. She is in the process of learning more than one language system. These interactions also serve to demonstrate Halliday's claim that while children are learning language they are also learning *through* the medium of the language. Hence language learning, for the young child, is central to developing cognition. In these extracts and exchanges Francesca is demonstrating her cognitive development in the strategies of: naming, categorizing, exophoric reference, questioning, modelling formulaic phrasing and accommodating her speech to different interlocutors. She is also demonstrating her ability to use the two language systems that she is in the process of learning. By accommodating to the maid, Elfie, Francesca switches from a Singapore variety of English to Malay/Bahasa Indonesia, thereby demonstrating an understanding that not all people use the same language.

Many of Francesca's in these extracts are formulaic, for example, the counting episode. However, young children learn through observation in their daily lives and through participation in ongoing activities. These routines facilitate learning and support language development. These extracts demonstrate the range of meaning potential achieved through relatively limited linguistic resources of a child aged between 23 to 28 months. Although somewhat limited by comparison with the adult repertoire, Francesca is displaying her ability to use the language as a resource to convey her messages and intentions to those around her and to thereby participate in the world in which she is learning to live her life.

5.8 Summary

Studies of young children learning their first words have shown that they do not simply copy the language they hear around them. In fact, they have a very specific ability to use what they hear to work out how their mother tongue(s)works. This ability enables most children to quickly become creative language users. Many linguists, and psychologists use this evidence to argue that language is not simply an invented means of communication, but that our capacity for learning and using language must be innate, an instinctive ability which is 'hard-wired' into the human brain. Other researchers have investigated the living relationships between language, society and the individual. They would argue that our brains may be designed for acquiring language, but, in order to become effective communicators, children have to learn a particular language and understand how it is used 'to get thing done'. Each living language is a cultural creation, which has emerged from the history of generations of a community of users. Children will only learn how to use the mother tongue – the local, specific version of the natural human communication system – by interacting with the people around them in the context of social events. Children are essentially social creatures who gain much of what they know from others. Some of the most crucial things that happen to children, or that children make happen, are achieved by employing the tool of language. Vygotsky's image of language as a tool is a helpful one because it emphasizes that language is used for practical purposes. Children may have an innate ability to acquire the language(s) of their home environment, but they still have a lot of learning to do about how to use language in particular ways within the community.

From the very earliest stages of a child's life we see the child trying to convey specific messages to the caregiver through the combination of different actions. In fact if we look at the developmental history of the child's ability to combine gestures we can discern three phases. The first phase is one in which the ability to use single gestures is developed. A second phase is where single gestures occur in sequences. Finally, there is a period in which several gestures occur together. A similar sequence is found in language development, the one-word-at-a-time stage, the two words in sequence and then multiword utterances. The indication is that the same system of communication is being developed for gesture and wording. In others words the child through gestures at this early stage is already mastering some of the fundamental skills of language.

As children get older they develop the more sophisticated communication system we call language. But it is a communication system, which fits into a context of use, initially within the family setting. In the process of learning the words and structures of the language or languages of the home, children are also invisibly learning the ways of being, doing and interpreting that are the ways of that particular community.

By around two and a half, the child will have developed the framework of the adult language system (Halliday 1978a) and for the subsequent years the system will be expanded to develop what Bernstein (1975: 99) characterized as the 'commonsense' knowledge of the home. That is to say that language provides the means of thinking together, for jointly creating knowledge and understanding. The inherent, open-ended flexibility and ambiguity of language makes it a very different

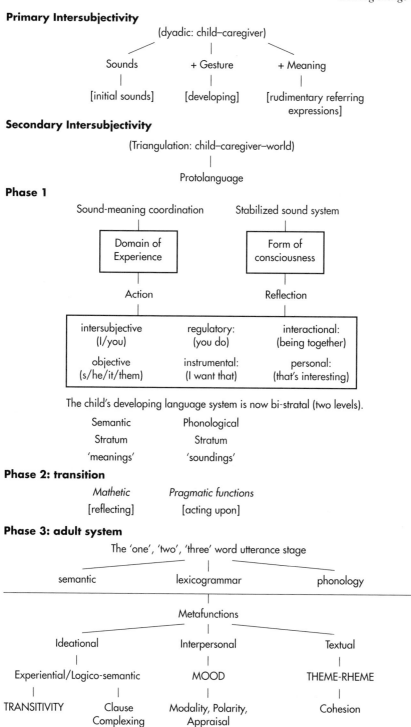

Primary Intersubjectivity

(dyadic: child–caregiver)

Sounds   + Gesture   + Meaning

[initial sounds]   [developing]   [rudimentary referring
expressions]

Secondary Intersubjectivity

(Triangulation: child–caregiver–world)

Protolanguage

Phase 1

Sound-meaning coordination   Stabilized sound system

Domain of
Experience

Form of
consciousness

Action   Reflection

| intersubjective (I/you) | regulatory: (you do) | interactional: (being together) |
| objective (s/he/it/them) | instrumental: (I want that) | personal: (that's interesting) |

The child's developing language system is now bi-stratal (two levels).

Semantic   Phonological
Stratum   Stratum
'meanings'   'soundings'

Phase 2: transition

Mathetic   *Pragmatic functions*
[reflecting]   [acting upon]

Phase 3: adult system

The 'one', 'two', 'three' word utterance stage

semantic   lexicogrammar   phonology

Metafunctions

Ideational   Interpersonal   Textual

Experiential/Logico-semantic   MOOD   THEME-RHEME

TRANSITIVITY   Clause
                Complexing

Modality, Polarity,
Appraisal

Cohesion

Figure 5.6 Summary of the stages of language development into the mother tongue

communication system from that of animals. It is not simply a system for transmitting information. It is a system for thinking collectively. Language is used for creating knowledge, so that language and the knowledge we create with it are resources for the development of the individual with the community and in the community. This is something we will discuss in more detail in the next chapter.

Activity

- Look at the following transcript in terms of the developing features of the child and comment upon the parent's attempt to interact with the child, particularly in the process of 'naming'.
- Following this you may want to try recording a child interacting with an adult or another child and look at some of the features of language that we have discussed in this chapter.

Francesca (28 months; 9 days old) Francesca and her mother are engaged in pretend play 'cooking' in the living room.

Mother:	Can you give me something to drink?
Francesca:	*Susu?* [Milk]
Mother:	Thank you. *susu?* ((M confirming with F))
Francesca:	Yes, OK?
Mother:	What is *susu*, darling? Is *susu* water?
Francesca:	Mmm ya.
Mother:	Is *susu* water?
Francesca:	*susu* water.
Mother:	Is *susu* water in English?
Francesca:	No
Mother:	What is *susu?*
Francesca:	Is milk, OK.
Mother:	OK ((M pretends to drink the milk)) Wah, very nice.

5.9 Further reading

There are many books available of child language and Halliday's own work in *Learning how to mean* (1975), London: Arnold has had considerable influence on the approach taken in this present volume.

Also Painter's (1999) *Learning through language in early childhood*, London: Cassell. This gives an extremely comprehensive coverage of the functional approach to language learning in early childhood.

One might also read Trevarthen C.T. (1979) Communication and cooperation in early infancy: a description of primary intersubjectivity. In M. Bullowa (ed.) *Before speech: the beginning of interpersonal communication.* Cambridge: Cambridge University Press.

On secondary intersubjectivity there is C.T Trevarthen and Penny Hubley's (1978) study: Secondary intersubjectivity: confidence, confiding and the acts of meaning in the first year. In A. Lock (ed.) *Action, gesture and symbol: the emergence of language.* London: Academic Press.

For a more general view of early language development of the young child Susan Foster's (1990) *The communicative competence of young children*, London: Longman, provides a good overview.

Fletcher P. (1998) *Child language acquisition.* London: Arnold. This volume also provides a good introduction into child language and the nature of language itself.

6 Language as a resource for learning

I will not go down to posterity talking bad grammar.

(Benjamin Disraeli)

6.1 Language and thinking

As we have indicated in the previous chapter, the child is surrounded by sustained modelling of language used in a variety of contexts. Older and more experienced language users unconsciously make visible to the child the functions and forms of language they are using (Ferguson 1977; Gallaway and Richards 1994; Painter 1999). In the 1920s, Vygotsky made some interesting claims about the relationship between language and thought and between individuals and society. As we have indicated in previous chapters, Vygotsky theorized that since tools were important for the beginnings of human society, it was the use of one distinctive tool – language – which had originally enabled human thinking and social behaviour to become distinct from other animals. Vygotsky described language as having two main functions. As a communicative or cultural tool we use it for sharing and jointly developing the knowledge, which enables organized human social life to exist and continue. He also suggested that quite early in childhood we begin to use language as a psychological tool for organizing our individual thoughts, for reasoning, planning and reviewing our actions. He came to believe that in early childhood a fusion of language and thinking occurs which shapes the rest of our mental development.

Vygotsky (1978) like Piaget believed that children are active in the construction of their own understandings and do not merely passively reproduce what is presented to them. However, for Piaget, cognitive construction occurs primarily in interaction with physical objects (Ginsberg and Opper 1988). People play an indirect role, for example, in planning the environment, which will cultivate or nurture the growth of cognition. In contrast, for Vygotsky, cognitive construction is always socially mediated. It is influenced by present and past social interactions. The basic principles underlying the Vygotskian framework can be summarized as follows.

6.2 Children construct knowledge

Vygotsky suggested that both physical manipulation and social interaction are necessary for development. For example, the children must touch, physically compare, arrange and re-arrange blocks before they can acquire the concept of the blocks, their attributes such as size 'big' and 'little'. The things an adult or peer points out to the child will influence what the child constructs. If someone points out that the blocks they are playing with are of different sizes, then this may help the child to build an overview or meta-construction. Adults frequently provide this type of guidance when talking to young children, pointing out features such as colour, size, and so on. This helps the child to construct concepts. It is through these dialogues that the adult or peers ideas mediate or influence what and how the child will learn.

6.3 Development cannot be separated from its social context

For Vygotsky, the social context influences learning more than attitudes and beliefs. Context has a profound influence on how and what we think. For example, the child who does not have these experiences may not only have a larger vocabulary but may also think in different categories and conceptualize the experience differently, perhaps even using language differently (Luria 1979; Rogoff, Malkin and Gilbride 1984; and Bernstein 1987). Social structures also influence the child's cognitive processes. For example, Sloutsky (1991) found that children raised in orphanages did not have the same level of planning and self-regulatory skills as children raised within smaller family units.

We have suggested in the previous chapter, following Vygotsky's theory that ways in which social and related contextual practices can and do influence language use and behaviour in which social experiences lead to the internal construction of schema and scenes. Luria (1976) worked in Central Asia with peasants who had not been incorporated into the large collective farms and found that their logic deductions were very different from a similar group who had been incorporated into the collective farms and had been exposed to new ways of farm practices and new cultural traditions. Cole and Scribner (1973) describe studies undertaken among the Kpelle people of Liberia, a culture very different from an urban culture. Their study found that the Kpelle people differed from those raised in an urban context. On some tasks the Kpelle people did not perform as well as those from urban settings but in others they were clearly superior. These findings are hardly surprising and suggest that people will be good at doing the things that are important to them and that they have occasion to do frequently. Donaldson (1978) calls this 'fields of intelligence' and suggests that we all have our own interests that we consider to be important and in which we can excel. Cole and Means (1981) and Scribner and Cole (1981) also suggest that societal practices influence the ways in which members of that society think; hence we can see that there is support from both psychologists and linguists for this view. More recent examples have been quoted by Bodrova and Leong (1996) who point out that the idea that culture influences cognition is crucial because the child's entire social world shapes not just what they know but how the child thinks. The kind of logic we use and the methods we use to solve problems are influenced by our cultural experience. For example, D'Ailly's (1992) study of children who regularly use an abacus demonstrates that they construct different conceptual frameworks of numbers from children who have not learnt to use an abacus. These studies all suggest that a child becomes a thinker and problem solver within their own cultural experiences. They learn from what they experience and what they need to know. Language is the essential performative tool in all learning. The child's thinking and communicating is a reflection of the social context in which the learning is taking place.

6.4 Learning can lead development

Learning and development are two different processes that are com-
plexly related to each other. While Vygotsky believed that there were
maturational prerequisites for specific cognitive accomplishments, he
did not believe that maturation totally determines development.
Inhelder and Piaget (1958) suggest that children must attain the stage
of concrete operations before they can think logically. In this view, the
internal reorganization of thinking precedes the ability to learn new
things. Thus, when information is presented at a higher level, children
cannot learn it until they are at the appropriate maturational level.
Vygotsky's view is different. His view is that not only can development
impact learning, but learning can actually impact upon development.
Adults can support through experience. For example, if a child is playing (he or she may be technically classifying objects) and the mother
intervenes and gives the child two boxes, one marked the word 'big'
printed on the side in large letters with the picture of a large teddy bear
and the other with the word 'little' in small print, with the picture of a
small teddy bear, then it is possible that the mother can actually support development by providing this experience. Eventually the child
may be able to categorize these and other objects without the external
support of the adult. As the child becomes becomes independent he or
she becomes capable of self-regulation (Vygotsky). In sum, social experiences can support learning and cognitive development and
the mother's intervention in the outlined scenario may hasten the
development of categorical thinking. There are of course dangers in
intervention. Programmes for accelerated development have suggested
the feasibility of teaching very young children, for example, babies to
read. The success of such accelerated interventions has not been easy
to establish but claims are strong from the creators of these programmes. However, the value of supported guidance that develops the
child marginally beyond his or her existing capabilities can be positive.
Bruner calls this guided intervention, scaffolding. We shall discuss it in
more detail later in this chapter.

6.5 Language plays a central role in cognitive development

Vygotsky's view is that language is a mechanism for thinking, a mental
tool. In other words, language makes abstract thinking possible.
Language is separable and independent from any immediate stimuli in

the environment. It is through language that cognitive processes, such as memories and anticipation of the future can be brought about. By using symbols and abstraction including concepts to think, the child is no longer dependent on the actual presence of the object in order to think about it. Language allows the child to imagine, manipulate, create new ideas, and share those ideas with others. Language frees the child from the confines of the immediate and the concrete. Since learning frequently occurs in shared situations, language is an important tool for appropriating other mental tools. To share an activity, there must be talk about that activity. Unless we talk, we will never be able to know each other's meanings. Language then is a universal tool that has been developed in all human cultures. It is a cultural tool because it is created and shared by all members of a specific culture. It is also a mental tool because each member of the culture uses language to think.

However, the acquisition of a specific cultural language tool for furthering mental development will depend on whether or not the tool lies within the child's zone of proximal development (ZPD). ZPD is a way of conceptualizing the relationship between the optimal and the potential of learning and development. Vygotsky chose the word 'zone' because he conceived it not as a point on a scale, but as a continuum of behaviours or degrees of maturation. By describing the zone as proximal (next to, close to), he meant that the zone is limited by those behaviours that will develop in the near future. Proximal refers not to all possible behaviours that will eventually emerge, but to those closest to emergence at any given time. Vygotsky suggests that the development of a behaviour occurs on two levels which form the boundaries of the ZPD. The lower level is the child's independent performance, what the child knows and can do alone. The higher level is the maximum the child can reach with help and is called assisted performance. The skills and behaviours represented in the ZPD are dynamic and constantly changing. What a child does with some assistance today is what the child will be able to do independently tomorrow. The level of assisted performance includes behaviours performed with the help of, or in interaction with someone else. For example, such an interaction may involve the scaffolder providing hints and clues, or rephrasing questions, asking the child to restate what has been said, demonstrating the task and so on. For Vygotsky the processes by which a child arrives at the solution provide a more accurate assessment of the child's intellectual capacity than merely assessing what the child already knows. He also saw this as being spiral with each stage of development dependent upon and reconstitutes the achievements of the previous stage.

In the course of the daily interaction parents and caregivers will develop a range of ways in which to support or scaffold the child through the ZPD. This may include various strategies such as:

1 providing the child with a new or appropriate words, phrases or chunks of language;
2 elaborating these chunks;
3 extending the child's interactions in various ways;
4 repeating the child's utterance;
5 prompting and guiding by asking questions;
6 jointly reconstructing shared experiences with prompts and frames like 'Do you remember when . . . ,' or 'Tell Auntie what you did today' or 'What did Auntie say?'

When such interventions are requested or initiated by the child then he or she is more likely to be receptive to the adult's intervention. Through this guided interaction, the caregiver is providing a scaffold which will be gradually withdrawn as the child becomes more independent, confident and competent in that area (Bruner 1978). Scaffolding is usually provided through language and social interaction on joint tasks.

6.6 Language development and learner strategies

It is not only caregivers, however, who employ a range of strategies in the language learning process. The learner, too, will develop various strategies to facilitate learning. In an earlier chapter we outlined Halliday's (1992, 1993) strategies that the child as an active agent brings into play in the development of the linguistic system as a resource for meaning and learning. What follows is a more detailed discussion of these learning strategies:

Strategy 1: Moving into new domains

The child will venture into new semantic domains when confronted with contextual demands. This is fairly frequent when there is more than one language. The following exchange between Saffiya and her mother is one example of this:

> *Mother*: *Tengah main dengan apa tu?* [What are you playing with?]
> *Saffiya*: Dough
> *Mother*: Dough *dalam Bahsa Melayu apa?* [What is dough in Malay?]
> *Saffiya*: *Tak tau* [Don't know]

Strategy 2: Refining distinctions

The child constantly elaborates the system networks by refining distinctions that have already been made and developing increasingly delicate options, both in terms of the grammar (e.g. moving from a 'yes/no' option in modality to shades of grey – 'maybe', 'might') and the lexis moving from the fairly generic 'got' to the more specific: 'walk', 'run', 'climb'.

Strategy 3: Deconstructing linked variables

The language and cognitive systems are in a constant state of construction, deconstruction and reconstruction as each new experience leads the child to make new connections, revisiting existing frames, scripts and schema. The strategy of 'disassociating associated variables' refers to the deconstruction of an already-formed opposition for example, AX/BY may become a recombination into two independent oppositions A/B and X/Y. This may be A = hot and B = cold with x = coffee and Y = tea. The disassociated associated variables may be deconstructed or re-arranged into independent oppositions of B/X = iced-coffee and A/Y = iced-tea or combinations for these concepts. Thus the opposition between 'hot coffee' and 'iced tea' may be recombined into 'iced coffee' and 'hot tea'. Halliday describes this as a 'simple but extremely powerful operation, one that is fundamental to all aspects of human learning' (Halliday 1993).

In addition to these three basic strategies, Halliday suggests a number of other moves made by the child in the further development of the meaning system or learning language. These are:

Filtering

This strategy is employed by the learners in constructing the adult linguistic system because children cannot learn the whole system all at once. The child tends to concentrate selectively on those aspects which are within their current language potential or slightly beyond that which they are currently able to process. This ability to recognize and work on a reasonable challenge accounts for language growth. Halliday surmises that the child's functional system serves as a grid, acting selectively on the linguistic input available to the child, filtering out those instances which do not resonate and capturing those aspects of the input which can be productively accommodated within the existing system Halliday (1992). For example in child talk instead of saying 'I am going home' a child at certain stages of development might say 'I going home'. This dropping of the copula is very common in early language development. It is also found in many colloquial varieties of English (Foley *et al.* 1998). One reason for this is that dropping of the copula does not hinder comprehension of the message and consequently can be filtered out by the child.

Trailer strategy

Every so often, in the course of learning, the child will venture into a new area, which is beyond the current level of ability. This is when the child anticipates a developmental step to come, then steps back in order to consolidate the step and build it into the overall learning process. This is what Vygotsky calls the spiral process in learning. For example, towards the end of the protolanguage stage a child may suddenly use a word or an expression in context which is clearly referential such as the word 'crane' uttered by a child living near a building site (one of the authors' own children at 13 months). This happened once and it may be some time, a year or so, before that child starts using the word crane more frequently within their system of referential meaning.

Magic gateway strategy

Halliday describes 'magic gateway strategy' as complementary to the trailer strategy. He proposes the use of the iconic sign as a gateway between non-symbolic and symbolic modes of action and the tendency to use the interpersonal gateway in developing new experiential meanings. Halliday's own example is taken of his Nigel data where the child was able to separate articulatory from prosodic features in the expression, thus enabling him to mean two things at once as this interaction between Nigel and his mother demonstrates:

'Mummy' [ama]	[ama] (tone mid level plus high level)
	meaning: 'where are you?'
	[ama] (tone high falling plus low level) meaning: 'there you are!'

Halliday describes this as the combination of 'proper name' (Mummy) with mood (seeking/finding), as a consequence, providing the magic gateway into the new level that of the lexicogrammar.

Strategy 4: Regression and reconstruction

There are times during development when the child might appear to regress. Halliday (1993) gives the example of children reinterpreting their experience in the new mode of written language. Children may be quite adept at discussing some semantically complex area of experience orally in commonsense terms. However, in writing about that same area, they can regress to an earlier level of development, while they reconstruct their linguistic system to cope with the new demands. This happens frequently when moving from oral recount to the creation of written narratives, or when the child is moving from a common sense understanding to a more technical education environment that demands a different kind of language use.

Strategy 5: Repetition

What is meant by 'repetition' here, is not the behaviourist approach in terms of drilling as a means of memorizing or learning by heart. Rather the repetition of 'chunks' of language allowing the child to 'model the language as a probabilistic system' (Halliday 1988a: 13). Each instance of language serves as evidence for construing the system that lies behind. Learning any system involves learning the relative probabilities of its options, thus building up a quantitative profile of the whole (Halliday 1993). In recognizing those options, which occur more frequently, the child is able to sequence the learning of grammar. So, for example, in English because certain verbs such as 'be', 'have', 'go' plus preposition allow a great flexibility in use they will have a high frequency of use and therefore high probability. Consequently, such verbal processes will appear relatively early in a child's repertoire.

Strategy 6: Chunking

In addition to revealing the probabilities of the system, the learning of large stretches of 'wording' as uninterrupted chunks plays an important part in language development. Much of what we say as adults is stored in ready-coded form as 'lines' – not all our utterances are freshly processed every time they are used. In language learning, familiarity with these chunks of texts allows the child to experience text grammar – the patterns of cohesion that are characteristic of adult language. For example 'How are you?', 'Where do you come from?', ' What's your name?' are all examples of formulaic chunks of language that are frequently used by adults.

We have so far emphasized how language develops through social processes and through learner strategies. There is another factor, which also contributes to the development of the child's meaning potential – that is the actual language system itself, the structure of the language or knowledge about the language.

By around two and a half, the child has developed sufficiently the framework of the adult language system to be able to use it as their main means of communication (Halliday 1978a). For the next few years the system will be expanded by means of the elaboration of existing elements and the extension of networks to the addition of new options. There is, as we have seen earlier in the Vygotskian theory, an integral relationship between language, culture and the social basis of language development. The idea that language development is complete by the age of four years is clearly not sustainable. Derewianka's (1995) longitudinal study of one of her own children indicates that the grammatical system is still developing at least up to the age of nine, and perhaps even beyond this age. For as long as the child is using language in new contexts of situation, enacting new social relationships, creating new kinds of discourses, the meaning system will grow in response to the new demands. However, for a number of developmental psychologists learning is conceived of in mentalist terms and it can be difficult to bring language into the picture. This view has been articulated, for example, in Bloom's (1993) study of initial word learning, in which she defines language as 'a system of expression, designed for taking the internal, personal, private mental meanings of individuals and making them external and public' (Bloom 1993: 19). Here, meaning is unequivocally located in the mental realm external to language and language is viewed as an expression form for non-linguistic thoughts. This is a position, which has been pervasive in the language acquisition literature, stemming as it does from developmental cognitive psychology. This can be further seen in the metaphors used such as 'mapping' language onto a non-linguistic representation of knowledge.

It is often argued that words must map onto concepts that have already been worked out non-linguistically (Markman 1989: 36) or that children could begin by mapping words onto pre-established conceptual categories (Clark 1993). However, even among cognitive psychologists there is no consensus. Schlesinger, (1977), Gopnik and Meltzoff (1986) and Nelson (1991) have argued that language may have a role to play in shaping rather than just expressing, cognition, and that which is to be recognized is not simply available ready structured for the child to perceive (Painter 1999).

Our view is that language development is closely linked with the process of children's socialization and interactions with others in the community in which they live. Through the process of socialization, children learn to develop their beliefs, feelings and behaviours appropriate to the particular role in the society as well as to learn about the language itself. Halliday has suggested that cognitive and linguistic processes are not two different things; they are two different ways of looking at the same thing. We can interpret such processes cognitively, as thought, or semantically as meaning – as one aspect of the total phenomenon we call 'language' (Halliday 1988b).

In this way, as Painter has pointed out, issues of cognitive development become issues of semantic development and can be addressed through an exploration of the child's language, since these are the actualizations of the child's meaning system. This view also consolidates support for the view that learning language includes learning appropriate social behaviour as well as learning how to think and view the world. In this sense, language plays a dual function as both the tool, and the focus of the learning. Learning language, therefore, is most appropriately considered as both social and cognitive.

6.7 Taking a closer look at what children say and do with language

Probably one of the most extensive studies to date of a child's language in use, with the aim of describing the way language is mobilized and developed as a resource for learning during the pre-school years comes from a study referred to earlier, Painter's (1999) study of her second child, Stephen, was two and a half when the research began and five when it was completed. From this study Painter identified a number of functions of children's early talk. These are:

Naming

Children's early talk is concerned with trying out and learning names as a means of interpreting their world. Children begin to understand that assigning names to things imposes meaning. Naming things is an important part of the child's identifying process, as the following extracts from Painter (1999) demonstrate.

(Stephen at 2;7 looking at a picture in a book with his mother)

Mother:	And do you remember what this is? (picture in book)
Stephen:	Mm.
Mother:	What is it?
Stephen:	It's a house.
Mother:	It's a house, special house and what's it made of?
Stephen:	Oh (pause) snow.
Mother:	Yes, that's right, it's made of ice.
Stephen:	Made of ice.
Mother:	And it's called igloo.
Stephen:	Igloo.

(Painter 1999: 85)

Perhaps more significant is another instance quoted by Painter when Stephen was aged 2;10.

(Stephen fiddling with raincoat in back of car)

Stephen:	I need a coat – a coat – what's it called? (it referred to a missing toggle)
Mother:	Raincoat (misunderstanding what S wanted the name of). You need a button on your raincoat.

(Painter 1999: 85)

Taxonomizing

One can often infer a number of taxonomic understandings from a spontaneously occurring text such as the following:

(Stephen at 2;7 with Mother and Hal, his older brother at breakfast)

Stephen:	Crocodiles die.
Mother:	Yes, crocodiles die.
Stephen:	And spiders die, and ants die, and giraffes die . . .

(continues through zoo animals seen two weeks before).

Stephen:	And aeroplanes die (looks at M).
Mother:	No, aeroplanes don't die, they just break.
Stephen:	Aeroplanes break . . . (continues catalogue of creatures + die).
Hal:	And Stephens die.
Stephen:	(indignantly) No, Stephen's not dying.
Hal:	Ye –
Mother:	Oh, don't start an argument.
Stephen:	Caterpillars die . . . (continues with parallel examples). And cars break.

> *Mother*:   Yes.
> *Stephen*:   And they drive all the way home.
>
> (Painter 1999: 88)

Only basic object level categories of things are named, but in naming different creatures and comparing these with different classes of vehicular transport, Stephen in interaction with what Halliday terms his coterie of significant others, his mother and older brother, is building this taxonomy of animate and non-animate things.

Causal relations

An additional way that language can be deployed to construe criteria for classification is by 'internal' causal relation (Halliday and Hasan 1976: 257). An example can be found of the cause link presented in bold in the following text:

> (Stephen at 3:7 with Hal and his mother. His mother says something about her 'best boys')
>
> *Hal*:   We have to be your best boys 'cause we're your only boys.
> *Stephen*:   And Daddy.
> *Hal*:   He's not a boy, he's a man.
> *Stephen*:   He is a boy, 'cause he's got a penis.
> *Hal*:   He's a male, we're all males.
> *Stephen*:   He's a man and a boy too.

As we can see the causal link is internal to the text, serving to explain the speaker's reason for inferring something. That is to say this internal relation elucidates the criteria for classification.

The construal of abstract meanings

Children begin to convey abstract concepts in a number of ways through language. They produce the formulaic chunks of language, expressions which sometimes convey abstract concepts. Also, everyday language particularly expressions of time introduces the child towards abstraction and ways of expressing temporal meaning. As the following example demonstrates:

> (Stephen at 3;5)
>
> *Stephen*:   He (referring to father) has to do it later cause – 'cause it hasn't – we haven't got time.
>
> (Painter 1999: 114)

Even before children begin formal education some begin to be aware of written language in their environment, as this extract demonstrates:

(Stephen at 3;9)

Stephen: Handbag has got 'b' and tummy has got 'm' and belly button is 'b'!

(Painter 1999: 115)

Before his fourth birthday Stephen has also become familiar with numerical symbols.

(Stephen 3;11 overhears his Father mention '50')

Stephen: Is 50 a number
Father: Yeah.
Stephen: How does it go?
Father: It comes after 49.
Stephen: A hundred comes after 49.
Father: A hundred comes after 99.

(Painter 1999: 115)

These examples demonstrate the ways in which Stephen is beginning to build taxonomies, categories and hierarchies of categories through language.

Learning from definitions

The following example illustrates Stephen's ability to draw an immediate inference from a definition.

(Stephen 4;4 discussing with his mother whether whales kill people)

Mother: There may be one kind of whale that can kill people, but most whales are nice creatures.
Stephen: They're not creatures, mum, they're whales.
Mother: Yes, creature is anything that's alive.
Stephen: Are we creatures?
Mother: Yeah.
Stephen: (laughs) No we're not!

(Painter 1999: 119)

In the above examples taken from Painter's (1999) longitudinal study we have only focused on the development of knowledge in terms of identification and classification of things and processes. To present a broader view of language development Painter also looks at how the child construes events, cause–effect relations and other abstract relationships.

Painter's study is of her own two sons, learning English in and English dominant society. Now we turn attention to language development in a multilingual environment. We have chosen Singapore as the multilingual setting partly because it is a context that we both know very well but perhaps more importantly because it represents important features of many new contexts. It is a new nation state. It is urban and is actively recruiting migrants to join its workforce, hence there are significant numbers of migrants complementing the already diverse linguistic population. In Chapter 5 Figure 5.5 we presented an overview of the linguistic environment of Singapore. Malay is the national language and there are three other official languages, Mandarin Chinese, English and Tamil. There are also a number of Chinese dialects spoken and there are new varieties of English and Mandarin emerging that are unique to Singapore. This combination of standard and colloquial varieties combine to create a rich linguistic environment for studying language use and development.

6.8 The child learning language in a multilingual environment

Often the target language(s) of the child may not only be one of several languages in the community but a diglossic variation within a language that is, using either the informal or formal variety. Interaction between the mother and child follows discourse patterns described in monolingual interactions (cf. Snow 1997). This pattern is:

---

clear orientation to the task → verbal feedback →, specific instructions → positive encouragement

---

Sharon 4;1

Linguistic background: parents speak mainly English and some Tamil to her. She spends two hours a day at an English-medium nursery. Sharon and mother are talking in the kitchen.

Mother:	You want to wash or not?
Sharon:	Yeah
Mother:	OK
Sharon:	*** put the soap
Mother:	Don't waste the soap ah.
Sharon:	OK

This one ah?

Why put on the big *panay* ['container' in Tamil]

Mother: Better, then you don't spill it, *intha* [here]

Sharon: Open the *thani* [water]

Mother: No, no, *thani vaenda* [don't want water]

You just wash it.

Sharon: I like *puttu* ((the red powder that Indians put on their forehead – Sharon has mispronounced it))

Mother: *Puttu?* Water *puttu*

Sharon: *Puttu* to put on my –

Mother: *Pottu da*. Not *puttu* * * *

Kudi [drink]

Sharon: Who use at their head?

Mother: Quickly drink up your milk

Don't spill it ma

Sharon: Who put *puttu*?

Mother: Oh some people use *pottu*.

(DELL Language Development Data 1985)

The caregiver and child are using two languages for their conversation about a cultural phenomenon within their particular society. There is clear support or scaffolding from the mother in this natural conversational dialogue. The combined use of two linguistic systems, the frame language (English) is followed by code-mixing that serves a functional purpose, clarifying meaning and focusing on the form of the language, correcting pronunciation.

Eliza

English and Cantonese are used at home where the child spends most of her time. In this particular event Eliza and the adult are looking at a picture book.

Through this interaction Eliza is learning about the world in which she lives. However, the focus is also overtly on language. Naming is taking place in two language: English and Tamil and there is also a focus on the form of the language with the mother repeating 'pottu' specifically to model the preferred pronunciation and specifically drawing Eliza's attention to pronunciation. In this exchange we have examples of three stages of language development:

Learning language–learning *through* language– learning *about* language

Adult: What is this?
Eliza: ***{ de } ((dress))
Adult: What about this?
Eliza: *fu* [trousers in Cantonese]
Adult: *fu*?
Eliza: Yes
Adult: Are you sure?
Eliza: *fu* so ((also)) – *f f*
           so ***
Adult: Are they the same?
Eliza: No
Adult: Why are not the same? Tell me
Eliza: This one cannot – this one can
Adult: Cannot what?
Eliza: Cannot to *jiok fu* – then so hard to *jiok* [to wear]
Adult: This one hard to *jiok*?
Eliza: Mm
Adult: This one is easy to wear? What about this one?
Eliza: This one can wear.

(DELL Language Development Data: 1983)

In this example Eliza is using her repertoire of languages as a resource for naming and therefore extending her commonsense knowledge. So for example, the Cantonese word for trousers *fu* gives the distinctive character-istic of the sort of traditional trousers frequently worn by some Chinese, particularly the grandparent generation. What is significant is that Eliza is using two linguistic systems, Cantonese and English, to name things she has observed and noticed. She is also building a taxonomy of cultural practices and artefacts of different clothes for different purposes. This cultural comparison is taking place through the guided conversation with her mother.

Michelle 4;2, Sally 4;2, Barbara 2;9

The next example shows children playing among themselves, where they use the colloquial variety of Singapore English. They codeswitch to Mandarin. The activity takes place in a playgroup. The three children are playing with Lego bricks. Michelle has just made a birthday cake for Sally. Barbara is another child in the playgroup.

Sally: Wah. My birthday so nice.
          My birthday nice ((Stands up))
Michelle: Baby (v) you like it?
Sally: ((nods))

Michelle:	Like it hoh?
Sally:	Ah. No. I sister
Michelle:	OK Mummy put flower first
	Flower, OK OK. Little bit put here.
Sally:	Ah. I don't want put there.
	I want put here ((Does so))
	So funny ah.
Michelle:	You like it or not?
Sally:	Wait first ah mummy (v) ((Goes off))
Michelle:	OK you mummy wait
Barbara:	*Wo yao qu* [I want to go to the toilet] ((Goes off))
Michelle:	Comes back the birthday
Sally:	You say what's the number? ((Walks back to M))
Michelle:	Five dollar
Sally:	Yah. Five dollar
Michelle:	((To S)) Ten . . . six dollar then can go
	You must give me six dollar money
Barbara:	((Runs back)) Sally (v) you got to wear shirt only
Sally:	Must wear uniform shirt ((Runs off))
Barbara:	You see, this wore shirt only
	((To M)) Michelle (v) wore shirt
Michelle:	((To S)) *Nimen kan shenme?* [What are you looking at?]
Sally:	((Whispers)) Uniform shirt wear
Michelle:	((Nods knowingly)) Ooh
Barbara:	Wore shirt only
Michelle:	*Na-ge bu-shi* Auntie T-shirt *ma*? [Isn't that Auntie's T-shirt?]
Sally:	Hah?
Michelle:	*Wo shi you kan mama kan meimei dai* [I've seen mummy
	and younger-sister wear it]
	Birthday *yao-bu-yao*? [Do you want birthday or not?]
	Yao ni jiu guaiguai [If you want, be good]
Sally:	*Wo chuan nide qian* [I wear your money]
	kan wo, wo chuan hen mei he? [Look at me, I look very
	beautiful wearing it, right?]
Michelle:	*Jiejie hen mei* [Elder-sister looks very beautiful]
Barbara:	*Wo mai xin-de* [I buy a new one]
Michelle:	Mm *Wo yao gei* Auntie May [I want to give it to Auntie
	May]
((Holds up the cake)) Wah. *So zhong ah*. [So heavy ah].
Sally:	I help you hold
Michelle:	Hold ah, *kuai-dian* [quickly]
	((Both Michelle and Sally get ready to walk off))

(Khoo 1987)

The children, here, are using a number of learning strategies and discourse strategies. Can you identify any of these?

1 contradicting ('Ah, I don't want put there');
2 taxonomizing ('shirt, uniform shirt, T-shirt');
3 linking cause and effect ('if you want, be good');
4 observation (*Jiejie hen mei*).

There is a movement from the Frame Language CSE into Mandarin. The main reason for this code-switching would seem to be that M is the dominant figure in the conversation and she frames her utterance in Mandarin Chinese *Nimen kan sheme?* [What are you looking at?]. As the first speaker she establishes the expectations of language use for the next (and subsequent) speaker(s). We can see from this interaction that these conversational strategies between the girls maintains the interaction and consequently the learning process.

Soon Ping 4;5 (male)

Soon Ping, a boy, has been raised in a linguistic environment where English, Mandarin and Hokkien, a Chinese dialect, are used. The first two languages are used by his parents with him while Hokkien is used by both his grandparents who were his major caregivers from the age of 18 months. He also has three sisters who are two years old and are triplets. The conversation takes place in his grandparent's apartment with LL, Soon Ping and his aunt. They are all engaged in pretend play.

In this extract we see an unconscious mixture of the colloquial variety of Singapore English (CSE), Mandarin and Hokkien. The aunt on the other hand is adapting her language and using the colloquial variety of Singapore English to accommodate to the child.

LL:	Some more? I very hungry you know. What else are you giving me?
Soon Ping:	Egg, nah, egg *hai yo* [and] . . . coffee.
LL:	*Hai yo leh?*
Soon Ping:	Hai yo, nah coffee.
LL:	Oh, not enough. I want something else. I very hungry you know.
Soon Ping:	*Ni yao nah shen mo fang shen mo fang ice yao bu yao?* [What do you want, do you want ice?]
LL:	Huh? Coffee *fang* ice [Coffee with ice]

Soon Ping:	((nodding his head)) Ah
LL:	((laughs)) Ice coffee ah?
Soon Ping:	Ah
LL:	OK loh, anything.
Soon Ping:	((finishes making coffee)) *Hao le nah, nah, nah.*
LL:	OK, what else you give me?
Soon Ping:	((Thinking)) Ah . . .
LL:	*Chui-kuch* ((Hokkien term for a cake normally eaten for breakfast)) ((laughter))
Soon Ping:	*Zhe mo tuo dong xi ya?* [So many things?]
LL:	Ah loh, very hungry.
Soon Ping:	OK. Nah, nah, nah ((pushes 'food' to LL)) *Hao le* [It's done]

(DELL Language Development Data: 1998)

What this extract shows is the child's development of knowledge in a social context that involves a language system where switching codes is something quite normal. SP shows an ability to interact and maintain a conversation with an adult although it is imaginary play. Of course the adult also has to adjust her language to fit the situation as well.

A number of the features of the profile of conversational ability proposed by Mc Tear (1985) can be found here. These include:

- turn-taking
- initiations and responses
- discourse devices for establishing and linking topics
- appropriacy markers
- conversational repairs.

Read the extract again and try to find specific examples of the children using these strategies.

Saffiya 5;0

This following extract is of an English–Malay speaking girl, playing with play-dough and talking to her mother and the researcher.

Saffiya:	I'm playing with the bun
Researcher:	Huh?
Saffiya:	Playing with the bun

Researcher:	What bun?
Saffiya:	This one lah
Researcher:	What's that actually?
Saffiya:	Dough
Researcher:	What is dough?
Saffiya:	Mama tell something dough dough dough dough flour lah flour flour
Researcher:	Then what are you making the flour into?
Saffiya:	Make people
Mother:	*Saffiya tengah buat apa?* [Saffiah, what are you making?]
Saffiya:	Er . . . *buat orang* [make person]
Mother:	*Buat orang? Tengah main dangan apa itu?* [What are you playing with?]
Saffiya:	Dough
Mother:	Dough *dalam Bahasa Melayu apa?* [What is dough in Malay?]
Saffiya:	*Tak tau* [Don't know]
((Saffiya is encouraged by her mother to describe what she is doing))	
Saffiya:	*Sekarang buat rambut* [Making the hair now]
	Sekarang buat buat rambut
	Panjang rambut [long hair]
Mother:	*Taruh rambut atas kepala* [Put the hair on the head]
Saffiya:	Oh huh
Researcher:	The hair no need to be black?
Saffiya:	No need
Researcher:	The hair black what?
Saffiya:	Then the dough white
Researcher:	Then cannot do anything?
Saffiya:	Don't have black flour
Mother:	*Rambut Saffiya warna apa* [What is the colour of your hair?]
Saffiya:	*Hitam* [Black]
Mother:	*Habis kenapa tak buat rambut hitam?* [Then why don't you make black hair?]

(Norwita 1987)

This is another example of how children and adults adjust and accommodate their language use and behaviour according to people they are interacting with, their fellow interlocutors. Subtle cues about their changing roles in different contexts demand this kind of accommodation. There are a number of roles an adult may adopt while interacting with young children. These may include a pedagogical role, as guide, teacher, instructor. While in a different context the adult may become the companion and thereby change the role-relationship and status between the interlocutors. Both types of interaction can involve the adult providing some kind of scaffolding to support the child, either directly or indirectly. This scaffolding can sometimes take the form of direct questioning that leads the child's attention.

> M: *Macam mana buat badan* [How do you make the body?]
> S: *Tak tau* [Don't know]
> *Ah, ini* press press [Ah, this]
> *Badan kan* round [Isn't the body round?].
> (Extract continues)
> . . .
> M: *Nanti boleh angkat* bag *angkat payung semua sekali. Nak?*
>   [Then you can carry your bag and umbrella]
> S: *Tak nak lah* [Don't want, Lah]
> *Nanti orang semua cakap eh empat tangan dia ada.* [Then people will say I have four hands]

Saffiya uses a loan words from English when speaking in Malay as in the following instances:

> M: *Tengah main dengan apa tu*? [What are you playing with?]
> Saffiya: Dough
> M: Dough *dalam Bahasa Melayu apa*?[What is dough in Malay?]
> Saffiya: *Tak tau.* [Don't know]
>
> Saffiya: *Habis tak ada colour hitam* [Then there isn't any black colour]
>
> Saffiya: *Dah tu taruk* body? [After that put the body on]
>
> Saffiya: *Ah, ini* press press [Ah, this press, press]
> Saffiya: *Badan kan* round? [Isn't the body round?]
> .
> Saffiya: OK, *sekarang* shoe [OK, now shoe]

However, when speaking English she only uses one Malay word in the transcript:

> Saffiya: Wait become *gila*. [mad]

But Saffiya does attach a Malay suffix and an English adjective to make a verb:

> Saffiya: *Kita* long-*kan* [Let me lengthen it]

In the following exchange Saffiya learns the Malay word for body *badan* and incorporates it into her repertoire later in the conversation. The following is an example of the ways in which the young child is learning commonsense knowledge while learning language. It is an example of learning *through* language. Children learn from this form of overt question and answer as a part of acquiring the commonsense knowledge of their environment.

> M: *Dah itu?* [After that?]
> Saffiya: *Dah tu taruh* body [After that put the body on]
> M: Body *apa?* [What body]
> Saffiya: (NVR)
> M: *Badan*
> Saffiya: *Badan.*
> Saffiya: *Badan kan* round [Isn't the body round?]
> N: After the head is what?
>   What are you doing now?
> Saffiya: *Taruh badan,* [Put (the) head (on)]

Saffiya demonstrates her growing knowledge about language and what she is able to recognize when she does not know a particular word. In the following extract she makes a specific request for linguistic information:

> N: Got toes or not to make after the legs?
> Saffiya: I don't know how to make toes
> M: *Ada jari tak?* [Are there fingers?]
> Saffiya: *Apa jari?* [What (is) jari?]
> M: *Jari kaki* [Toes]
> Saffiya: *Kita tak tau buat* [I don't know how to make]

Saffiya generally maintains the interaction by responding appropriately to the questions asked and endeavours to maintain the interaction even when the frame language changes from CSE to Malay.

> N: The hair no need to be black?
> Saffiya: No need
> N: The hair black what
> Saffiya: Then the dough white
> N: Than cannot do anything?
> Saffiya: Don't have black flour
> M: *Rambut Saffiya warna apa?* [What is the colour of your hair?]
> Saffiya: *Hitam* [black]
> M: *Habis kenapa tak buat rambut hitam* [Then why don't you make black hair?]

Saffiya: *Habis tak ada* colour *hitam* [Then there isn't any black colour]
M: *Dah itu?* [After that?]
Saffiya: *Dah tu taruh* body [After that put the body on?]
M: Body *apa?*
Saffiya: (NVR)
M: *Badan* [Body]
Saffiya: Badan
M: *Macam mana buat badan?* [How do you make the body?]
Saffiya: *Tak tau* [Don't know]
Ah, ini press press
Badan kan round? [Isn't the body round?]
Press press press
N: After the head you put what?
Saffiya: *Tak tau* [Don't know]

Saffiya is also aware of and can employ conversational strategies such as backchannelling to maintain the interaction and to keep the channel of conversation open:

M: *Taruh rambut atas kepala* [Put the hair on the head]
Saffiya: Uh huh
N: Now are you putting on the legs, is it?
Saffiya: Uh huh
M: *Kenapa kaki pendak sangat?* [Why are the legs so short?]
Saffiya: Uh huh lah

Saffiya also demonstrates her developing cognitive understanding in her ability to categorize the parts of the body in terms of a relationship of meronymy. This she is developing through two linguistic systems, Singapore colloquial English (CSE) and Malay:

(Superordinate)   orang (people)

(Meronymy) | badan [body] | tangan [hand] | Rambut [hair] | kaki [legs] |

Saffiya says at one moment in the dialogue that if she makes a doll with four hands, then people will say that she has four hands, thus displaying some commonsense knowledge of the world. It is also worthwhile noting that Saffiya in order to argue her point has to use a clause complex in Malay.

Nanti *orang semua cakap eh dia empat tangan ada* [Then people will say that I have four hands]

6.9 Summary

In this chapter we have proposed that it is from the conversational exchanges in specific contexts of family and peer group life that the child's understanding and use of language develops. Language is used as a tool, not just to communicate but also to develop the growing cognitive abilities of the child. The immediate contexts in which the child participates provide linguistic opportunities and challenges for learning language. In language learning the child needs to gain control over an ever expanding range of domains, beginning at home but quickly expanding to explore the unfamiliar and new. As we have seen, in each new domain, the child is confronted with new phenomena which need to be named. Each new experience helps to build new connections that extend and modify the child's developing taxonomies, changing understandings of how their world is organized. New social roles, new relationships require the child to learn new language forms and to expand their existing semantic range of meaning potential. While learning language the child is also learning about their world through language.

In the early stages, much of what a child hears is observed in their environment, allowing the child to make tangible connections between what is said and the significance of the utterance. The context of situation, however, is not seen simply in terms of the objects and the events of the external world. Rather, it is a configuration of semiotic patterns concerned with the field of activity, the negotiation of roles and relationships, and the channel of communication. There is a relationship between the child's communicative experience and the language system itself. The language system, as proposed in systemic theory sees language processing as a collaborative effort. The interactants are partners in the accessing and constructing of meaning. Children learn through their interactions with more experienced others (cf. Bruner). In most cases, such teaching is achieved not by explicit metalinguistic explanation, but by 'making the potential visible in text' (Painter 1984: 23). Invisible learning is taking place through interaction and language.

Much of what the child hears will be incidental as members of the meaning group go about the business of everyday life. Thus the child is surrounded by sustained modelling of authentic language, from a range of people, in a variety of social contexts. Older language users unconsciously may make explicit reference to language and thereby make some language functions and forms more transparent for the child. The child may choose to engage in this ongoing linguistic endeavour, or the adult may attempt to accommodate to the child's level (Painter 1984). The primary caregiver, because they have shared the contexts of growth of the child's meaning system and unconsciously tracked its progress, are able to gauge the appropriate linguistic level appropriate to what the child is capable of comprehending, and more importantly, what would constitute a reasonable challenge for the child. The child's ability to switch between linguistic systems in order to cope with this challenge is an important asset in the learning process.

As we have seen in the earlier part of this chapter, it is not only caregivers however, who employ a range of strategies in supporting the language learning process. The learner, too, will develop various strategies to facilitate learning using the languages available. For children, the overall context is one of survival, and they develop semiotic strategies to use their meaning potential as they are building it and build it as they are using it (Halliday 1975). If therefore, we return to the various strategies that children might use to facilitate learning and apply these to some of the data discussed in this chapter, we can see how children are active agents in their own language development.

Moving into new domains

The child will venture into new semantic domains when confronted with new contextual demands. We saw this in the previous chapter. A very young child, like Francesca switched from Malay to English and avoids the question that her mother poses such that the mother is being controlled by the child.

Mother:	What colour is the elephant? What colour is this? What colour?
Francesca:	*Pupu Pupu* [butterfly] ((pointing to a butterfly mould))
Mother:	Make *kupu*? Butterfly say!
Francesca:	*fi*:

Refining distinctions

The child constantly elaborates the system networks by refining distinctions that have already been made and developing increasingly delicate options both in terms of grammar and the lexis. We saw some of this happening with Saffiya when she says: *Nanti orang semua cakap eh dia empat tangan ada* [Then people will say that I have four hands]. Not only is Saffiya trying to reason something out but in order to do this she has to develop her logico-semantic aspect of language through clause complexing.

Deconstructing linked variables

The system is in a constant state of construction, deconstruction and reconstruction as each new perturbation leads the child to make new connections, often forcing the adjustment or relinquishing of previous knowledge. In the following extract, the conversation between Eliza and the adult shows the child having to readjust her thinking process to accommodate new knowledge.

Adult:	What is this?
Eliza:	***{ **de** } ((dress))
Adult:	What about this?
Eliza:	*fu* [trousers in Cantonese]
Adult:	*fu*?
Eliza:	Yes
Adult:	Are you sure?
Eliza:	*fu* so ((also)) *f f*
	so ***
Adult:	Are they the same?
Eliza:	No
Adult:	Why are not the same? Tell me
Eliza:	This one cannot – this one can
Adult:	Cannot what?
Eliza:	Cannot to *jiok fu* – then so hard to *jiok* [to wear]
Adult:	This one hard to *jiok*?
Eliza:	Mm
Adult:	This one is easy to wear? What about this one?
Eliza:	This one can wear.

In another example, Man Ling (3;2) a Chinese Singaporean girl asked her aunt for a little cooking oil and then requested black sauce but this she could only describe in Mandarin. Man Ling's knowledge in certain domains seems to be restricted to one language in this case Mandarin as this is her dominant language.

Man Ling:	Give me the *yi dian* you [a little oil.]
Aunt:	*Yi dian* you, *zai na li*?[A little oil, where is it?]
Man Ling:	*Gei wo leh.* [Give me] leh. *Li mian hai you leh* [There's more inside] *leh. Li mian* [inside.]
Aunt:	You *shenme*?[Have what?]
Man Ling:	You you. *Zhe ge mei you le* [Have oil. There's no more of this already.]
Aunt:	What's that?
Man Ling:	*Yi dian* you [A little oil.]
Aunt:	Enough
Man Ling:	Enough. *Wo yao hei hei de* [I want the black black one.]

Aunt:	What's that?
Man Ling:	*Hei hei de* [Black black one.]
Aunt:	Black sauce. Chilli? Put Chili?

(Tan 1998: 137)

Chunking

In addition to revealing the probabilities of the system, the learning of large stretches of 'wording' as uninterrupted wholes plays an important part in language development. As in the case of Soon Ping (4;5) in his imaginary play with the aunt (LL).

LL:	Okay. *** return home already
Soon Ping:	And I go home already.

Or another example:

Soon Ping:	*Ni yao nah shen mo fang shen mo fang ice yao bu yao?* [What do you want. Do you want ice?]

Repetition

The repetition of chunks of language allows the child to 'model the language as a probabilistic system (Halliday 1988a). In learning which options occur most frequently, the child is able to sequence the learning of grammar. Repetition would need a much more extensive database than that which is presented here, but as an indication of what happens, we can see Saffiya interacting with Norwita (the researcher) and using 'chunks' of language in this case the verb 'buy' in various grammatical structures.

Norwita:	*Saffiya nak kasi bunga tak?* [Saffiya, do you want to give flowers?]
Saffiya:	*Kita nak tapi mama tak beli* [I want but Mama didn't buy any.]
Norwita:	*OK mama belikan nak?* [OK shall Mama buy them?]
Saffiya:	*Kita beli?* [I buy?]
Norwita:	*Kenapa tak boleh?* [Why cannot?]
Saffiya:	*Dia beli lah kasi kita kasi cikgu* [You buy for me to give to the teachers].

Decontextualization

Role play according to Vygotsky, is important in a child's development. He writes:

> In play, thought is separated from objects and action arises from ideas rather than from things: a piece of wood begins to be a doll and a stick becomes a horse.
>
> (Vygotsky 1978: 97)

For Vygotsky an object becomes a signifier for something else, a pivot through which children detach themselves from immediate sensory experience (Cloran 1999). Wertsch (1985) sees this detachment from sensory experience as a stage in the process of decontextualization or of being context-independent. And as we shall see in the next chapter this is crucial for entry into educational knowledge.

Lemke (1993) describes, language as a 'dynamic open system' which is metastable in character that is to say that such systems persist only though constantly changing in interaction with the environment. The system is the potential for a generation of new instances, and the instances produced in each unique environment make incursions back into the system. As the child engages in particular contexts of situation, certain demands are made upon his or her linguistic resources. The child's language develops in response to the current challenge. On the basis of these encounters, the child constructs transitional micro-paradigms which are specific to the contexts of situation in which he or she is engaging (Halliday 1975). With each new change in context, the child may need to renovate these micro-paradigms by processes of addition, modification or complete reconstruction.

The expansion of the child's meaning potential, then, is not simply a matter of constantly adding new options to existing sub-systems, but rather involves the constant reconstrual of the system in the light of new linguistic experiences. Painter (1992) points out that developments within the child's meaning potential enable new ways of thinking and learning, and that in the course of using the enriched language system, the learner may be alerted to new possibilities for meaning. Language development is thus seen as a series of implication sequences – certain options need to be available within the system before further development can take place, thus the importance of Vygotsky notion of 'spiral development'. The argument then is that the bi/multilingual child increases these options by being able to use more than one language to further development not only at the linguistic level but also at the cognitive.

Activity

Can you identify any of the functions and strategies suggested by Painter (1999) or Halliday (1993) that Man Ling is using? Look at the following transcript and decide what learning processes (for example, those described by Painter) are being developed in the interaction. In this example the child, Man Ling at the age of three years two months code-mixes in Mandarin, knowing very well that her aunt speaks both English and Mandarin.

Man Ling 3;2 female

Man Ling is an only child. Man Ling's maternal side of the family speak Teochew, a Chinese dialect, Mandarin and English. On the paternal side of the family Hokkien and a little Mandarin with English is used mainly. Man Ling also went to a nursery where both English and Mandarin were taught and used by her teachers. As is common within the Singapore context Man Ling spent various periods of her first years with the paternal grandparents and then with the maternal grandparents. Her working parents might only see her at night or sometimes at the weekends depending on their work commitments.

In the following extract she is talking to her aunt.

Aunt:	Find the pieces yourself. See, they are all here what.
Man Ling:	Cannot, I cannot play.
Aunt:	Why not?
Man Ling:	Because *wo re si liao* [I'm too hot.] ((ML is complaining about the hot weather.))
Aunt:	Ha?
Man Ling:	*Re si liao* [It's too hot].
Aunt:	*Shenme*? [What?]
Man Ling:	*Re si* [Too hot.]
Aunt:	*Re si ah*? [Too hot it?]
Man Ling:	Ah.
Aunt:	What is that?
Man Ling:	*Wo tou re si liao, zheme wan*? [I'm already too hot, how to play?]
How to play	fini: I don't know. What so you want to cook?
Man Ling:	*Wo yao yi dian you xian. Yi dian you.* [I want a little oil first. A little oil.]
Man Ling:	Give me the *yi dian you* [a little oil: *Yi dian you, zai na li*? [A little oil, where is it?]
Man Ling:	*Gei wo leh*. [Give me leh] *mian hai you leh* [There's more inside leh] *Li mian*

[inside].

Aunt:	You *shenme*? [Have what?]
Man Ling:	*You you. Zhe ge mei you le* [Have oil. There's no more of this already: What's that?
Man Ling:	*Yi dian you* [A little oil.]
Aunt:	Enough
Man Ling:	Enough. *Wo yao hei hei de* [I want the black black one.]
Aunt:	What's that?
Man Ling:	*Hei hei de* [Black black one.]
Aunt:	Black sauce. Chilli? Put Chilli?

(Tan 1998: 139)

6.10 Further reading

Painter, C. 1984: *Into the mother tongue*. London: Pinter.

Painter, C. 1989: Learning language: a functional view of language development. In Hasan, R. and Martin, J. (eds) *Language development: learning language, learning culture. Meaning and choice in language: studies in honour of Michael Halliday*. Norwood, NJ: Ablex.

Painter, C. 1999: *Learning through language in early childhood*. London: Cassell.

7

Language development in the school

I kept Monica at home today because she was not feeling too bright.

(Richard Lederer)

7.1 The transition from commonsense knowledge to educational knowledge

Learning within the family is a matter of building up what Bernstein (1975: 99) has termed as 'commonsense knowledge'. However, with the move to school the child is expected to learn new roles and new ways of relating to others. The familiar roles of the child interacting with siblings and neighbours are complemented by those of a wider community, which normally for example, would consist of other children in the class, the school and the wider friendship peer-group. No longer can the child expect the undivided attention of adults or the comfortable familiar routines of the household. No longer the primary focus of attention, the child must learn appropriate interaction patterns within much larger, more formal groupings. Behaviour such as raising the hand to ask questions, not making direct demands, taking part responsibly in group discussions all need to be learnt. New relationships also have to be negotiated as the child learns the nature of pupil and teacher roles, makes new friendships, interacts with a wider range of adults and generally extends the scope of their participation in the world. Bernstein (1975: 99) referred to this type of knowledge needed for school learning as 'uncommonsense' in nature.

The school is necessarily concerned with the construction of official guided construction of knowledge (Mercer 2000).

As we have seen from the descriptions of the first few years of language development, the development of cognition parallels the development of commonsense and this is engendered in the processes of everyday dialogue. The language of the school however is of an increasingly uncommonsense kind. Indeed it is a very specific kind of learning that Halliday has termed 'educational knowledge'. The institution of the school exists to initiate children into more consciously designed, systematized and explicit ways of reasoning about the world.

Painter has categorized the differences between two kind of knowledge, commonsense knowledge and educational knowledge as follows:

Commonsense knowledge	Educational knowledge
Relevant to a specific context	Universalistic in orientation
Based on personal/shared experience	Distant from personal experience
Based on language mediated observation	Based on semiotic representation and participation
Concrete non-technical meanings	Abstract and technical meanings
Negotiated in spoken language	Constituted in written language
Built up unconsciously	Built up consciously
Built up slowly and gradually	Built up rapidly
Pace of learning at discretion of learner	Pace of learning at discretion of instructor
Built up piecemeal, fragmented way	Systematically presented, logically sequenced within a topic
Lack of insulation between topics	Disciplinary boundaries may be maintained

(Painter 1999: 71)

So far, much of the focus in this book, has been on the interaction within the home, mainly between caregiver and child exhibiting features of what we have identified as commonsense knowledge. This commonsense knowledge, can and often does, help to facilitate the child's transition into literacy and the sort of learning that takes place in the more formal school setting.

Hasan (1983 and 1986) following on from Bernstein's earlier studies in the 1970s has underlined the importance of language and social context in gaining commonsense knowledge. Hasan and Cloran (1990) in their study of mother–child interactions in Australia show that the selection and organization of meanings is regulated by social relationships. They categorized the families into two sociological categories: the HAP families who enjoyed a high degree of autonomy and control over their time at work and the Lower Autonomous Professions (LAP) families who did not. HAP parents worked as librarians and engineers, for example, while the LAP parents were employed as school-canteen assistants and factory workers. Their study of the interactions between the mothers and their children showed that both groups have different ways of behaving in their interactions with their children. Their choice of language and the organization of the discourse differed in a number of ways yet both exercised what Hasan and Cloran describe as invisible control over their young children during their conversations together. The HAP mother–child interactions can be characterized in the following ways:

The HAP mothers are:

- highly likely to issue indirect and suggestive commands, so that the coercive nature of authority is opaque and invisible;
- inclined to elaborate both commands and reasons so as to prepare the ground for both commands and reasons;
- likely to give more inherent reasons for the commands issued;
- were likely to give commands that were prefaced by some remark, not viewing the child as an extension of self but as a separate being;
- likely to make supportive assertions, thereby contributing to the positive self image of the child;
- were likely to keep any challenge to the child to a minimum thus positively avoiding conflict.

(Hasan and Cloran 1990)

These distinctions in use of language are of course not absolute. There would be occasions when the LAP mothers also demonstrate some of the features of the interaction ascribed to the HAP mothers and vice-versa. What Hasan and Cloran were showing was that the semantic choices made by the mother affected the ways of reasoning and of learning. That this was possible because the grammar and the lexical features of these semantic patterns were quantitatively foregrounded. This leads to the probabilities of the child actually learning these patterns of language and using them eventually in their own linguistic repertoire. We can illustrate this by taking a few examples from Hasan and Cloran (1990) data:

> *Mother*: put it (= the torch) up on the stove and leave it there
> *Karen*: why?
> *Mother*: cause
> *Karen*: that's where it goes?
> *Mother*: yeah

The LAP mothers offer no extended reason beyond 'cause' in answer to the child's *Why*-question. Interestingly, it is Karen who provides a possible adequate answer to her own question.

In a later exchange between Karen and her mother we have the following dialogue:

> *Karen*: you . . . you . . . try guess a name alright?
> *Mother*: um . . . there's John . . . isn't there?
> *Karen*: who else?
> *Mother*: I don't know. I can't remember.

In this exchange Karen's mother's last two utterances disclaim knowledge of the fact, and use failure of memory as the reason for not being able to provide the requested information. Hence this exchange stays at a minimal level of interaction.

By contrast the short exchange this time Nathan and his HAP mother is quite different:

> *Nathan*: ah . . . yes where is it (= toy ladder) standing
> *Mother*: I don't know darling. I'm just suggesting perhaps you look there (= downstairs), it could be there . . . go and have a look.

Here although the mother begins by denying knowledge of the whereabouts of the toy ladder, she does not evade answering but gives her opinion of where it might be. Rather she elaborates on her possible reply (Hasan and Cloran 1990).

The proposition put forward is that the development of the child's growing commonsense knowledge into educational knowledge is essentially structured around this scaffolding from the adult to support the young learner through what Vygotsky has termed the 'zone of proximal development'. Hasan and Cloran's study shows for example, that in picture reading sessions at home the LAP mothers tend to provide minimal information over and above what could be seen in the picture, while on the other hand the HAP mothers tend to give more information and to expand on the child's own questions. What this means is that where additional information is typically not given, access to knowledge of the world is not available at the level of the choice of wording used by the mother. Children need to be guided, supported or scaffolded in their learning and one of the main tools available for this is language and social interaction.

In schools, explicit verbal formulation in discourse (e.g. 'Can you explain what you mean?') is used by teachers as a fundamental tool in the development of educational knowledge. In Hasan and Cloran's study the LAP mothers' semantic network (that is the choice of wording), was found to be the least like that of teachers while the HAP mother would have significantly greater similarity with the discourse patterns of the teacher. Thus HAP mother–child interaction was considered to be more explicit preparation for school-type learning.

The families of Hasan and Cloran's study were, monolingual and living in Australia. How far such characteristics of mother–child interaction can be applied to other societies is an issue to be explored. For example, in a number of the more affluent economies of Asia, the primary caregiver in the early stages of a child's life can often be someone other than the mother or father. Although the mother and father might well fit the sociological profile of the HAP parents, the profile of the actual caregiver is far more likely to be like LAP mothers, baby sitters, elderly relatives, or cheaply employed live-in domestic help, frequently, migrants who are generally less well educated than the child's parents. It is therefore likely that the selection and organization of meaning in the language or languages used with the child will be more direct and not exercise such a high degree of invisible control. Indeed, it may not even be the dominant language that is used in the education system. Ko and Ho (1992) report on a large study of 2418 children aged between three and six in Singapore. The study indicated that on a number of cognitive tasks related to their language (English, Chinese, Malay and Tamil) the interaction between caregiver and the child, particularly between mothers and their children, was confined to language regulating or monitoring behaviour functions rather than encouraging talk. In other words although a number of the families in the sample would correspond to the Australian HAP sociological profile, their use of language(s) was more like that of the Australian LAP mothers.

The indications from the Ko and Ho study are that many pre-school children spend a great deal of time with caregivers other than the parents. There are several possible reasons for this, but the most common cited is that increasingly, both parents go out to work and buy professional care for their children. This means that the children may only be in contact with the parents for very short periods or time in the late evening or even only at weekends. This may limit the range of activities and functions which the parents and children share together. This is not merely a question of language but also the emotional and social development of the child. There are some in Singapore, for example Lee (1992), who regard this as a negative alternative to direct parent care as the following statement suggests:

> as more and more of our pre-school children will be 'farmed out' on either a weekly or daily basis to other caregivers besides the parents and the immediate family due to changes in the economic situation of the homes, the emotional and social development of our children is perhaps more pressing than the intellectual needs.
>
> (Lee 1992: 129)

Consider the child care arrangements in your own context.

Points to ponder

- How much are birth parents actively engaged in the process of child rearing?
- Does this apply equally to both parents?
- What do you consider to be the consequences of these arrangements for the young child's language learning?

Through early interaction the young child is learning language, commonsense knowledge and some suggest preparation for later educational knowledge which because of the role it plays in society is mainly accessed through a linguistic process. As Halliday wrote:

> all education takes place through the medium of language. I don't mean all learning: human beings learn a great deal without the medium of language. But all educational learning is mediated through language . . . Language is implicated in some way or other in all educational activity.
>
> (Halliday 1991: 1)

This suggests that becoming educated is essentially a linguistic process. Language is seen as 'the essential condition of knowing, the process by which experience becomes knowledge' (Halliday 1992), and in order to become educated, the learner must develop control over the language of educational knowledge.

In the early years of schooling, there should normally be no dramatic discontinuity between the commonsense knowledge of the home and the type of knowledge being developed in the school classroom. The curriculum seldom introduces unfamiliar fields in the first couple of years as the child is coming to grips with new interpersonal and textual skills. Furthermore, the pre-school child has already developed a sophisticated array of semantic strategies in making sense of the world. It is not as if the school needs to teach children how to compare, contrast, classify, hypothesize and so on, as we have already noted in our studies of young children. The role of the school in the initial stages of the guided construction of knowledge appears to be more of consolidating, formalizing and systematizing this commonsense knowledge, bringing the familiar to consciousness as an object of explicit investigation.

However, it is also true that in many societies it can happen that children have to learn a new language when they begin school because the language of instruction or the official language may be different from the language of the home environment. Such a situation can have considerable implications for a child's development of educational knowledge and consequently, may affect the child's overall development throughout primary education. This is something educators have to take account of when trying to mediate educational knowledge through a language, which may not be the child's home language.

7.2 Classroom talk

One of the main factors that will affect the child's development on entering into the formal education system is what actually goes on in the classroom. While the process of formal education has some special characteristics which we need to take account of, it is also useful to see classrooms as just one of a range of real-life settings in which knowledge is jointly constructed and in which people help others to develop their understanding. Mercer (1995) gives as an example someone having their first driving lesson.

Marie, the aunt is sitting beside Rebecca the teenage niece in the car, Rebecca is behind the wheel.

Marie: Right. You have to know where everything is first. Umm.
Rebecca: Umm, yeh.
Marie: Right, do you know what the footpedals are for? No?
Rebecca: Yeh but I cant remember which way it goes.
Marie: It goes, um, that one on the right, accelerator. (*R presses it*) Yeh

> *Rebecca*: Yeh, accelerator, brake, clutch, ABC.
>
> *Marie*: That's right. Yeh. So you move that foot from one to the other, so you don't have it on both, right? Do you know what the clutch is for?
>
> *Rebecca*: Change gears.
>
> *Marie*: Right, go on then, try changing gears without the engine switched on. Put your foot on the clutch and . . .
>
> (Mercer 1995: 9)

As Mercer points out, much of the learning process in driving would involve non-verbal activities (pointing and manipulating the controls) or what Rogoff (1990) calls a sort of guided participation. But, as we have already indicated, language plays a crucial role in the classroom and because of this talk and the quality of that talk is vital. By quality talk we mean how effective the communication is whether teachers and pupils appreciate each other's intentions and expectations and whether misunderstandings are recognized and dealt with. Developing an awareness of the talk that goes on in the classroom requires much more careful observation of what goes on, than in normal everyday circumstances. Compared with the more formal patterning of teaching and learning in secondary and higher education, much of the communication in early school such as primary level is made up of teachers' communication with relatively small groups of children and much is generated by unplanned events. This model of primary education has dominated pedagogy and education in many contexts, notably the northern hemisphere. However in many parts in the world, the classroom can still be a highly regulated environment and the process of communication is often uni-directional, directed by the teacher and treating the class as a single unit rather than a collective of individuals. So different kinds of classroom talk need to be learnt by new pupils. This includes talk with peers, communications with teachers initiated by children, and what children use talk for outside the tasks set by the teachers.

Taking this perspective of education in a formal setting we can define it as a sort of superimposed second-order culture which consists of schemes of conceptual organization and behaviour designed to supplement the first order processes of the primary socialization of family upbringing. Consequently, the language of the classroom (both spoken and written), which gives access to educational knowledge is both a tool for learning and learning itself. However, such educational knowledge engenders special varieties, patterns of language that are specific to learning in school including not only teacher-talk but also the language of textbooks and other learning materials. Children have to learn these new ways and uses of language and the new means of invisible control inherent in these texts.

7.3 Oral genres

Classroom discourse, oral and written is one of the main tools for the construction of educational knowledge. Language is seen as the primary tool for developing pupil ability to move from the world of commonsense knowledge, everyday language, to the kinds of technical and academic discourses required by the school syllabus. Pupils have to be apprenticed into the kind of writing valued by the educational community; that is, pupils must not only be aware of the language requirements of the reading and writing tasks asked of them but also be given the tools with which to complete them successfully.

A key element in providing the tools to acquire educational knowledge is that of instructional scaffolding. Scaffolding sees learning as a process of gradual internalization of routines and procedures available to the learner from the social and cultural context in which the learning takes place. New skills are learnt by engaging collaboratively in tasks that would be too difficult for the individual to undertake alone but can be completed successfully in interaction with the caregiver (in an educational setting this will often be the teacher). In this interaction, the role of the teacher is to provide the necessary support to allow the child to complete the task and also in the process to provide the child with an understanding of the problem and the strategies available for its solution. This is the zone of proximal development (ZPD) discussed earlier. In education this notion would explain the difference between the child's actual developmental level, as measured by an IQ test, for example, and the child's potential developmental level. To assess the potential level of development, it is necessary to present the child with a problem, the solution to which is just beyond his/her mental capacities, and allow him or her to interact with another person while working out the answer. The processes by which the child arrives at the solution will provide a more accurate assessment of the child's intellectual capacity than merely examining what he or she already knows. Formal instruction, therefore, is the mechanism whereby the child can grow intellectually and internalize the processes necessary for such development (Garton and Pratt 1989).

Allied to this notion of ZPD is Bruner's (1978) notion of the spiral curriculum. He suggests that by couching new information and ideas within the previous experience of the pupils it is reasonable to expect that they will be able to achieve the outcomes as stated in the syllabus. So when children go to school and become literate, they are not simply extending their powers into a new medium (reading and writing); they are learning a new way to learn.

Education engenders special varieties, patterns of language that are specific to learning in school – including not only teacher-talk, but also the language of the textbooks and other learning materials used. Christie (1989) has pointed out that the institutionalization of language in the schools can be seen as a series of teaching/learning episodes that have a distinctive overall pattern or shape and that these may be thought of as also having a generic structure. Since the processes of school learning are mainly encoded in language, all the discourse produced by the children and their teachers in any one class over the day may be thought of as discourse. However, even within the classroom, the situations are different so they produce different discourses. The shifts in learning activities spread over the day are themselves encoded in shifts of behavioural patterns and these are reflected in the language. These shifts in language are the curriculum genres, that is the genres produced orally by teachers and pupils. Christie in the Australian context has analysed a number of curriculum genres and has demonstrated that patterns of interaction between teacher and pupil are reflected in the written genres produced by the pupils. The findings that pupils use particular written genres because of the context in which they are learning means that even when the teachers are not conscious of what they are doing, they have a powerful effect, not only on the pupils' writing development but on the kinds of knowledge being constructed in the classroom.

The institutionalization of language in the school can be shown to have a distinctive overall pattern or shape, and that they may be thought of as a genre, a staged, goal-oriented, purposeful activity in which the speakers and writers engage as members of a culture (Martin, 1984).

For example, picture talk activity is conducted in many lower primary classes. Its main purpose is to improve the pupils' oral skills although this is often expressed in terms such as 'Now say that in a complete sentence'. Picture talk, which is commonly referred to as oral comprehension by the teachers is an activity where a picture is talked about. Either a large picture is placed by the blackboard, or each pupil has the picture to be described in their reader. Each discussion begins with the teacher instructing the pupils to describe the picture, Now you are going to tell me what you can see. Using the picture as a reference point, the teacher may direct the pupils into slightly different activities such as recalling an experience, 'Justin, can you come out and tell us what dreams you have had?' Or, mapping out a procedure, 'How does your mummy cook brinjals?' At the end of these lessons, it is often the case that the children are instructed to write sentences about the picture.

A number of instructional strategies have been identified to describe the curriculum genre of picture talk. These are:

1. The focus

The pupil's attention is deliberately concentrated on the picture or on a particular participant feature in the picture. The teacher guides the pupils through instructions and questions. The focus stage of the lesson is realized in the grammar either as a polar interrogative or an imperative, involving the process of perception. Reference to the picture and participants is made using definite nominal items, such as 'the picture' and 'this lady'. Thus the stage is almost entirely context-dependent and the exchange between the teacher and the pupils relies heavily on the picture artefact.

Teacher: Now look at the picture carefully. Can you see the picture?
Pupils (in unison): Yes.

2. Instruction

The instruction from the teacher gives an indication about what the pupils' role is going to be in the social process 'Tell me and you are going to tell me'.

Teacher: Now can you tell me something about the picture?
S1:   There are two monkeys there.
Teacher: Now you (are) going to tell me what you can see.

The instructional stage is realized through interrogatives or statements that concern verbal processes. Both the interrogatives or statements function as commands and are produced only by the teacher. Sometimes this stage may be absent from the lesson because one picture talk lessons assume a similar structure. Once pupils are familiar with that, the teacher may assume that the pupils know what is expected of them and may hence omit this stage. The teacher assumes that the pupils' frame of expectation for the lesson includes this introductory focus stage.

Point to ponder

- Do you consider this to be a fair assumption? Consider the difficulties this may pose for some learners.

3. Identification

In this instructional strategy, the participants, both animate and inanimate in the picture or the location are identified and named as in the following:

Teacher: OK, tell me where the people are
SS: Fair, fair
Teacher: Eh?
SS: Funfair
Teacher: Fair?
SS: Funfair. Right. Good. These people are at a funfair, right.

Identification uses several ways of naming. There is the frequent use of circumstantial elements of location. Very often identification is the response to the teacher's *wh*-interrogative. For example, the teacher asks, 'What is he holding in his hand?' or 'What is that item here?' The answers to this rely entirely on the pupils' understanding of the picture. Sometimes through identification the teacher takes the pupils through the process of creating taxonomies:

Teacher: What prize would you win if you threw a ball into – what
           prize would you win? Yes, Meng Lin.
ML   A bear
Teacher: Only a bear. What kind of bear?
SS: Teddy bear
Teacher: A real bear? A grizzly bear?
SS: A teddy bear
Teacher: A teddy bear. You're sure it's a teddy bear?
SS: Yes.

4. Description

The description strategy can encompass two options. Either, a participant in the picture can be described or a comprehensive overview of the picture as a whole can be described. Possessive and intensive relational processes are the most common realization forms when a participant's appearance or feelings are described. Although a picture gives a static representation of actions, the commentary-like description treats the actions as actually happening at the moment of utterance. The pupils' use of the present tense is important here as their description is a commentary on the actions that are considered ongoing or incomplete.

S: The genie is very big
S: The man is afraid of the monster very much.

The questions from the teacher also provide some scaffolding and prompts for the pupils. These include questions that engage the pupils in the events as participants.

> *Teacher*: What are the man and woman doing in the picture? Liang Choo?
> *LC*: They are watching television.
> *Teacher*: Watching television.

However, description also include requests for more speculative responses that require the pupils to project or speculate and that cannot be verified by perceptual evidence. These may be signalled with by the use of the projecting clause, 'you think':
For example:

> *Teacher*: All right. What do you think the man is explaining?

There is also the possibility that some pictures involve describing what caused the action as well as describing the actual scene. That is to say events that led to the picture and that took place before the action depicted in the picture have to be inferred. These may be hypothetical or may demand the pupils' use of background knowledge. The pupils may also be invited to speculate. The tentative nature of the inferences is reflected in the grammar with the use of modal operators such as 'be able to', 'must' or verbs such as 'think'.

> *Teacher*: Now do you think the burglar will be able to get away without being seen? Do you think the burglar will be able to go away and these two people won't be able to – won't realize that the robber was in the house?
> Do you think so?
> Do you think he will be able to escape?
> *S6*: No.

5. Explanation

The description strategy is usually followed by the teacher eliciting explanations for the description given. These reasonings form a substantial part of picture talk. Explanation does not take place independent of description. At the level of the grammar the teacher's demand for a reason is achieved by a *why*-question and the response is usually a clause-complex where the reason is subordinated using 'because'. Frequently the projecting clause 'What do you think?' is used as the explanation strategy. Modulation by adjuncts such as 'probably' and verbs like 'could' are also found here:

Teacher:	Now what could have caused the fire?
	Ek Keng
	Shaidah
S6:	Uh, maybe the baby is playing with matches.
Teacher:	Baby?
	[Children laugh]
	Look at the baby.
	Could it be possible that babies play with matches at that age?
	All right, give me a more reasonable explanation
	These are possible reasons, right?
	Possible reasons.

Also, in this exchange, we see the use of what might be termed the pupils' background knowledge required for their responses.

Teacher:	And what is the policeman doing this side?
S6:	Blocking, blocking the people from coming.
Teacher:	Blocking the people from coming?
	Why? Yes?
S7:	Because if you crowd round you.[?], its harmful to the boy.
Teacher:	Yes, probably because if you are going to crowd around the injured person, maybe the person needs air and all that.

Closely related to this is the use of inference based on what appears in the picture. It is an example of one event or state that can be explained by another in the picture. In the following text the teacher probes the cause for a certain event. The first reason given, that the girl was crying because she had nothing to play with, is an inference based on the observation that the other children in the picture are involved in some sort of pleasurable play activity. The second reason is by direct reference to the picture. There is a causal relationship. Something in the picture is seen as the logical cause of something else that is happening in the picture.

Teacher:	Look. Why do you think she is crying?
SS:	I know, I know.
S2:	Because he nothing play.
Teacher:	Right. OK.
S1:	The balloon fly away.
Teacher:	Ah, maybe her balloon fly, flew off!

	Yes or no?
	She was playing with the balloon.
	Then suddenly the balloon –
SS:	Fly
Teacher:	Right, flew away. OK.

Point to ponder

- Consider what else this teacher is doing through language in this interaction?

6. Justification

The justification strategy is the basis for inference. During a justification sequence attention is directed at the process of making a claim and this process is questioned by the teacher:

Teacher:	OK Hussein, where do you think this place is?
Teacher:	At the beach?
	OK, why do you say its at the beach, Muzbul?

Though explanation and justification are quite different, there are occasions when these two strategies combine. For example, a teacher's probe for justification may yield an explanation as a response.

Teacher:	How do you know he was afraid?
S10:	Because the monster is very ugly and is chasing him.

The inference that has been made is that 'he was afraid' and instead of providing evidence for the inference, the cause of his fear is given based on the other features of the picture. The linguistic structure or form of the appropriate response for explanation and justification strategies may be similar.

7. The closure

The curriculum genre of an English lesson often ends with a writing task.

Teacher:	Now go back and write a few sentences for me.

Sometimes the task is outlined on the blackboard or the pupils under the direction of the teacher give a verbal account of the text that they later write up.

The curriculum genre of picture talk is an oral interactive classroom genre with the following characteristics:

1 the pupils have the possibility of contributing to the activity;
2 they can build up their linguistic and commonsense knowledge and skills;
3 strategies of their natural use of language are exploited and
4 problems are solved jointly through interaction between the teacher and the pupils so that the young learners can become more competent users of the language.
5 Picture talk also leads to the production of written texts so it can also be considered a writing negotiation genre.

Picture talk curriculum genre provides insights into the range of text-types that primary school pupils are socialized into as part of their school learning experiences. The picture talk curriculum genre places emphasis on oral/spoken language, although the lessons are dominated by the teacher–pupil interaction with the teacher taking a central role, guiding the discourse. Lesson also lead to writing activity and the creation of a written text. The oral interaction is meant as an introduction and preparation for the writing activity. This approach is based on the assumption that oral language is the basis for writing texts. The picture talk curriculum genre can be characterized as being the use of a number of strategies. These include:

● a high proportion of labelling, naming and comment/observation strategies
● some appeal to background knowledge
● identification and description strategies
● inferencing and hypothesizing strategies.

However, this suggests that the teacher rarely exploits the full range of language and ideas demonstrated by the pupils during the oral interaction events of the lessons. From the extracts presented it is clear that pupils need to develop ways of behaving appropriate to being a pupil in a classroom. They need to learn what the teacher expects of them, linguistically and in their social behaviour. Very often the teacher does not give direction or explicit guidance on these expectations. This is part of the invisible pedagogy that Bernstein describes and which pupils have to learn if they are to be successful in school learning.

However, the classroom is not just made up of production skills (speaking), but also of reception skills (listening). Listening skills are often listed as a high priority by teachers. This quite understandable concern arises from observations that some children seem unable to retain, or comprehend, information spoken to them by the teacher. On the other hand, other children do seem to retain information and appear to understand. The conclusion often drawn is that the former lack listening skills. It is certainly true that individual children do vary in their aptitude for different intellectual pursuits, but there might be other reasons worth considering. The successful retention and comprehension of information by children may depend on such matters as: the motivation of the both the teacher and the child to attend to and communicate with each other; the extent to which the teacher and child have a shared understanding, a common framework of language and concepts. To have this common framework the following points would need to be considered:

- What do children need to know about classroom talk?
- How can established patterns of communication in the classroom be modified to assist children's learning?
- How well do they understand the purpose of what they are doing in school and the criteria for success in school work?
- How does the wider social context influence patterns of communication in the classroom?

What do children need to know about classroom talk?

Early studies into the discourse of classroom talk (Sinclair and Coulthard 1975; Mehan 1979; Willes 1983) have concentrated on the structure of the discourse created by teachers and pupils. One of the main conclusions drawn, as we have seen was that much of the discourse falls into very regular patterns. One very common pattern of exchange often termed IRF is 'initiation' (by the teacher), a 'response' (by the pupil), and further evaluation or 'feedback' from the teacher on what the child has said. A typical example would be the following extract from a maths class:

Teacher:	OK, Troy, the first one (**I**)
P:	(undecipherable) 0.8 (**R**)
Teacher:	0.8 correct (**F**)
Teacher:	Second one, Craig (**I**)
S:	I haven't even started (**R**)
Teacher:	Quick, do it in your head. (**F**) 6.6 divided by 3. (**I**).

(Veel 1999: 211)

It is easy to see why this kind of pattern develops as a teacher wants to find out what a pupil knows, and offer confirmation, correction or guidance. Using a whole series of exchanges, a teacher can lead pupils through a set procedure, checking their understanding as the lesson progresses. This can enable a teacher to work with a group, or even a whole class, in such a way that all the children involved can attend both to the questions and to the answers either given by the teacher or the individual pupils.

Through the language of the classroom, most children encounter many new features of language when they go to school, and one aspect of this will be the new words, and the new meaning of some words they know. If our aim is to broaden the children's experience of language, and to develop their language repertoire so that they can express themselves more adequately, then vocabulary enrichment can be an important part of this development. This growth in language helps to scaffold through the interaction in the development of educational knowledge. However, there are a number of problems that children may encounter. One is that some words, or some meanings of words, will be encountered only by the children in school and their out-of-school experience may offer little opportunity for them to develop their understanding of these words. Another is that many words with which the children are familiar outside school may rarely if ever be part of the school vocabulary. In multilingual settings, the segregation of the language experience in the home and in the school domains may mean that an opportunity for school to make an important contribution to one aspect of their language development – helping them develop the sophisticated translating skill of communicating ideas from one language into another is being missed.

Patterns of communication in the classroom assist children's learning

Teachers in schools and other educational institutions use language to pursue their professional aims and goals. One of their aims is to guide the learning activity of their pupils along directions required by the syllabus, and to try to construct a joint, shared version of educational knowledge with their pupils. There are certain common techniques that teachers use to try and achieve this. The techniques (no matter how subconscious) are goal-directed ways of talking, which reflect the constraints of the institutional setting. This is what Bernstein (1996: 26) called framing: the controls on communication in local, interactional pedagogical relations.

The patterns of communication, which can be observed in most classrooms are that of one teacher trying to keep in touch with all the individuals in the class, while the pupils typically only have to communicate with the teacher. But the IRF pattern of interaction not only reflects the relationship between the teacher and the pupils. This pattern has come to define that nature of the relationship in many classrooms. The question to explore now is, can the children's learning experience be enhanced through a different pattern of classroom talk?

Teacher–pupil interaction

Although we have seen that there are good educational reasons for the emergence of some typical patterns of teacher–pupil discourse (the IRF teacher–pupil discourse), it seems that once learnt, these kinds of patterns quickly become habitual. They can dominate classroom talk to such an extent that they allow little opportunity for different patterns of communication to emerge. Studies such as Wells (1984), Legaretta (1977), Bialystok (1978), Ramirez et al.(1986), Nunan (1989), Brumfit and Mitchell (1990), Mercer (1995) and Foley et al. (1998a) all show that pupils have very little opportunity to ask questions and that they rarely initiate exchanges. This is true of primary, secondary, the EFL and foreign language classroom. The pupils' contributions to discussions, on the basis of their own knowledge have to be tailored to the teacher asks, pupils reply, teacher comments format. At the very best, this limits the opportunities for learners to develop and practise a broader range of communication skills, such as how to ask effective questions, how to present one's ideas clearly and how to comment on the statements made by other people. Whether the quantity of teacher talk is a good thing or not, will depend on what one believes about the role of input in the learning process. If one believes that learners learn best by doing, then the classroom activities will be structured so that the amount of learner talk is increased at the expense of teacher talk.

In the following example (Mercer 1995) a class of fourteen year olds were engaged in an extended computer-based communication with children in a nearby primary school. In a fantasy adventure, the secondary school pupils were pretending to be stranded in space and time. Explanations of their predicament and requests for solutions were emailed to the primary children. In this sequence the teacher was questioning one group of girls about the most recent interaction by email.

Teacher: What about the word dimension, because you were going to include that in your message, weren't you?
Anne: Yeh, And there's going to be – if they go in the right room, then they'll find a letter in the floor and that'll spell dimension.
Teacher: What happens if they go in the wrong room?
Emma: Well, there's no letter in the bottom, in the floor.
Teacher: Oh God! So they've got to get it right, or that's it! (*everyone laughs*) The adventurers are stuck there for ever, And

Cath can't get back to her own time. What do you mean the letters are in the room, I don't quite follow that?

Emma: On the floor, like a tile of something.

Teacher: Oh I see. Why did you choose the word dimension?

Anne: Don't know (*the three pupils speak together, looking to each other, seeming uncertain*)

Emma: It just came up. Just said, you know, dimension and everyone agreed.

Sharon: Don't know.

Teacher: Right, because it seemed to fit in with, what, the fantasy flow, flavour?

Sharon: Yeh.

(Mercer 1995: 30–1)

By observing and monitoring the patterns of dialogue, which go on in the classroom, the teacher can ensure the opportunity for pupils to increase and make more varied contributions. In the sequence we have just seen, the teacher uses questions to draw out from the pupils the content of their recent email message, and also some justifications for what they include in it. In some ways the teachers' language is classical teacher-talk. Most of her questions are ones to which she does not already know the answers; but she certainly evaluates the answers she receives. There are the recognizable IRF exchanges. Like many effective teachers she is using her enquiries not only to monitor children's activity, but also to guide it. Wells (1984) suggested that such activities as creative and open-ended tasks whose outcomes are not entirely defined in advance by the teacher and which draw on the children's own experience are among the most effective examples of teacher-pupil communication.

Communication between children

It is a characteristic feature of progressive or learner centred teaching for teachers to organize their pupils into groups for task based activities. One criticism often levied at this practice is that even when the pupils are organized into groups they often work individually on the task set. There are some obvious organizational advantages in group work for the teacher. The pupils become actively engaged in the tasks set and they talk about things among themselves. Yet many language classrooms have not given high priority to collaborative activities requiring talk between the learners. This may be because are not entirely clear of convinced of the educational benefits of collaborative learning and small group activity. Traditionally, talk between learners in the classroom has been discouraged and treated as disruptive or even subversive. Although ideas may be changing, pupil–pupil talk in the classroom context is still regarded suspiciously by many teachers. So while the experience of everyday life supports the value of collaboration educational practice has implicitly argued against it.

Part of the reason for this is that some of the more prominent theories of children's cognitive development over the last hundred years have been too individualistic. As Donaldson (1978) pointed out, the children's performance in the experimental tasks used by Piaget were strongly influenced by the social context and their understanding of their relationship with their experimenter. Under varying social circumstances, children's apparent level of cognitive development would therefore seem to vary. As we have seen cognitive development is inextricably tied up with social development. Translated into classroom practice, this means (among other things) setting up more structures, which enable children to communicate with each other and to practise and develop their communicative abilities. The concept of socio-cognitive conflict was used to take account of how a child's understanding may be shifted by interacting with another child who has a different understanding of events (Bell *et al.* 1985). The idea is that when two contrasting world-views are brought into contact, and the resulting conflict has to be resolved to solve the problem, it is likely to stimulate some cognitive restructuring – some learning, empathizing that can lead to an improved understanding.

Collaborative learning and small group activities have been foregrounded particularly in EFL/ESL studies (Brumfit 1984; Long and Porter 1985; Nunan, 1989; and Ellis 1997). These studies found that pair work and small group work afforded more opportunity for language production and a wider range of language use in such areas as initiating discussion, asking for clarification, interrupting, competing for the floor and joking. There has been the argument that exposure to incorrect peer input may lead to fossilization (Plann 1977) and as Pica and Doughty (1988) point out the interlanguage talk produced by the learners is less grammatical than teacher talk. The same argument is also used against the use of the mother tongue or home language(s) in the classroom. This argument has been particularly strong against pupils whose home language is a vernacular, dialect, or non-standard variety. Hence, practice to date has rarely supported pupils' bidialectism.

If we were to summarize what research has indicated as the benefits of small group work to encourage among other things, communication between learners they would seem to be the following:

that the children talk more freely

they take greater risks with their thinking

they take greater initiatives in posing questions

they relate their own experience to the new learning

they draw on more of their linguistic range however limited

they carry the support and the help they often give each other in their social relationships into their school learning.

The argument that group teaching, as opposed to whole class teaching, provides language learners with more opportunities to talk. This is based on the assumption that talk, irrespective of the focus or form, is of intrinsic benefit in school learning.

Being in school is a unique experience for children; they do things there that they would never do in the rest of their lives. School has its own rules for how they should talk and act and very rarely are these rules, or aims that underlie them, made explicit. Bernstein (1996) has termed them invisible pedagogy. Children are taught how to do specific things, like how to read and write but the underlying ground rules are something that they have to try and work out for themselves. Their conception of what they are doing and why may differ from that of the teachers.

According to Bernstein any particular form of pedagogic discourse is constituted by three types of rules which are hierarchically related, that is 'distributive rules' regulate the 'recontextualizing rules', which regulate the 'rules of evaluation'.

Distribution rules regulate who may have access to what knowledge and therefore who may have access to discursive power. In many classrooms the distribution rules come from the teacher, although he/she may have received them from other sources such as the syllabus or the textbook.

Recontextualization rules provide a means for understanding the embedding of discourses which are produced in sites outside formal schooling (such as the interpretation of important historical events). A significant question for cultural production and reproduction is: in what form should this knowledge be reproduced in pedagogic discourse? The move from the original documentation or the interpretation of the documents/events to reproduction in pedagogic discourse requires selection and ordering of the content according to some set of principles. For example how these historical events are presented, we will see in a later chapter how the whole episode of Christopher Columbus and his impact on the Americas has only recently been re-contextualized in a light that is less flattering than before. Even this re-contextualizing can carry with it a conscious or unconscious bias.

In educational knowledge what we are often evaluating is the re-contextualized knowledge of subject areas, such as history, geography, physics, maths and so on. In other words our assessment of whether or not educational knowledge has been transferred to a particular group of children is through formal examinations and/or assessments. Such assessment is often based on the criteria which may have been set by the school or an official body such as the government setting a series of standards to be attained as in a national curriculum. In a foreign language situation the criteria are set by proficiency examinations such as the TOEFL/IELTS. The question of how well do children or even older pupils understand these criteria for success should perhaps be rephrased in terms of how valid these criteria are for determining the amount of educational knowledge attained by the learners at their various stages of learning. The validity of these criteria is to show that the learner has sufficient knowledge to proceed to the next level in the educational process. However, it is doubtful that these criteria are in fact valid in the first place. This has been well illustrated by how poorly A-level results predict degree results at university or equally how unsatisfactory the TEOFL/IELTS scores are as an indicator of the learner's ability to use English in real situations.

How does the wider social context influence patterns of communication in the classroom?

Communication in the classroom as elsewhere, involves much more than exchange of words (written or spoken) between teachers and children. Non-verbal communication such as body gestures, facial expressions and tone of voice are all integral parts of non-verbal communication signals. It is often the non-verbal signals that convey our feelings – our moods, attitudes towards the person we are talking to. More than 30 years ago Good (1970) found that pupils who teachers expect to do well received much more verbal praise and other signs of approval than those for whom they had lower expectations.

For example Bourne (1992) found that teachers dealing with children they consider as bright seem to model their better pupils with self-directive, reflective, questioning. As for their choice of language the teachers expressed solidarity with the pupils and encouraged further interaction.

Example

Teacher: Right. Where's! This is the first bit! up to, oh up to there. So that first bit is about what then?
Tuk: (inaudible)
Teacher: Its about the little shell?
Tuk: (inaudible)

Teacher: Uh huh. What's the next bit about then? I tell you what, why don't you go and get me the shell and then we'll know what were talking about. (pause)

Teacher: Now where's this little shell? (pause – Tuk shows her.)

Teacher: That looks like a whelks shell, like Nicola's. Gosh. And the second/Is this the second bit? What's that about?

Tuk: (inaudible)

Teacher: Uh huh. And what's your next bit? What's that about?

Tuk: (inaudible)

Teacher: But then you've said here some of the lines are. You're still talking about the lines. And here you're talking about the spikes again.
That's a new section. And here you're talking about the spike again. I think all this is about what the shell looks like. Yeah. Except this bit.

Tuk: That's what lives in it.

Teacher: That's what lives in it isn't it?

> (Bourne 1992: 543–4)

In contrast, teachers dealing with children who are regarded as less able produce a different interaction. They use more direct questions; the discourse does not use the inclusive 'we' but 'you'. There is little or no direct reference to the text itself. In interaction with these children teachers focus much more on content.

Example:

Teacher: What does that mean? What did you mean by that? You don't know! (pause) Let's just . . . If I just write some of this again. Up to that bit.
(Pause)
My . . . You read it for me as we go.

Somiron: My shell is a brown . . . (hesitates)

Teacher: Venus

Somiron: Venus shell and it had vertical stripes on it.

Teacher: Just a minute, just a minute: vertical stripes on it . . . (writing)
(. . .)

Teacher: Right. Now I'm going to put a full stop there. Now you tell me what you wanted to say next. Don't look at that (referring to the child's previously written text she is holding). Tell me what you wanted to say next about the shell.

> (Bourne 1992: 547)

The evidence presented here suggests that, contrary to the concept of pupils being alone struggling to express themselves, the teacher's intervention in the process of constructing text in the classroom can have a very powerful effect. Consequently, we need to ask how far differential teacher intervention might work to produce pupils at different levels of attainment.

Of course, this is far from being the whole picture. There are many ways in which teachers' and children's experience of the wider social world outside school influences the taken-for-granted patterns and content of classroom communication. Three social factors which have been given attention by researchers are gender, race and culture. Again it has been well established in a number of studies in the early 1980s (for example, Stanworth 1981; French and French 1984) that there was more attention given to boys than to girls in class. The indicators were that the boys get more verbal and non-verbal indications from teachers that they are important, likeable, and capable of making valuable spoken and written contributions in class.

How much of this is a reflection of society is a debatable point (Coates 1994; Mills 1995; Cameron 1998). There is certainly an asymmetrical representation of women and men in society at large. For example, the following appeared on a News Broadcast (3 January 1995) in the United Kingdom with references to changes in the laws regarding children in licensed drinking bars.

> For decades, pubs have been man's best friend. He could take his wife, his girlfriend, but not his children. But now that's all about to change.
>
> (As quoted in Thomas and Wareing 1999: 68)

Also, different arguments and explanations have been put forward about how the various factors of language variation, cultural background and racial attitudes influence the behaviour of both teachers and pupils in their classroom (Heath 1983; Barton 1992; and Saxena 1994). Some of these explanations, while sharing a strong concern for the educational futures of ethnic minorities, sometimes seem in apparent opposition (see Rampton 1995 for an extensive discussion on this issue). It is certainly the case that growing up in an ethnic minority community, or speaking a language or dialect other than the standard variety, will mean that some children will come to school with a culturally specific style of communicative behaviour which is different from that of the teachers and the education system. This will not only make for different interpretations of specific aspects of communication like tone or voice, purpose of questions and non-verbal signals, but may also lead to behaviour which the teacher is liable to misinterpret. So for some children using the language of the dominant community can be regarded as denial or even betrayal of their own cultural and ethnic identity.

> My sister, she's a right little snobby . . . if she came here now she'd speak plain English, but she can speak Patois better than me. She speaks it to me, to some of her coloured friends who she knows speak Patois, but to her snobby coloured friends she speaks English. She talks Queen English, brebber. She's the snotty one of the family.
>
> (Edwards 1986: 121)

When issues of equality are discussed in terms of how they can influence interpersonal communication (see Cameron 1995 for a discussion of the factors involved), it is not uncommon to hear people (and in particular teachers) assert that they treat everyone as individuals and that they respond to individual children's personalities. Such assertions are naïve. Communication is a mutual affair even if most teachers do not consciously intend to talk differently to different children. Children quickly acquire their own expectations of how they should act and talk. With these matters, as with other aspects of teaching, teachers can only feel confident about what they are doing in the classroom if they have made real efforts to observe and monitor what really goes on and not just assume that their best intentions are reflected in practice.

7.4 Summary

In this chapter we have been looking at the transition from common-sense knowledge to educational knowledge with a particular focus on the use of spoken language in the classroom. Bernstein's studies in the 1970s and Hasan's in the 1980s underlined the importance of language in the home environment, particularly in preparing the child for the more formal setting of classroom language. In spite of cultural differences, it was noted that the language and interaction of the home environment remains a key influence in the development of a child's language.

However, language in the school is institutionalized as Christie has pointed out. That is to say it can be seen as a series of teaching/learning episodes that have a distinct pattern. These Christie has called curriculum genres which are mainly oral in nature especially at primary school level. We further examined one such curriculum genre, that of picture talk. Although this study was done within the specific context of Singapore, it was felt that the finding would be applicable to many primary school situations. The teacher often did not often seem to exploit the range of language or ideas that had been developed in the oral interaction especially when it came to the writing output of the children. In other words the teacher did use the spoken language of the children as a gateway to develop educational knowledge and exploit the potential within the zone of proximal development.

We also discussed the fact that language in the classroom is not just about speaking but also about listening. In general, listening skills are often listed as a high priority by teachers, but the careful retention and comprehension of information by children in their listening depends on a variety of factors. Such factors were found to include: the motivation of both teachers and children, the extent to which the teachers and children shared a common framework of language(s) and concepts (such as criteria for success in school work). Lastly we looked at the importance of the wider social context of gender, race and culture and the effects these have on developing educational knowledge.

Activity

Read the following extract from the writings of Margaret Donaldson, an educational psychologist, and note down your own thoughts on what she is saying, with particular reference to your own country, community or region.

> In the first few years at school all appears to go very well. The children seem eager, lively, and happy. There is commonly an atmosphere of spontaneity in which they are encouraged to explore and discover and create. There is much concern, on the part of teachers, with high educational ideals. These things tend to be true even in parts of the community, which are far from being socially privileged in other ways. However, when we consider what has happened by the time the children reach adolescence, we are forced to recognize that the promise of the early years frequently remains unfulfilled. Large numbers leave school with the bitter taste of defeat in them, not having mastered even moderately well those basic skills which society demands, much less having become people who rejoice in the exercise of creative intelligence.
>
> (Donaldson 1978: 13–14)

7.5 Further reading

Mercer, N. 1995: *The guided construction of knowledge, talk amongst teachers and learners*. Clevedon: Multilingual Matters.

Mercer, N. 2000: *Words and minds: How we use language to think together*. London: Routledge.

8 Developing language through writing

> Mine was the kind of piece in which nobody knew what was going on, including the writer, the publisher and the reader. Consequently, I got pretty good notices
>
> (adapted from Oscar Lavant)

In previous chapters we have focused on ways in which children have to learn new ways of behaving and speaking appropriately when they enter formal education. In this chapter we explore how children learn about language through writing. We shall explore frameworks for understanding written texts that help learners towards a critical understanding of these models and frameworks that describe writing.

Children arrive at school already highly competent and sophisticated language users. As children enter school their linguistic repertoires has to broaden from the common-sense functions of language they have learnt to use with their coterie of more familiar others to include different types of language with different functions. These include educational and specialist subject technical texts. As pupils, young learners need to be able to both create and understand these new forms of language. Central to school learning and the education-linguistic repertoire is learning to be literate, that is, learning to read the texts that others have created, and learning to create texts for others to read. Levels of literacy are a key public, political and educational issue in societies all around the world. Levels of literacy among the population are frequently used as a measure of national development. Learning to be literate is used a key measure of educational success and learner competence. One of the key differences between common-sense texts that children already speak and understand when they begin their formal education and the educational and technical texts central to school learning, is the ways in which children learn these different facets of their repertoire. By the time children arrive in school they have already learnt a great deal about language. It is likely that their linguistic repertoire will be highly developed and that oral language skills will dominate. Literacy will be less well so but this does not mean young children have no experience or understanding of written texts. To understand how we become literate it is important to consider the differences between spoken and written texts. The following table lists features of written and spoken language or texts. In written texts the linguistic features of the language, in this case English, are realized in different ways. Halliday (1992: 31) suggests a number of differences between spoken and written forms of English.

Here follows a comparison of written and spoken texts.

Spoken texts	Written texts
Prosodic features	Marked by punctuation
Sounds	Marked by spelling
Phonology	Marked by punctuation
Words	Marked by the letters of the alphabet
Utterances	Marked by strings of letters as words
Highly rule bound	Highly rule bound
First language – naturalistic	Usually requires a teacher

8.1 Components of the structure of written texts

- Letters of the alphabet.
- Is combined in strings to become morphemes.
- Is divided into units of words.
- These combine to become sentences.
- Sentences combine to become texts.
- Texts include features such as:
  - Cohesion
  - deixis
  - anaphoric and cataphoric referents

These features all apply to written English. Some are more general features of texts written in other languages. In addition, the following can be regarded as identifying features of written English:

- Left-to-right orientation.
- Top-to-bottom orientation.
- Capitalization of letters is significant.
- Spelling conveys meanings (cf. hair and hare).
- Punctuation is significant.
- Deixis and cohesion are important.</BL>

Consider other writing systems with which you are familiar.

Point to ponder
- What are the characteristic features of other writing systems, for example, Chinese, Arabic, Japanese?

The language that children learn to read and write in school may not always be the same language of their aural repertoire. In some cases it may be a different variety of the language. Hence young learners will need to expand their linguistic repertoire to learn these new varieties. For some this will mean developing on from the colloquial variety that forms part of their aural repertoire to learn the standard variety for the written texts that are central to school learning. As English increases in influence as the global language of formal education around the world (Graddol 1997) for some being a pupil will require learning a new language for school learning. Learning to be literate increasingly means learning to read and write the English language.

A great deal of educational debate during the last decade has centred around methods of teaching reading. Educationalists have been polarized: those who advocate that learning to read and learning to write should emulate the learning to talk, and those who advocate the teaching of skills specific to written texts. In many ways, this debate reflects the one that has characterized approaches to child language development. Is it a cognitive process or social activity? The list above identifies ways in which written and spoken texts are simultaneously both similar and different. This contrast between spoken and written texts is more apparent in some languages than it is in English. For example, Arabic where the standard written forms (SWA) differ in structure, lexicon, and so on from the colloquial varieties spoken in Arabic speaking countries geographically dispersed from Morocco to Saudi Arabia and the Gulf region. While the SWA is mutually intelligible in all communities (at least for those who are literate) for the colloquial varieties this may not necessarily always be the case.

Written texts in English have uniquely defining features that differ from other written language systems, for example, Arabic and Chinese characters. English written texts are characterized by left-to-right orientation across the page and top-to-bottom layout on the page (directionality), capitalization and letter formation, conventions of spelling and punctuation, deixis, coherence and cohesion, and features such as collocation and to be literate, learning to read and learning to write. Debates around how best to teach children to read and write have followed the debates held elsewhere in the literature on language development, namely whether it is a social or cognitive process. This debate can somewhat simplistically be characterized as a process-product divide with some insisting that the product, that is the text produced being the important thing, while others suggesting that it is the processes by which the text is created that is important for understanding more about how children learn to write.

Maley (1993: 04) provided the following comparison between product/genre and process approaches:

Process	Genre
Individual	Social
Creative	Conformist
Exploratory	Prescriptive
Invention	Convention
Process	Product
Evolving meaning	Codified meaning
Finding the way	Knowing the destination
Problem-solving	Solution-stating
Education	Training

Britton *et al.* (1975) and Graves (1983) were amongst those who expressed support for a process model because of the perceived negative impact of a product/genre driven approach particularly for young learners. Their view was that if the surface structure of the text was to be the main focus of attention it could stifle creativity in the young writers. Britton (1982) spoke of 'spontaneous inventiveness' and 'shaping at the point of utterance'. He likened the writing process to one of hearing an inner voice dictating forms of the written language appropriate to the task in hand (Britton 1982). Bereiter and Scardamalia (1987) favoured conferencing, a process whereby learners talked about their writing with their peers or talking together in a focused way to create joint written texts. All favour writing as a cognitive process. Britton, Bereiter and

Scardamalia all stressed the centrality of meaning in the writing process. Widdowson (1983: 38) explained 'Meaning is a function of the interaction between participants . . . mediated through language', emphasizing the importance of audience and socially appropriate forms of text. This is a view similar to that of the genre theorists (cf. Christie, Halliday, Martin). Process writing stressed individual creativity, ownership of the text and the expression of personal experience through 'a voice of one's own', which Bamford (1992) regards as an inner rather than outer orientation. The link between individual creativity and social interaction was also made by Freire (1972) who suggested that teaching literacy is concerned with the construction of social realities and only secondarily with the technicalities of how this is achieved through written forms. However, he held the view that writers should create their own texts and that these should express personal identity and personal realities, and in this way contest the dominant society's overdetermination of the writer's reality. In sum, process writing theory is concerned with *how* writing takes place.

It was an approach favoured by many primary school educators and led to an almost sole focus on one particular type of text, creative writing, story or narrative, with little or no exposure to and experience of other forms of writing such as expository or factual writing. Thus writing in the classroom was seen more as a form of creative expression rather than an across-the-curriculum tool for learning. Yet factual or expository writing is central to all subject study in secondary school. An early attempt to re-focus the teaching of writing was the *Language in Use* (Doughty *et al.* 1971) programme for secondary school use which developed as a follow-on to the *Breakthrough to Literacy* programme in the United Kingdom. A continuation of the linguistic and pedagogical principles on which these programmes were based was developed in the Department of Linguistics at the University of Sydney. One of the main concerns of this research was with construing instructional and pedagogical (both instructional and regulative) discourse as genre. This concern was eventually developed into several other school projects including the *Language and Social Power Project* in the 1980s and the *Write it Right Project* in the 1990s in the Metropolitan East Region of Sydney's Disadvantaged Schools programme (Rothery 1994). Recognition of the central importance of expository texts in classroom learning led by researchers including Martin and Rothery (1980, 1981, 1988), Martin (1992, 1997a), Christie (1984, 1995, 1999), Derewianka (1990), Collerson (1994) focused on textual aspects of writing and helped to bridge the divide between the process-product approaches. Their approach combined a focus on textual features with the social and cultural contexts in which the texts were produced.

It was Halliday's appointment to the chair of linguistics at the University of Sydney in the mid-1970s that gave impetus to the development of the systemic-functional model of text and genre descriptions in Australia. This coincided with wider interest in genre that emphasized the significance between becoming literate as a means of accessing social power and thereby gaining social equality, as well as a linguistic interest in the predictable forms, structures and purposes of texts. The systemic-functional model has been enhanced by wider interest from other groups including:

- The English as a Foreign Language (EFL)/ English for Special Purposes (ESP) model;
- the social process model;
- the 'new rhetoric' model.

8.2   Genre

Genre analysis has a long-standing tradition in EFL, especially in ESP. Richards *et al.* (1992: 156) described a genre as 'a particular class of speech events which are considered by the speech community as being of the same type'. Their examples include prayers, sermons, songs, speeches, conversations, novels and letters. They point out that a single genre may contain instances of other genres. These they term complex genres. EFL teaching has been interested in genre as a tool for analysing and teaching the spoken and written language required of EFL users, especially in academic and professional settings, thus the emphasis in the area of ESP (cf. Bhatia 1993; Hopkins and Dudley-Evans 1988; Swales 1986, 1990a, 1990b; Thompson 1994, amongst others). Swales' work which has been seminal in shaping genre theory in ESP describes genres as 'communicative events that are characterized both by their communicative purpose and by the various patterns of structure, style, content and intended audience (Swales 1990a: 58). Analyses of ESP texts have paid particular attention to detailing the formal characteristics of genres and less on the specialized functions of texts and their social contexts. Thus, descriptions of language patterns and audience expectations in the ESP approach to genre analysis are described as being characteristic of a particular genre, rather than being features by which the genre might be defined.

Genre as a social process model

In an article entitled 'Towards a social theory of genre', Kress and Threadgold (1988) proposed an account of text as a number of partially independent intertextual systems and processes. Threadgold put this into a wider perspective:

> A theory of language as a social semiotic and of language and ideology has to concern itself with language as a form of social interaction, a meaning potential in and through which subjects and the social are constructed and reproduced and cultural and human conflict are negotiated.
>
> (Threadgold 1986)

Both Kress and Threadgold regard Halliday's notion of register as a starting point but stress more the modalities of the social interactions that form and accompany texts.

Texts have their way by which they were created. This model focuses on developing a detailed analysis of the often hidden ideological effects and outcomes of texts. This will be discussed in more detail in Chapter 10, particularly with reference to multi-literacies. Kress stresses the social elements of genre rather than the surface features of the text, such as the organization, structure, and grammar. Key questions for those working within a social process model is 'What is going on in the text?' and 'What social dynamics are at play here?' While SF theorists such as Martin approach the text more in terms of, 'What stages has this text been through to reach its purpose?' These differences are not merely theoretical. They have significant implications when using genre theory to develop pedagogy for teaching writing in the classroom.

The new rhetoric model

Research emerging from what has become known as 'new rhetoric' studies (Bazerman 1988, 1994; Coe 1994; Freedman and Medway 1994a, 1994b; Miller 1984, 1994) reflects another approach to conceptualizing and analysing genre. These studies from a variety of disciplines concerned with L1 teaching, including rhetoric, composition and professional writing have focused more on the situational contexts in which the genres occur than on the forms. They have placed special emphasis on the social purposes or actions that these genres fulfil within these situations. Miller (1984) argues that a rhetorically sound definition of genre must be centred not on the substance or the form of the discourse but on the action aims to accomplish. New rhetoric frequently uses ethnographic rather than linguistic models to understand texts (Bazerman 1988; Schryer 1994; Smart 1993). Miller says that a genre represents 'a conventional category of discourse based on large scale typification of rhetorical action' (Miller 1984: 163). The examples that she quotes are letters of recommendation, progress reports, lectures, public proceedings and sermons. Bazerman further extends this view when he argues that expected features and understanding of a genre vary through time, place and situation. A genre does not exist apart from its history, which continues with each new text invoking the genre. These genre theories are part of a wider social empowerment model (see Gee 1990 for an overview). Other models include critical language awareness models (cf. Fairclough 1989, 1992 and Baynham 1995) who emphasize the social purpose and contexts but subject them to critical analysis as part of the educational process. This aspect of language awareness will be discussed in the next chapter.

Genre theorists, however, place their theory of language within a framework which connects with socio-political contexts. The outer layer, language as social practice, incorporates ideologies with discourses and institutional environments (Fairclough 1989; Kress 1989). The next layer, language as social process, incorporates the ways in which language is interactionally accomplished in contexts of situation or what Martin and Rothery (1980, 1981) defined as staged, goal-oriented social processes. The inner most level is language as text, which links into the semantic, lexico-grammar,

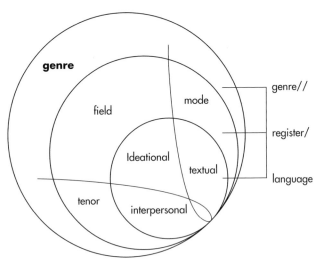

Figure 8.1 Genre, register and language (Martin 1997a: 11)

phonology/graphology features of language. Diagrammatically the three layers are represented in Figure 8.1 representing overlapping configurations.

The purpose of genre theorists is to provide a holistic approach to language initially by examining the core text-types used in education settings. It is believed that this approach to learning to write is better preparation for life beyond the classroom and school domain.

However, Martin (1997a) suggests that genres cannot be divided into types with categorical precision. He proposed a set of criteria for establishing degrees of nearness or proximity texts in the same category. He proposes a range of parameters which define similarity and differences among the text-types or genres (Martin 1997a: 15 quoting Lemke). For example, from the typological perspective, the categorical differences between historical recounts and personal accounts is difficult because many texts use a combination of sequential and causal relations. In reality there is more of a 'cline' towards one rather than the other. This topological perspective on genre is particular useful in educational contexts because it facilitates the development of learner pathways in that it outlines what kind of developmental sequence that might help students move smoothly from the control of one genre to another. It also helps teachers and students to recognize types of genres in their reading and which may not always be prototypical examples of canonical genres (Martin 1997a).

8.3 Core-genre in the development of educational knowledge

In terms of language development and the growth of educational knowledge the following is a list of genres that are typically found in western educational systems where English is the medium of instruction. Obviously such genres can also be found in the EFL/ESL classroom. There are two broad elements: essential i.e. those without which the genres would not achieve its purpose, and optional. It is possible, of course, to find unexpected elements or stages in a text. One genre may even be embedded within another, for example, information reports often contain explanations. However in exploring and analysing texts, we need to look at the function of each stage and ask what roles it is playing in helping the text achieve its purpose. The main text types found in the school syllabus are outlined in the following table overleaf:

The main generic structures used in school settings: (^) optional element, (*) recursive (Foley 1994: 295).

Main generic structures used in school settings

Observation/ comment:	Orientation (^) Event Description (^) Comment (^)
Recount:	Orientation (^) Event (*) Re-orientation (^)
Narrative:	Orientation (^) Complication (*) Resolution (*) Coda (^)

Report:	General classification,
	 Description – parts [and their functions] ⎱ not necessarily
	               qualities ⎰ in this order
	               habits/behaviour/uses

Procedure:	Goal Steps (*) Diagram (^)
Explanation:	General statement Sequenced explanation (*) Final state of being or thing produced.
Exposition:	Thesis Position Preview Argument (*) Point Elaboration Reiteration of thesis
Discussion:	Issue | Argument (*) — for/against | Recommendation (^)

[The main generic structures used in school settings(^) optional element, (*) recursive]

The following examples of these text types or genres are taken from multilingual environments where English is the medium of instruction.

Text type 1: recount genres

Recount genres reconstruct past experience. A recount is the unfolding of a sequence of events over time. Language is used to keep the past alive and to help to interpret past experiences.

Purpose

To tell what happened.

Types of recount genres

Personal recount: the retelling of an activity that the writer/speaker has been personally involved in (e.g. oral account, diary entry, a letter).

Factual recount: the recording of particulars of an incident (e.g. an historical account, a newspaper account of an incident).

Imaginative recount: taking an imaginary role and creating details of events (e.g. a day in the life of . . .).

Text organization is important. It focuses on a sequence of events which relate to a particular occasion. It can be organized in the following way:

Orientation (optional): giving the reader/listener the background information needed to understand the text (i.e. *who* was involved, *where* it happened, *when* it happened).

Event 1: the recount unfolds with a series of events.

Event 2

Event 3 . . . and so on

Re-orientation (optional)

It may include some personal comment on the incident (e.g. 'We had a wonderful time').

Personal recount

This is an example of a personal recount text written by a seven-year-old primary 3 pupil in Singapore.

Textual theme	Topical theme	Rheme
Orientation		
		Tuesday January 9th.
	In the holidays,	I <u>went</u> to Malacca for my holidays.
Events		
	We	had my Mum's birthday.
	We	<u>went</u> into town
and [then] of		<u>saw</u> the oldest temple in the whole south east Asia.
Then	we	<u>went</u> to the Church of Christ.
Then	we	<u>went</u> back to the PSA bungalows.
A few days after that	we	<u>went</u> to St John's fort.
	There	were some cannons there.
Then	we	<u>went</u> back to the Portuguese square to have lunch.
Reorientation		
Yesterday	we	<u>went</u> home.
	We	had a wonderful time.

Language features

1 Personal recount: use of first person pronouns: (I, we).

2 Use of the past tense, as a feature of the reconstruction of past experience; (i.e. went, had).

3 Use of action verbs (material processes): that help build the events

    e.g. I <u>went</u> to Malacca.
We <u>went</u> into town.
We <u>went</u> to the Church.
We <u>went</u> back.
We <u>went</u> home.

In this particular text there are one or two relational processes because the child is talking about her own experience: e.g. 'had my Mum's birthday', 'We had a wonderful time'.

There is a tendency to put the narrator in unmarked topical theme position, so that this becomes one of the organizing principles by which the text is carried forward (e.g. 'We had', 'We went', 'We went to', etc.). However, the opening clause has a marked topical theme 'In the holidays', while the final clause is more of a comment.

The use of temporal conjunctions in the position of textual theme, helps to carry forward the events, for example: 'Then', 'A few days after that', 'Yesterday', 'and [then]'. What appears in [ ] does not appear in the actual text but is used to distinguish and [then] from and [therefore], and so on.

Factual recount: Rongotai claims Ablitt Cup

This is an extract from *The Straits Times*, Singapore, Monday 5 November 2001, and in contrast is a more mature example of Recount as found in newspapers.

Textual theme	Topical theme	Rheme
	Rongotai	captured the Ablitt Cup with a 42–7 thrashing of the Australian Legends in the Singapore Cricket Club International Rugby Sevens Tournament at the Padang yesterday
	Rongotai	took control of the match from the starting whistle, with Roy Kimikinilam and Esava Tuki.
	Kimikinilam	used his pace to great effect.
Meanwhile,	Tuki	was doing what he did best, stopping every attack his opponents could put together.
Time and time again,	his excellent positional play	broke up the attacks mounted by the opposing team.
From one counter-attack,	Tuki	fed the ball to team-mate Scott Waldron to bring the score to 15–7.
	The second half	saw Rongotai in the same commanding form and scoring two more tries.
In the dying minutes,	the Kiwi side	scored more tries to complete the rout.

Language features include:

- Details are usually selected to help the reader reconstruct the incident Ablitt Cup, Singapore Cricket Club International Rugby Sevens.
- Sometimes the ending describes the outcome of the incident (scored more tries to complete the rout).
- Details of time and place, and specific participants may need to be stated (Roy Kimikinilam, Esava Tuki, 42–7).
- The passive voice may be used in phrases such as 'it was reported . . .'.
- Textual markers of time give a chronological flow to the whole text ('Meanwhile', 'Time and again', 'In the dying minutes').

Narrative genres

The elements of the narrative genre are based on those proposed by Labov and Waletzky (1967) in their study of oral narratives. It is not suggested that narratives have only one schematic structure (see Toolan 1988). In many cultures the narrative genre may have a much more complicated structure than that offered here. However, the basic pattern will have beginning or orientation, complication and resolution.

The schematic structure of narrative genre is:

- Orientation
- Complication [recursive]
- Resolution [recursive]
- Coda [optional].

Orientation is where the characters are introduced in some setting, often of time ('Once upon a time') or place ('There lived on the mountain'). There has to be a complication, where a problem or series of problems are set. The resolution, is some sort of solution to the problem. The complication-resolution part can be recursive. An optional element is that of the coda where some comment is made on the significance of the story. The essential difference between narrative and recount genres is the complication. As we have seen, recount often has an orientation but is followed by a list of events. Narrative has this basic tripartite structure of orientation, complication and resolution. Young children in oral and written stories will often use the recount genre before developing the full narrative genre. The following text is an example of a narrative written by a primary 5 pupil aged 11 years. English is a foreign language (FL).

An unforgettable evening: narrative genre (primary 5, age:11 FL = E)

Textual theme	Topical theme	Rheme
Orientation		
	Last Sunday evening,	Joe told Raman
that	he	could not go over to Raman's house to play chess
because	his uncle	
	who lived at Rose-Hill	was going to England
and	Joe	would go to meet him.
	The next day	Raman would have the English test.
	He	was reading an English book in a room near the kitchen
and		was thinking about the English test.
Complication		
While	he	was reading
	he	heard a noise in the kitchen
	he	was a bit afraid
because	his parents	told him
that	they	will come home at eight.
When	he	entered the kitchen
	he	saw a thief breaking the window pane to open the door from inside.
	He	cried for help at the top of his voice.
Resolution		
	His friend who lived	
	next door to him	heard the shout of Joe.
	He	ran to telephone the police.
When	the policeman	arrived
	they	caught the thief.
	One of the policemen	went to telephone Joe's parents.
When	they	came home
	the Joe's parents	went to thank the boy.
Coda		
Since that day in	they	never leaved Raman alone the house.

Language features

1 Mainly action verbs there are 16 material action verbs. These include 'to pay', 'was going', 'to meet', 'will come', 'entered'.
2 There are often verbs which refer to what the participants felt or thought: two mental e.g.'was thinking', 'was . . . afraid'; eight verbal (e.g. 'heard', 'told', 'to telephone'). This demonstrates a mix of processes being used by the writer.

Normally narrative uses the past tense for example, 'came home', 'caught', and so on. In this text the past tense is used although there are a number of modals. However, these are inappropriately used for example, 'would go', 'would have'. Also 'will come' is used when it ought to be past tense. The past continuous is used 'was going', 'was reading', 'was thinking' but a 'leaved' and 'to thanked' are frequently found in young FL learners' texts, and in young native speakers of English.

- In more developed narratives dialogue is often included to give the sense of immediacy and the tense can change to the present or future.
- There tends to be much more descriptive language in narrative to enhance and develop the story by creating images in the reader's mind.
- The first or third person can be used. Here the young writer has used the third person throughout.
- Specific references are often used, again a common characteristic for narrative ('Joe', 'his uncle', 'Raman'. The major participants are human, or sometimes animals with human characteristics can be used.
- Several types of textual connectors are for example, 'while', 'when', 'since', 'because', 'then', 'and'.

In this text cohesion is lost because the pronominal reference is confusing. The overuse of 'he' and 'him' means that sometimes the nominal referred to (Joe, Raman) is unclear. Indeed towards the end of the narrative, the writer seems to have confused the referent himself. This leads to a serious breakdown between the writer and the reader's comprehension of the text.

Factual writing

Report genre

The term 'report' is used in everyday language to refer to many different types of factual texts – news reports, science reports, weather reports, and so on. In the example we give here the report is more 'informational'. The function of an information report is to document, organize and store factual information on a topic. Information reports classify and describe the phenomena of our world. We use them to talk about a whole class of things, as in our example 'Reptiles'.

Text organization

> *General classification*
> *Description*
> > parts (and their functions)
> > qualities [not necessarily in this order]
> > habits/ behaviours/uses

So the topic of a report is usually introduced by an opening statement or general classification, followed by facts about various aspects of the subject.

Reptiles (aged 14: secondary 2: FL = E)

Textual theme	Topical theme	Rheme
General classification		
	Common reptiles	<u>are</u> snakes, lizards and crocodiles.
	They	<u>have</u> scales on their body.
	They	<u>lay</u> eggs.
Description (specific qualities)		
	Some of the Mauritian lizards	<u>live</u> on trees and <u>have</u> beautiful blue, green and red colours.
	They	<u>are</u> so beautiful that people abroad <u>keep</u> them as pets.
	There	is a law now which forbids the export of these coloured lizards
because	they	<u>are</u> unique to our island.

Textual theme	Topical theme	Rheme
Description (specific behaviours)		
	We	have other lizards in the house but
	they	are not so pretty.
	The house lizard	can walk on the ceiling
		because they have special pads on the toes.
Description (specific)		
Another	lizard	we have is the cameleon.
Description (specific qualities)		
	Apart from lizards	we have couleuvres.
	There	is no need to be afraid of them since
	they	are completely harmless.
	On Round Island,	there are two types of snakes which are found nowhere else in the world.

Language features

- Generalized participants: a whole class of things (e.g. common reptiles, Mauritian lizards).
- Normally there are many linking verbs that are used in description relational processes of 'being' and 'having', together ('live', 'have', 'are' etc.).
- The descriptive language tends to be factual and precise rather than imaginative (colour, shape, size, body parts, habits, behaviour).
- The language for defining, classifying, comparing and contrasting is used ('have scales', 'have blue, green and red colours', 'walk on ceilings', 'have special pads'). The use of the first person pronouns would normally not be found in this sort of writing because the writing tends to be formal and objective in style.
- There is a noticeable lack of time connectors.
- In the sample text the textual themes are built around: 'and',' because' 'but', 'since'.

Procedure genre

This is a factual text designed to describe how something is accomplished through a sequence of actions or steps. It is an important genre in our society because it enables us to get things done, and is equally common in oral and written mode. Typical examples would be recipes, instructions, game rules, appliance manuals, directions to reach a destination.

Text organization:

- goal
- materials listed in order of use
- steps to achieve the goal
- diagram [optional]

The text may include comments on the usefulness, significance or danger of the activity.

Heading, subheadings, photo numbers are often used to make the instructions clear and easy to understand.

Text (aged 6: Primary 2: MT=E)

The house game

Goal: how to play the house game.
Steps: the rules: numbered in sequence

Textual theme	Topical theme	Rheme
1.	Stand	behind the beanbags
2.	You	must not get a ball into the zero
if	you	do
[then]	it	is the end of the game.
3.If	you	get two, three, four, five or six
[then]	you	have to get the ball in that number to make the number.
Then	it	is the end of your turn.

Language features

- Generalized participants referring to a whole class of things (ingredients, utensils for example in a recipe).
- The reader or person following the instructions is referred to in a general way (you/one) or sometimes not even mentioned at all.
- The verbs will be mainly action type verbs, material processes (i.e. 'stand', 'get', 'do', 'make').

- The tense if often timeless ('You get') or imperative ('Stand behind').
- In a more elaborate text than the one cited here, there could also be factual descriptions (shape, size, colour, amount, etc.).
- Detailed information (adverbials) on how and where and when to do things can be quite widely used.
- The textual theme in this particular text is linked together by numerals, in other texts temporal conjunctive relations would be found (one example here is 'Then').

Explanation genre

This is the type of factual text used to explain the processes involved in the evolution of natural phenomena or how something works. Explanations are used to account for why things are as they are. Explanations are more about processes than things. In the school curriculum, explanations are often found in science and social science studies.

Schematic structure

1 A general statement to position the reader, then a sequenced explanation of why/how something occurs (usually a series of logical steps in the process).
2 Explanations have a 'process' focus rather than a 'thing' focus. Thus the concern with logical sequence.

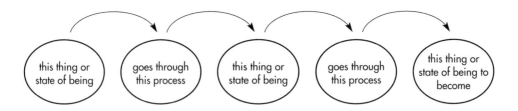

This sequence continues until a final state of being or thing is produced.

Text (aged 15: secondary 3: FL = E)

The making of sugar

Textual theme	Topical theme	Rheme
General statement to position reader		
	Sugar	comes from sugar cane and sugar beet.
	Sugar cane	needs a hot climate
but	sugar beet	does not need a hot climate.
	We	are going to talk about sugar cane.
Sequenced explanation of why/how something occurs		
	Sugar cane	grows in fields
and		needs lots of sun and lots of water.
	It	takes 6 months to ripen.
Then	the cane	is cut
and [then]		brought to a factory.
	Big cranes	carry the canes to a metal platform.
From there	the canes	fall on a conveyor belt
where	sharp knives	cut them into pieces.
	The pieces	are crushed by heavy rollers to get the juice.
	Water	is sprayed over the crushed cane to remove any juice left.
	Bagasse	is then removed.
	The juice	is heated.
	Lime	is added to clarify it.
	The juice	is then boiled.
	A very thick syrup	called massecuite is obtained.
	The massecuite	passes through separating machines which are called centrifugals
where	sugar crystals	are separated from molasses.
	The sugar crystals	are dried
and [then]		stored in big tanks.
From there	it	is loaded in sugar boxes.
	The sugar	is taken away by lorry to the bulk sugar terminal for export.

Language features

- The topical thematic development comes through generic, non-human participants (e.g. 'sugar', 'sugar cane', 'sugar beet', 'water', 'lime', 'bagasse', 'the massecuite', 'the juice', 'the sugar crystal', etc.).
- Time relationships ('first', 'then', 'following', 'finally').
- Other variations can have a cause-effect relationship ('if/then', 'as a consequence').
- The use of mainly material processes, (e.g. 'comes', 'grows', 'takes', 'brought', 'fall', 'crushed', 'to get', 'sprayed', 'remove', 'boiled', 'passes through', 'separated', 'loaded', 'taken away'. The dominance of material processes is necessary because of the carrying forward of the action.).
- Passives might also be used (e.g. 'is heated', 'is added', 'is boiled') as agency is removed from the process.
- Timeless present can also be found (e.g. 'grows', 'needs', 'takes', 'passes through').

The textual theme comes from temporal and causal conjunctive relations e.g. 'and then', 'Then', 'From there', 'where'.

Technical vocabulary: there are certain terms such as 'bagasse' and 'massecuite' which relate to the local sugar-cane industry.

Exposition genre

This type of factual text is used to put forward an argument or a point of view. For example we would find this genre being used in an essay, a letter to the editor, where the sequencing was logical rather than temporal.

Schematic structure

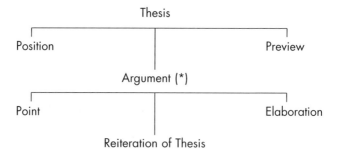

Thesis
Position — Preview
Argument (*)
Point — Elaboration
Reiteration of Thesis

The following text is an example of exposition genre. Should smoking be banned in Singapore for those below eighteen years of age?

Textual theme	Topical theme	Rheme
	Smoking	has become a bad habit among the teenagers in Singapore.
	A survey	conducted by a local teenagers' magazine shows that one out of ten teenagers under the age of eighteen takes up smoking.
	I	strongly feel that smoking should be banned in Singapore for those below eighteen.
This is because	I	feel that smoking definitely has many bad effects on the smokers.
Firstly, in the teenage years	health	is the most important factor.
When	a smoker	smokes a cigarette,
	the tar of the nicotine in the cigarette	would be taken in by the smoker
and		trapped in the lungs.
Hence	diseases like throat cancer and lung cancer	would show effect.
And	smoking	would definitely makes the teeth dirty and yellow.
Since	smokers	are prone to many illnesses and diseases,
therefore,	indirectly, smoking	would affect the growth of a teenager
as	the smokers	are more likely to fall sick than the non-smokers.
	Without good health	teenagers cannot grow well.

Textual theme	Topical theme	Rheme
In conclusion,	I	would like to emphasize that young teenagers should spend their money and time wisely and not on smoking.
	A good health, a good management of time and a good impression	are three very important factors that will help the teenagers to survive in this world later on in their lives.
Therefore,	the teenagers	should take not take up the bad habit of smoking.

Language features

- General participants, sometimes human but often abstract such as issues, ideas, opinions (e.g. 'smoking', 'a survey', 'teenagers', 'cancer', 'health', etc.).
- Possibility of technical terms relating to the issue ('tar', 'nicotine').
- A variety of verbal processes: relational in terms of linking ('has become', 'is', 'are', etc.); material ('conducted', 'smokes', 'shows', 'take up'), mental ('feel', 'like').
- Mainly timeless present tense when presenting a position or points in the argument ('shows', 'is', 'smokes'). However, if the historical background to the issue is being given, then the tense will change (conducted). If predictions are being made, the tense would change to the future.
- Connectives associated with reasoning ('because', 'hence', 'therefore').
- Persuasive texts often employ emotive words ('strongly feel', 'definitely', 'very important') and a great deal of modality ('should', 'would', etc.). Strong emotive language is generally more appropriate in spoken debate, and essays are often more successful if the writer seeks to convince the reader through logic and even understatement sometimes.

Discussion genre

The function of this genre is to present information about and arguments for both sides of a topical issue, often concluding with a recommendation based on the weight of evidence. This generic structure is:
Discussion

The following text of a group discussion about advertisements demonstrates this.

Advertisements

Textual theme	Topical theme	Rheme
Issue		
Advertisements		
	There	are many reasons for both sides of the question,
	'Should we	have printed advertisements?'
	Many people	have strong views
and		feel that ads are nothing more than useless junk mail,
while	other people	feel it is an important source of information.
Arguments for		
	Here	are some reasons why we should have advertisements in newspapers and magazines.
One	reason	is ads give us information about what is available.
	Looking at ads	we can find out
	what	is on sale
and	what	is new in the market.
	This	is an easy way of shopping.
Another	reason	is that advertisements promote business.

Textual theme	Topical theme	Rheme
When	shop owners	compete against each other
	the buyer	saves money,
	more people	come to their shops
and	they	sell more goods.

Arguments against

On the other hand,	some people	argue ads should not be put in newspapers and magazines for these various reasons.
Firstly,	ads	cost the shopkeepers a lot of money to print onto paper.
Also	some people	don't like finding junk mail in their letter boxes.
	People	may also find the ads not very interesting.
	ads	also influence people to buy items
[that]	they	don't need
and		can't really afford.
	ads	use up a lot of space
and	a lot of effort	has to be made to make the ads eyecatching.

Recommendations

After looking at both sides of the issue,	I	think
	we	should not have advertisements
because	they	cost a lot of money to print onto paper.
	ads	also take up a lot of room in the papers
and	I	don't think
	I	find some of them interesting.
	I	mainly disagree
because	it	is junk mail.

Language features to note include:

- Use of material ('saves', 'come sell', 'compete', 'print', 'make'); relational ('have', 'are', 'is'); and mental processes ('feel', 'don't like', 'looking', 'think', 'don't think', 'influence', 'find', 'disagree').

- The simple present tense is used: 'are', 'have', 'feel', 'is', 'give', 'promote', 'compete', 'argue', 'cost', 'influence', 'make'.

  – The topical thematic development has a focus on generic human and non-human participants: 'many people', 'other people', 'reason', 'some people', 'ads', 'people'. There is also some use of the impersonal 'we'. The only time the topical theme becomes personalized is in the recommendations where it would be expected.

  – The textual theme uses logical conjunctions: 'while', 'why', 'and', 'on the other hand', 'firstly', 'also', 'after', 'because', etc.

8.4 Changing features of writing on entering secondary school

What has been outlined in the various genres described above, is not an exhaustive list. However, it allows us to see that control over a relatively small set of genres can enable pupils to succeed in the subject areas in which they engage in formal schooling. However, students would also need to see the role of different genres in relation to each other in a learning area. The pupils' learning would be facilitated if they knew why a particular genre was used. It is argued that approaching genre in terms of function-in-a-subject best enables students to extend skills across discipline boundaries. Such an approach is particularly necessary in secondary schooling and is becoming increasingly important for subject study in primary school.

One immediate and very important feature of secondary school texts is what Halliday (1994) called grammatical metaphor. Many of the texts we have cited from young children and foreign language learners of English create their texts by producing a series of clauses, each of which construct a particular event and then link through conjunctive relations. The tendency to build experience in this way represents a congruent way to build meaning. That is to say, one clause is used for one event, where the event is realized essentially in a process with accompanying participants and sometimes accompanying circumstances. For example:

Since that day	they	never leaved	Raman [alone]	in the house
Circumstance	*Participant*	*Process*	*Participant*	*Circumstance*

This is a feature of less experienced writers while in texts by more mature writers the grammar is rearranged to create fewer clausal structures using grammatical metaphor. It is control of grammatical metaphor that is important as pupils move into secondary education, and into the need to construct the language of educational knowledge.

The following example given by Halliday (1998a: 202) is typical of the sort of writing found in scientific textbooks:

> The absolute indistinguishability of the electrons in the two atoms gives rise to an 'extra' attractive force between them.
> (Layzer 1990: 61, quoted in Halliday 1998a)

We can unpack the metaphors in the clause and produce a more congruent rewording such as the following:

> They attract each other 'extra' strongly because the electrons in the two atoms are absolutely the same.

Note what has happened:

- one clause has become two;
- conjunctive relationships between clauses (because) build a sense of logical relationships between the messages of the clause;
- the one process used in the original clause (gives rise to) is a relational process, creating a relationship between the two 'things' or entities which allow description.

> Halliday (1998a: 203–4)

Overall the one clause of the original version is much denser than the more congruent or spoken form. This is because there is a tendency, especially in science or technological writing to compress information by use of the nominal group. However, it should be noted that the extent to which a text uses grammatical metaphor is in part a condition of the field of knowledge or experience being constructed. Many school subjects use grammatical metaphor to make their meaning and this, as we have indicated is especially true of science texts. The reason for this is that science involves trying to understand a phenomenon by looking at it through a technical framework, turning commonsense understanding into technical understanding. Nominalization by the use of grammatical metaphor facilitates the setting up of technical terms. This further allows an arranging of the terms taxonomically and then using that framework to explain how the phenomenon came to be as it is. Furthermore this process is recursive in that technicality once established can be used to create further technicality, and so on.

Halliday (2001: 186) has pointed out that the evolution of the grammar of scientific English can be traced back to Chaucer and Newton's writings. By the eighteenth and nineteenth centuries nominalization had become well established. Modern stylists who object to this form of clausal construction cannot deny, however, the fact that it has developed as a feature of discourse because it was found to be useful.

Several studies (Wignall 1998) have been undertaken on the discourse of science, the discourse of the humanities, the discourse of the social sciences and their distinctive strategies. In order to interact with these types of discourse the pupil must be aware of what these strategies are. The following are some examples:

The strategies used in the discourse of science

- Defining in the sense of a technical term identifying some phenomenon: (technical term shown in *italics*):

    Water vapour   is   the invisible gas which ends up in the air when water evaporates.

    An *embryo*   is   an organism in a very early stage of development.

- Classifying, as well as naming things, science reorganizes things by arranging the technical terms into taxonomies (part/whole and class/sub-class).

    The *ecosystem*   has   two parts – the *physical environment* and the *biome*.

- Explaining: explaining how things happen is typically done through implication sequences. A sequence of events is outlined by using material processes and clause enhancement (sequence in time, cause and effect, condition).

    Frontal uplift   occurs   when cold air meets warm air forcing the warm air to rise.

    (Wignall 1998: 299)

The strategies used in the discourse of the humanities

Whereas science uses technicality the humanities use abstraction to understand and interpret the world. Abstraction involves moving from an instance or collection of instances, through generalization to abstract interpretation.

For example, in history initially we might find individual people doing things in time and space (using tense and temporal conjunctions to order events), then a move to generic classes of people participating in general classes of activities set in time (using circumstances of location), then a shift away from the people to a focus on events (nominalized as participants) and finally an interpretation of what the events mean (nominalization of events and reasoning realized through grammatical metaphor). So such a movement involves shifts in mode; the more interpretative a text, the more abstract it is in terms of mode (Wignall 1998: 301).

The strategies used in the discourse of the social sciences

Wignall (1998) has suggested that the discourse of the social sciences has evolved from a synthesis of the discourses of the humanities and science. Social science is a technical discourse in that it also uses 'defining' and 'classifying'. Technicality begins at the most superordinate end of the taxonomy and proceeds downwards. Wignall illustrates this in an example from sociology:

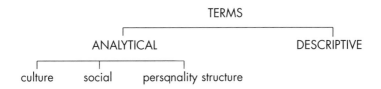

In addition to technicality, there is also the use of abstractions and metaphors. One discourse strategy is using an established technical terms (so congruent for the specific field) as part of the defining process together with nominalizations ('things') which are realized as abstractions or metaphors. For example, '*Roles* are *positions* made up of *performances* which respond to a bundle of *norms*' (Wignall 1998: 321). What we have is an existing technical term 'norms' (congruent in this particular field) as part of a syntactic structure using a grammatical metaphor 'performances' and an abstraction 'positions' to define another technical term 'roles'.

If we relate this to the development of writing research in secondary schools (Christie 1995, 1999) it shows that pupils vary enormously in their ability to use all the grammatical resources with which to produce written language of the kind we have been reviewing. The process of preparing pupils for control of written language should commence in the primary school, and where pupils receive plenty of guided assistance from their teachers in studying and using models of literate language, they will be in a strong position to enter secondary schooling. However, whatever pupils know at the end of primary school, needs to be consolidated and extended at the secondary level. Where teachers are aware of the particular linguistic requirements of their particular subject area, they will be able to anticipate their pupils' needs, and to direct their learning by drawing attention to the features of language being used.

8.5 Summary

In this chapter we have outlined a genre-based approach to written text composition and identified a number of different text types frequently found in the primary and secondary school syllabus. We have suggested that textual structures are not fixed and unchanging but develop as cultural and social practices change over time. It is not intended that teachers encourage pupils to learn the stages mechanically, but rather to focus on the features of the text to enable learners to create text types in a meaningful way. In secondary schooling knowing the generic structure of texts in specific subject areas of sciences, the humanities and social sciences will help pupils to write more appropriately for these subjects. Writing linguistically appropriate texts is central to school success and educational knowledge. It is suggested that a genre based approach to teaching literacy provides a compromise between the product–process divide. Focusing on textual features and text structure allows learners to be creative within a supportive scaffold of text-type structure.

Activity

Letters follow certain conventions but they can also present features of different text-types or genres. Try and identify in the following letter to a local newspaper the sections in the letter that are characteristic of different text types and then decide which text type this letter primarily belongs to.

15, Wastwater Cres.
Wath Brow,
Cumbria

12.5.2002

Dear Sir,
As I was taking a stroll near St. Mark's school yesterday, I noticed four youths casually walking to school well after school had started. They were talking and laughing and seemed to be in no hurry to get there.

It was reported in yesterday's *Evening Mail* that today's young people have never worked harder at school. This certainly was not borne out by my observations. I believe that punctuality and self-discipline are crucial for a decent upbringing. All young people need to learn a modicum of discipline and punctuality before they leave school.

As parents, we must:
– first of all set a good example
– be punctual ourselves
– help the community to instil discipline through our school system.

Yours faithfully
Josh Lowther

8.6 Further reading

Christie, F. (ed.) 1999: *Pedagogy and the Shaping of Consciousness*. London: Cassell.
Martin, J.R. and R. Veel (Eds.) 1998: *Reading Science*. London: Routledge.

9 Critical language awareness

> Each one of us has this ability (to use language) and live by it; but we do not
> always become aware of it or realize fully the breadth and depth of its possibilities
>
> (M.A.K. Halliday)

Halliday wrote this in his Introduction to *Language in Use* (Doughty *et al.* 1971: 10) and it remains a recurring concern of those interested in explanations of language development ever since. Children learn the values of the culture in which they are being raised implicitly through the language they are learning and though the social relations they form. All interactions transmit the values of the prevailing culture and language is the medium of that process of transmission. However, awareness of the power of language has to be taught explicitly. This teaching has become established within the school curriculum as language awareness or critical literacy. Both emphasize slightly different things. Luke (1992: 10) suggests that:

> A critical literacy entails not only a rudimentary control of the linguistic and semiotic codes of written text, but also understandings of the ways in which literacy has shaped the organizations and values of social life and the ways in which the texts of everyday life influence one's own identity and authority. Literacy is therefore as much about ideologies, identities and values as it is about codes and skills.

While Hollindale (1992: 250) describes it as developing 'the ability to evaluate, control and avoid manipulation by the language systems of one's culture'. In the editorial of the first issue of the journal *Language Awareness* it was suggested that:

> . . . it has to do with finding things about language, with becoming conscious of one's own and others' uses of it in speech and in its written forms, with developing a sensitive relationship to it, with being able to talk explicitly about one's insights into it.

Fairclough (1989) in his writings has drawn attention to specific ways in which assumptions about language and society are reflected in traditional sociolinguistics. Previously, many sociolinguists understood social processes arising from individual's behaviour and their interactions were determined by each pursuing their own strategies and goals. Holmes (1992: 16) emphasizes description over explanation. She writes: 'Sociolinguists aim to describe sociolinguistic variation and if possible, explain why it happens'. Fairclough discussing the place of language in society sees language as social practice determined by social structures and holds the view that discourse is determined by socially constituted orders of discourse, or the sets of conventions associated with particular social institutions. In this sense orders of discourse are ideologically shaped by power relations in social institutions and in wider society. He suggests there is a two-way influence operating. Discourses impact upon social structures and are simultaneously determined by them. In this way, language can contribute both to social continuity and to social change.

While there is difference in emphasis, two principal points emerge from descriptions of critical language awareness and critical literacy. The first is the belief that ideologies or values can be analysed through their linguistic realizations, language and social interaction. Since this is not explicit, language awareness can help to uncover the underlying ideological content which remains implicitly. For Fairclough the ideas of Bakhtin (1981) are central to critical language awareness. Bakhtin views language as a 'site of struggle' that operates at every level of language use between centripetal and centrifugal forces. The 'centripetal' forces in linguistic terms work towards a uniform language system and at the social level are connected with what Bakhtin calls the 'authoritative discourse' which includes religious dogma, scientific truth and the political and moral status quo. These are characteristically inflexible and fixed. These centripetal forces are however, in constant tension with, and interpenetrated by, centrifugal forces with the result that language, at any given moment, is being stratified and diversified into different genres, professional groups, age-groups and historical periods. This creates a constant tension when spoken or written language is used between the pull towards the standardization of language use, meaning and authority, and a drive in the opposite direction which acknowledges the diversity of individual experience, perspective and meaning. For Bakhtin, it is the dynamic tension between centripetal and centrifugal which keeps language both simultaneously dynamic and amenable to new meaning potential but also constant. In this way a balance is maintained between over-rigid, authoritative discourse at one extreme and fragmentation to the point of disintegration of meaning and communication at the other. The second focus is a view of discourse as social practice that suggests that in order to account satisfactorily for both the production and interpretation of text one needs an integrated analysis of text, interpretative processes and socio-historical context (Clark *et al.* 1990), what can be called context of culture or context of situation.

However, Lemke has pointed out that:

> Every text, the discourse of every occasion, makes sense in part through implicit and explicit relationships of particular kinds to other texts, to the discourse of other occasions.
>
> (Lemke 1995: 27)

In other words, this intertextuality is the knowledge which readers mobilize when they try to make sense of texts. It comes from previous experience of other texts, particularly other texts of the same genre. If we have once read a story which begins 'Once upon a time', we have begun to build a schema of expectation of what a new text that also begins in the same way, can be about. Technically we are building a schema of fairy tale genre. The intertext is the sum of all the other texts that we have previous experience of. These will vary from reader to reader, from community to community and even within communities. In educational settings the notion of intertextuality is important because it helps to develop learners' reflective practices. Macken-Horarik (1998) suggests three requirements of critical language awareness within schooling:

1 contextualization
2 meta-level awareness of texts
3 acquisition of both of the above within visible pedagogies marked by explicitness.

9.1 Contextualization

Critical language awareness or critical literacy practices emphasize relationships between textual meanings and social practices and stress that students need to learn how to analyse and critique these relationships. Contextualization is a key element in the understanding of text. So what kinds of contextualization are germane to literacy practices? A critical orientation situates any given text within possible alternative discourses. Learners must be able to contextualize a text in terms which are obvious before they can be expected to reframe it in alternative terms.

9.2 Meta-level awareness

The competent literate is presumed to be able to answer questions about the text after an initial reading. These might include:

1 What is the topic?
2 Who is writing to whom?
3 How is this topic being written about?
4 Why is this topic being written about?
5 What other ways of writing about the topic are there?

(Macken-Horarik (1998: 80–1)

A study of the generic structure of the text is one way to access intertextuality. The metalanguage of theme–rheme, lexical cohesion, transitivity relations, and so on, show how the writer(s) construct the text within the framework of a particular genre. These compositional features of the text enable the reader to disengage from the text and see above and around what the writer is saying.

Explicitness

Students have to learn to contextualize texts in alternative ways and to apply the metalevel awareness of how the language is being used. Many students will not gain access to these resources without a visible pedagogy i.e. being taught how to do this. In order to do this the teacher has to make explicit the structure and language of different genres and the relationship of the text to different purposes and contexts.

9.3 Taking a closer look at text types

Looking at language critically requires questioning conventions that are normally taken for granted. It can help to make people more sensitive to language, more aware of the sociolinguistic worlds they inhabit, and be more critical of these. It can help to empower, in the sense of giving greater conscious control over aspects of our lives. It helps to make transparent the ways in which language shapes or constructs social subjects and thereby affects various aspects of their social identities. School as one of the main agents of cultural transmission can play a role in this process of empowerment. However, it is a challenge for teachers who frequently have to work within prescribed curricula with prescribed texts and inflexible examination systems that often rely on abstract and formalist views of language. The following texts are taken from a variety of sources and demonstrate that critical language awareness can be applied to a range of texts:

Example 1

Kress (1999) uses this text from a small card advertising 'Italian Leather'

ITALIAN LEATHER
ANNAPELLE

- Annapelle is a 100% Australian owned company specializing in the manufacture and importing of quality handcraft leather handbags

and accessories.

- This fine produce which is made in Italian leather was manufactured in the People's Republic of China under strict supervision, and the packaging and quality inspection was carried out in Melbourne, Australia.
  - MADE IN CHINA

There are a number of points to note:

- The discourses here seem to work around the nationalism of Australian ownership, with an emphasis on incorporating Australian values and practices.
- Racism and certainly ethnic differences underline what is suggested here (nervousness about standards of manufacture in China) and by contrast the positive evaluation of European manufacture and Australian quality assurance.

- Aesthetic values: the evaluative adjective 'fine' and the valuation given to the mode of production: 'handcrafted'.
- Economics and business: the 'jargon' of the business world: 'quality inspection', and so on.
- Heritage: with indirect reference again to the invocation of European as Italianness.

(Kress 1999: 127–8)

What we are seeing here is more than the mention of topics, but the manner of the respective evaluation of these factors in a web of values. Such values stem from stereotypical sociological representations as seen through a particular cultural perspective.

Example 2

The following extract is taken from the *Asian Wall Street Journal* (23.04.01).

A Party without vision
With no sign of real reform ahead, the Vietnamese are bored to tears by the Ninth Party Congress.
By Barry Wain

HANOI – Vietnam is a one party state, and it is ruled by the Vietnamese Communist Party, which holds a national congress every five years to select new leaders, adopt fresh policies and determine future directions. The country is politically and economically paralysed and badly in need of rejuvenation. So why is the lack of public interest in the party's Ninth Congress to be held as early as next month after more than 18 months of preparation, so palpable?

'Is it the ninth? I've lost count,' says an educated and successful young woman in Hanoi. 'For people like me in business, it doesn't make any difference one way or another.'

The state owned press, which enjoys a monopoly, has carried extensive extracts from documents to be presented to the meeting, as well as officially inspired upbeat commentary. But many of the Vietnamese with enough interest to plow through the columns of grey type have joined the ranks of the already apathetic. Nothing suggests anything will change in a way that brings hope to a nation of 80 million that has underperformed for too long. The prospect is for five more wasted years.

Martin (1997b) and White's (2000) work on appraisal is pertinent here. They see appraisal (alongside negotiation and involvement) as elements in the interpersonal metafunction of language; and they subdivide appraisal into 'affect' (a matter of emotional responses), 'judgement' (a matter of moral evaluations) and 'appreciation' (a matter of aesthetic grading).

There is obviously a considerable amount of appraisal in this extract both in terms of 'affect' and 'judgement'. The reader of the *Asian Wall Street Journal*, are business people and with some sympathy towards a capitalist rather than socialist or egalitarian world. The setting of the scene in presenting Vietnam as a 'one party state and 'communist' presents a negative image. Lexical items as 'politically and economically paralysed' 'in need of rejuvenation' are forceful judgemental terms. The writer (who is not from Asia) also points out that this lack of interest is reflected in the ordinary people's attitude. The quote from the 'educated, young and successful business woman' represents the future of Vietnam. Other phrases which convey a negative judgement are 'plow through columns of grey type', 'joined the ranks of the already apathetic', 'underperformed for too long', 'five more wasted years'. The accumulation of this negative appraisal provides the reader with the view that the Ninth Party Congress is irrelevant for the real world, the world of business.

Example 3

This example (see Carter 1996) is taken from an interview with a politician on Radio 4 in the United Kingdom. A close examination of what is said reveals a slippage in moving from inadequate literacy practices through slovenly language, to slovenly habits to the eventual logical outcome, crime. However, such *non sequiturs* of discourse when politicians are speaking, are all too common.

> We've allowed so many standards to slip . . . Teachers weren't bothering to teach kids to spell and to punctuate properly . . . If you allow standards to slip to the stage where good English is no better than bad English, where people turn up filthy . . . at school . . . all those things tend to cause people to have no standards at all, and once you lose standards the there's no imperative to stay out of crime.
>
> (Norman Tebbitt, BBC Radio 4, 1985).

The connection between the slipping of 'standards' to 'spelling and punctuation', to 'good' and 'bad' English, to 'hygiene' and eventually to 'crime', demands several jumps in the logic of the argument, which might go unnoticed to the casual listener. Once such a text is transcribed and looked at more closely, the naivety of the argument becomes all the more apparent. Unfortunately we rarely examine closely what we hear in this way.

Example 4

This next example concerns the language of 'officialdom' which is often impenetrable or at least confusing in terminology for the audience addressed.

The letter quoted in Wareing (1999) refers to a previous letter complaining about the language used in Ofsted reports on schools and pupils. (Ofsted is the organization responsible for monitoring standards in schools in the UK, OFfice of STandards in EDucation.)

> Ofsteadspeak
>
> Lucinda Bredin's concern about the language of Ofsted reports (Review, August 24) is justified. The mysterious world of Ofstedspeak can be difficult to penetrate.
>
> The word 'satisfactory' which smacks of mediocrity, is discouraged by Ofsted. The word 'sound' is encouraged instead.
>
> The bright and shining ones at Ofsted have also given thumbs down . . . [to] the word 'ability'. Inspectors are asked not to refer to pupils' different levels of ability. They must instead write about levels of attainment, meaning what pupils can do in relation to what might be expected of them.
>
> That happily relieves everyone of having to say of any child that he or she lacks ability. Poor attainment may be the result of poor teaching, or inappropriate curriculum or, come to that, government policy.
>
> As the second wave of inspections takes place, reports will be written in a different language than before. In particular, where a first wave report has said that pupils are performing well in relation to their ability, that will be out of order in a second wave report.
>
> There is real danger that Ofsted language will become so arcane as to be unintelligible to ordinary citizens.
>
> Peter Dawson
> Ofsted registered inspector
> Derby
>
> (The *Daily Telegraph*, 7 September 1997,
> quoted in Wareing 1999: 3)

For the general reader, personal bias will influence the interpretation of what they read. Obviously, for some people naming things does matter. The discourse of the British school education system might seem impenetrable to anyone outsiders to the system. Yet the 'ordinary citizens' should have a direct interest in what is going on in the schools.

All this presupposes that one accepts the judgements made by the writer of this letter in the first place. There is a lot of writer 'appraisal' in this text where the writer is persuading the reader to adopt the point of view he expresses. Many of the words used indicate a strong bias, for example: 'mysterious world', 'smacks of mediocrity' 'The bright and shining ones at Ofsted'. Readers have to balance this negative appraisal with what they might know from other sources. If they have no other sources to refer to, then they might be inclined to accept the information provided in this letter as the reality.

Example 5

The next example is a history text: *Christopher Columbus, the discovery of the New World* Evans Bros, London 1993 designed for 9–13 year-old learners. The reason for selecting this example is because several writers have pointed out that history is one of the fields that young learners find most difficult to study. History is full of judgements and valuations or what Martin (1997b), Coffin (1996) and Veel and Coffin (1996) term appraisal. Goom's (2003) detailed study of this text underlines how much judgements and valuations are sometimes explicit, but often implicit in the writing of history. They are derived, consciously or otherwise, from the grand narratives of the history writer's and history learner's culture or possibly the grand narratives of other cultures. Many teachers in the upper primary school are not necessarily specialists historians or history teachers. Even in lower secondary school it is common for teachers of geography and English to teach history classes. While history specialists may be very good at making explicit judgements and valuations in history texts not all history classes are taught by history specialists.

This coupling of knowledge as projected by and through culture and personal reactions can be expressed explicitly with evaluative lexis or without. Moreover:

> Every institution is loaded with couplings of this kind, and socialization into a discipline involves both an alignment with the institutional practices involved and an affinity with the attitudes one is expected to have towards these practices.
>
> (Martin 1997b: 19)

Insiders in these institutions, are those who have successfully conformed, mentally and socially. Outsiders are those who cannot or will not or who do not have insider experience. Group identity, inclusion and exclusion are central to historical accounts.

For example in the following extract Columbus is described as follows:

> He was also ambitious and greedy. In return for discovering a sea route to Asia, Columbus demanded that he should be knighted, and made an admiral. He also laid claim to ten per cent of all the riches that he might bring back from the voyage.

How does one judge 'ambitious' and 'greed', in present terms or those of the period? Was Columbus any more ambitious or greedy than Francis Drake? What value can we put on 10 per cent? By modern day standards this seems a reasonable return for services rendered. So how does the novice reader appraise these judgements made by the writer? Certainly a lot more background knowledge is required and yet these judgements could have an influence on the perspective the readers have of Columbus (Goom 2003).

As Bernstein (1996) has pointed out school texts are recontextualizations from the academic field and history textbooks are no exception. In some cultures, the academic field of history traditionally sees itself as autonomous, strongly disapproving of academic history, where elsewhere that is overtly tied to the support of the political status quo. However, national bias within the academic field is generally acknowledged, even though it is generally in the form of the other writer's transgression. As Davies writes:

> National states are themselves 'imagined communities' they are built on powerful myths, and on the political rewriting of history.
> (Davies1996: 44)

For the last half-century or so academic history has come under attack on the grounds of hagiography and ethnocentrism. This attack has been under two influences. The first is the rise in importance of social historians, accompanied (within the field) by the continuing shift from narrative to analysis and (externally) by the general rise of the social sciences. The second is the articulation of viewpoints not included in the traditional all-white hegemony of Western Europe and North America. For an example of this one might read C.L.R. James's, (1938), treatment of Christopher Columbus.

As Goom points out, this attack at the level of overt debate, has made considerable headway. Davies says of hagiography:

> The really vicious quality shared by almost all accounts of 'Western civilization' lies in the fact that they present idealized, and hence essentially false, pictures of past reality. They extract everything that might be judged genial or impressive; and they

filter out anything that might appear mundane or repulsive . . . judging from some of the textbooks, one gets the distinct impression that everyone in the 'West' was a genius, a philosopher, a pioneer, a democrat, or a saint, that it was a world inhabited exclusively by Platos and Marie Curies. Such hagiography is no longer credible.

(Davies 1996: 28)

Within general history for young learners biographical narrative as iconic exemplification is constituting the social process by reconstructing unshared vicarious experience; whereas the surrounding historical generalization is constituting the social process by construction. In other words, the writer has more choice with respect to historical generalization than with respect to biographical narrative; but this greater choice is still, of course, constrained by the context of culture.

Where a book is entitled by the name of an iconic individual such as 'Christopher Columbus', the writer can choose to give more, or less, space to historical generalization, and to make the relationship between generalization and the choice of icon more, or less, explicit (Goom 2003).

9.4 What young readers might not know

Goom in her study treats this question under three headings: General (non-historical) knowledge, historical knowledge, and linguistic and textual knowledge.

General knowledge

Goom claims that the authoritarian-sounding experts are now much less fashionable in schools. Teachers are more likely than they were half a century ago to give reasons for disciplinary decisions and perhaps more likely to aim not just at transmitting information but at elucidating approaches to knowledge. Some textbook writers share these concerns for demystification; others do not. A writer's attitude with respect to his or her own role will have implications for the organization of the text. Texts will give more, or less, space to reporting debate; they will be more, or less, open in quoting sources. They will be more, or less, open in inviting readers' opinions on any aspect of the topic or related question.

History texts will also vary in what play they make with solidarity: the use made of 'we' and 'our' and how clearly the referents are defined apart from the degree of sympathy between 'us' and the various historical participants.

A significant feature of school textbooks is that they are often multi-modal, in the sense that their physical layout, illustrations, typeface, and so on, are important factors to be considered in the appraisal of the text. This is especially important in books written for children and is an area that needs to be discussed at length, something we will do in the next chapter. For the present the focus will be on the 'recontextualizations' from the academic field of history.

In all texts there is bias as Davies remarks, in a discussion of the effects of national bias on historical texts:

> The problem of national bias is probably best observed in the realm of school textbooks and popular histories. The more that historians have to condense and simplify their material, the harder it is to mask their prejudices.
>
> (Davies 1996: 33)

However, Goom suggests that general acceptance of anti-hagiographic and anti-ethnocentric arguments might lead to a recontextualization, and a children's book would reflect this acceptance. Such an expectation might be suggested by the following statement (on the back cover of the book, for example):

> The year 1492, when Columbus first landed in the New World, as America was then known, marks one of the great turning points in history: Europe, America and the rest of the world would never be the same again!

Reading a text about history also requires the reader to have some historical knowledge.

Historical knowledge

The book begins with the following sentence:

> The result of this introduction was the creation of what Europeans called the 'New World' – a land of dreams and opportunity, and also a land of nightmares and destruction.

For those who are initiated into the history of the Americas over the last 500 hundred years, this sentence is a clear predictive signal for the whole text: there will be happy events recounted and unhappy events. Alternatively, for those with no historical background but a good knowledge of how texts operate, the predictive signal will also work. For those without the historical background, and without the textual knowledge, the signal will fail. The

'New World' is glossed, but in a dense cluster of nominalization. Actions, both planned and realized, are represented as nouns, all the participants (both the happy, and the unhappy, the doers and the done-to) can be elided from the text. This formulation will fail to convey to many young readers that white American society was built on the ruins of native America, and that an additional cost was the forced disruption of the life of many Africans. Even a brief reference to the doers and done-to (a land of dreams and opportunity for some, a land of nightmares and destruction for others) would alert young readers.

Although it is pointed out in the Introduction that 'Columbus . . . lived in times very different from our own' (p.5), children must often bring the relevant differences to the text for themselves.

Linguistic and textual knowledge

Goom's examination of the linguistic and textual knowledge also addresses the lexical density. Inexperienced readers are likely to have more difficulty with high-density texts and the lexical metaphors, as well as abstract, grammatical metaphors.

It is not difficult to find sentences with a high lexical density – that is, the number of lexical items divided by the number of ranking clauses (Halliday 1994: 351).

Here are some examples:

(a) The result of this introduction was the creation of what Europeans called the New World – land of dreams and oppor-tunity, and also a land of nightmare and destruction (p.4)
lexical density: 12

(b) New ideas about art, science and religion, and new inven-tions such as printing, had combined to produce an atmosphere of change (p.4).
lexical density: 12

(c) The only way for Christian kingdoms to increase their power and wealth was to turn their attention to the grey waters of the Atlantic Ocean (p.8).
lexical density: 13

(d) With a single daring voyage, Christopher Columbus opened up a whole new world of exploration and overseas trade for Europe (p.24).
lexical density: 12

In the light of Halliday's (1996) finding that typical lexical density in technical texts for adults is 6–10 these figures are quite high.

Lexical metaphor abounds. For example, the lexical metaphor in (b) is chemical: elements combine to produce a new compound (a gas creating: 'atmosphere of change'). In (c) the lexical metaphor is a continuation from the previous sentence; 'The blue waters of the Mediterranean Sea were besieged by the rival powers'. 'Waters besieged'; it might even be questionable as to cultural availability. Lexical metaphors add colour more than aid clarity. They are a recurrent strand operating in those parts of the text with high lexical density.

Goom's conclusion that writing history for young learners is a demanding task because there is so much implicit learning, is supported by Painter as quoted in Derewianka 1995: 247:

> If this model of implicit learning is adopted within the school, then there is every likelihood that the successful language learner will be unresistantly co-opted into the cultural values and assumptions which lie implicit in the texts which constitute the sources of school knowledge. Without explicit ways of reflecting on educational texts and other public forms of speech and writing, the school will be apprenticing children into particular ways of looking at the world and of dealing with experience, without simultaneously giving them tools for being conscious that this is so, and for making choices about whether and how they will make use of this learning.
>
> (Painter 1999: 66)

In this History class, it is one of the major roles of the teacher to make explicit what is implicit, not just in the written text but also in the surrounding illustrations, diagrams and visual lay-out which project additional information.

Example 6

Our final example is taken from a series of romance novels published for the English speaking market in South-East Asia. These novels with such titles as: *Coming home*, *Kiss me, Kat*, *City girl* and *The right track* all present the female protagonists are successful, independent, modern intelligent and emotionally strong. This is congruent with the image often presented of the ideal English speaking bilingual female in the growing economically powerful countries of South-East Asia. A critical analysis of the texts, however reveals another picture.

Our main focus will be on *Coming Home* the first in the series of romances set in Singapore. The author, Joan Anderson was, in fact, a writing partnership of two Americans who taught part-time in a university in the USA.

The target audience as described by the publisher's general manager (also a woman) is three groups: teenagers (12 to 15 year-olds), young office workers (16 to 25 year-olds) and middle-aged housewives. The contextual situation of this series of novels was described in the following terms:

> It . . . would seem to be more subdued and understated than that of the more outspoken culture of most countries in the West. Thus it would require more skill to draw out the intricacies of feelings and relationships.
>
> (*The Straits Times* 14-8-92)

The novel is set in modern day Singapore with two principal characters. Mei Leigh, a 'Eurasian' having her own legitimate escort business, as travel agent and protocol adviser for foreign businessmen and Gregg Holden, an American investment specialist on an assignment in Singapore. The storyline is built around a series of misunderstandings such as the nature of the escort service provided and more importantly, the feelings of the characters. A crisis is caused by the intervention of the Singapore Internal Security accusing Mei Leigh of jeopardizing state security. This is a *deus ex machina* in the story, which has little rationale except to create a situation where Mei marries Gregg to escape from the Security Services and thus legitimize the more intimate scenes in the novel. However, to maintain the element of pseudo-suspense Mei insists that it be a marriage in name only so that this device keeps the reader waiting. The consequent removal of Mei to the USA and the selling of her business adds to the growing tension and mutual suspicion. This carries the novel forward to its final resolution and expected happy ending.

The themes that underlie the novel are: male–female sexuality with the male the dominant partner in contrast with statements about the series. The Eurasian woman in Singapore society; the need to marry outside of the community; the perspective of men; the idealized male–female encounter depicted are stereotypical of the genre. As the target readership is mainly young English-medium educated females, the essential purpose is to have created realism, a sense of being involved with situations and people in the story. However, the realism here is really more like consistency, in that characters and events are consistent – not in reference to reality, but to the conventions of the genre in which they are operating (Cranny-Francis and Palmer Gillard 1990).

This romance genre overlaps with the adolescent trade paperbacks. The common threads we find in these adolescent romances and the romantic fiction are:

1 Romance is seen as a transforming experience giving life meaning and structure.
2 It is essential about male power and control.
3 Romance is an assemblage of feelings and emotions.
4 Romance is a way for girls/women to manage gender relations.
5 A precondition to romance is beauty which develops physical presence as a characteristic of femininity.

(Christian-Smith 1989)

In *Coming Home* the design on the front cover focuses almost exclusively on the physical aspects of the female character and the jacket blurb is fairly explicit:

> Admit it. You're not selling sightseeing tours. You're peddling sex.

However, *Coming Home* maintains this juxtapositioning by the writers of the female–male stereotyping as the following extracts demonstrate.

Text 1 (pp.3–4)

> When the first passenger exited through the automatic doors, she lifted a neatly lettered sign high above her head. On this was printed the name of Gregg Holden, the investment specialist she had been hired to meet.
>
> Though Mei had no idea what the man looked like, experience told her that any consultant retained by Tradewinds Investments was bound to be as dynamic as he was competent. She was well acquainted with the type. As founder and sole owner of a company that specialized in services for the visiting executives, she had squired around her share of VIPs.

The effects of the writers' choice of lexis presents Gregg Holden as a highly successful man who is asked for advice on important issues while Mei is in the service industry, albeit her own boss.

The female character is highlighted and the targeted readership is supposed to identify with her, especially as the impression given is that of an independent and resourceful person, therefore a possible role model. However, there is also an indication that she is being presented as not just an actor but someone who is going to be acted upon. The male character is clearly going to be effectively the principal actor as his distinguishing characteristics are already marked out for this role at this early stage in the novel.

Text 2 (p.5)

> Gregg spotted the sloe-eyed beauty just as the couple in front of her broke away to greet an elderly man. In her sleeveless red dress, she stood out like a brilliant cardinal among a flock of sparrows. Despite a stiff Mandarin collar, her simple sheath managed to be more alluring than innocent. The fitted bodice hugged her slender form, and narrow slits up both sides of her skirt revealed a tantalizing glimpse of shapely golden thigh. He wondered if she was aware of how saucy she looked or of how much skin she exposed by her off-centre stance.

In this extract the verbal processes have the effect of presenting the female as primarily something to be looked at ('spotted', 'stood out', 'fitted', 'hugged', 'revealed', 'aware', 'exposed'). Added to this is the nominalization which directs the semantic connotations and hence the reader.

The female is treated here as an object. The aspect of appraisal is not in personal terms but as an object. The writers present the female as seen through the eyes of the main male character and the overall impression given is that of an object. However, it must also be noted that the description is a culturally biased very western view of the Asian female. The precondition for romance presented exclusively in terms of physical presence and femininity is established from the outset.

Text 3 (p.6)

> He wasn't at all what she'd expected. With his thick sandy hair, broad shoulders and boldly masculine face, he looked as though he'd be more at home on an athletic field than behind a desk. Yet his eyes told a different story.
>
> Sharp, observant, assessing, they left no doubt that here was a man who preferred to play his games in a boardroom.

The male character is described mainly through relational processes ('was', 'looked', 'be', 'was') and comes over as 'boldly masculine' and 'athletic' but also 'clever'. The nominalizations process also focuses on both the physical and mental prowess of the male.

The underlying message is that you can never judge a man by his initial appearance. The subjective judgement made by the writers through the eyes of the female is presented as fact and therefore not to be questioned or doubted. These are the 'given premises', which are established in the reader's mind from the beginning.

The male character is marked out as having a beautiful body and a good mind by the writers, something noticeably lacking in the text where the female was described only in terms of her appearance. Overall the dialectic of evaluation is effectively construed by the writers to establish a fixed image of the main characters.

A question to be posed is whether these initial impressions conveyed by these sample extracts are representative of the text overall.

As has been pointed out by Carter and Nash (1990) 'realistic realism' is often a key element in narrative, sartorial detail, topographical exactness, these together with the physical attributes of the actors are characteristics of romance novel genre.

Further investigation was undertaken by Foley (1998b) and Phoon (1998) into the selection of lexical items and the connotations these build up.

There are also verbal processes used to convey certain effects to the reader. These are writers' devices for creating a value system.

The author's use of the lexical network of choices forces the reader to enter into the authors frame of reference. What is presented is an essentially male dominated power-base. Any notion in the novel of gender equality is mere tokenism. Female gender equality is postulated but the whole attitudinal approach as reflected in the choice of language used portrays the female as an object of physical attraction.

Frequently, in order to achieve and maintain commercial viability the writer needs to address a specific market, one that knows and buys the genre. That is to say the market consists of readers who have knowledge of the generic forms and have very precise expectations. So the demands of the readers are very powerful constraints on what some writers do. Writers must reproduce the significant features of the genre, and have limited opportunity for any challenge to the constraints of the genre and its meanings (Kress 1988).

Exemplification shows support for the argument that there are different ways of using the resources of language and thus give different modes of interpretation. It is also certainly true that for all kinds of reasons connected with the complexities inherent in our social structures, individuals view their social world from different positions and construct their interpretations through different choices in the linguistic network. However, since the processes of categorization and selection are often problematic, they may function as the site of contestation, where participants attempt to impose their own modes of interpretation on others or negotiate a way through the social tensions that inevitably arise from difference in interpretation.

It is interesting within the Singapore context to juxtapose the attitudinal stance of the authors of this novel as reflected in their choice of wording and recent advertisements produced by the Family Life Education Programme. These government backed advertisements are meant to encourage marriage between Singaporeans of similar educational background. Lazar (1999) argues that there is double talk in the advertisements, equalizing gender relations on one hand while reaffirming the existing inequality between sexes on the other. What is significant is the advertisement addressed to females could be an exact description of the heroine of this novel.

Are you giving men the wrong idea?

PICTURE OF BUSY FEMALE EXECUTIVE

It's wonderful to have a career and financial independence.

But is your self-sufficiency giving men a hard time? They say that you expect a lot from them and have become rather intimidating and unapproachable.

Surely that can't be true. You really are a warm and friendly girl and look forward to a home of your own and a family.

Perhaps it's time to give the guys a break. By being more relaxed and approachable. Friendlier and more sociable. That way they'll get to know you – which is how relationships begin.

After all you don't want to give men the wrong idea.

As Lazar points out sustaining sexism by such advertising maintains the societal needs of male interests with the primary supposition that the woman role is essentially that of becoming a mother. Of course one of the major roles of women in society is the procreation of children but there is a big jump from that to the notion of 'quality breeding' as proposed by this advertisement. There is also the presupposition that it is only in the domestic arena that a woman has a place within society.

By reading these 'romance' novels, the targeted audience which remember is mainly made up of young teenagers and women under 25 according to the publishers, are learning society's narrative about society. This audience is learning not only not to question anomalies or injustices but also learning not to see them. They are learning to accept ideological justifications for the 'way things are' (Cranny-Francis and Palmer Gillard 1990).

9.5 Summary

The key issues raised in this chapter are that writers use language in a variety of ways to convey values and meanings. Readers need to learn:

1 How texts convey particular ideological messages
2 How texts position people in certain ways
3 Resources for resisting such positioning
4 That the wider social processes and institutions shape the language we use and the meanings we create from it.

Our general argument is that being aware of how language conventions and language practices are invested with unequal relations of power and ideological processes should form part of any educational programme. The examples cited cover advertising, journal articles, broadcasts on the radio, letters in a newspaper, primary school history textbooks, and romance novels. A critical approach to language awareness implies an understanding of the relationships of power encoded in language. Society itself, is structured according to unequal relationships of power, thus an awareness of what people do with language will allow others to be able to participate better and gain access and perhaps be agents of change in society.

What does all this mean for the teacher in the school? If we consider formal education as schemes of conceptual organization and behaviour designed to supplement primary socialization of family upbringing, then the raising of critical language awareness is of paramount importance. Romance novels like *Coming Home* construct femininity stereotypically, as are class and race ideologies. Consciously or unconsciously such novels are being used to guide young minds at a very vulnerable time in their lives. Young girls are reading these ideologically constructed narratives in an experiential sense, seeing this characterization of women and their interactions as a guide to behaviour in their own lives as Cranny-Francis and Palmer Gillard have pointed out (1990).

The range of examples given illustrates that awareness of how language is being used and how it is an essential component of the continuous process of language development that goes on in our lives.

This development should not just be considered in terms of the written or spoken text but also in terms of the other forms of multimedia communication which is growing exponentially in our societies, something that we will address in the next chapter.

Activity

> ### Points to ponder
>
> Select a 'Mills and Boon' type romance genre novel or a romance story from a magazine and do an analysis of the lexis used by the author, following the guidelines suggested by Carter and Nash (1990) on sartorial details and the physical attributes of the main actors. Then see to what extent are the main characters presented as stereotypes or individuals. What ideological message is there consciously or unconsciously expressed in choice of lexis?
>
> Alternatively, you could take a 'letter to the editor' from a daily newspaper and examine how the writer uses appraisal in the letter. See how a particular view point is conveyed by the writer.

9.6 Further reading

Cameron, D. 1995: *Verbal hygiene*. London: Routledge.
Fairclough, N. 1989: *Language and power*. London: Longman.
Fairclough, N. 1992: *Discourse and social change*. Cambridge: Polity.
Open University 1994: *Language and literacy in social context*. Milton Keynes: The Open University.

10 Multiliteracies

10.1 Television

> it's just like on TV. And that is the most superlative compliment Archie can think of for any real-life event.
>
> (Zadie Smith: *White Teeth* 2000: 444)

Texts in today's society are multi-semiotic. Language is being increasingly interwoven with other semiotic forms, as can be found for example in films, television, photographs and magazines. Words and images have always been closely related in text (Smart 1993). Indeed modern writing itself seems to have arisen from iconic symbols and pictograms. For example, in the middle ages, illuminated manuscripts brought words together with image, colour and other forms of decoration. We could go much further back in history to find other examples of multi-modal forms of communication (Graddol 1994).

In more modern times, as Graddol again points out, media texts such as television or film, but also other forms of text such as magazines, have different semiotic threads that relate to each other in different ways. It is this interplay between different semiotic threads that is an important part of textual strategy and therefore of what makes a 'text' multi-semiotic.

In this chapter our main focus will be on television and popular magazines as these two multi-semiotic forms of communication play a substantial role in our everyday lives. The media has revolutionized the way we think about ourselves, each other, and about our world. Television for instance is probably the most popular medium available today (DeFleur and Dennis 1994). It plays an important role as both part and product of modern, everyday living, which influences and is influenced by society. The way in which television represents the world affects our beliefs and values that in turn can change the way we think about ourselves and our relations with others.

But the idea that television offers 'a window on the world' in which events and places 'out there' are unproblematically made available to viewers in the home is highly questionable. For example the popular television programme in the United Kingdom, *The Royle Family* often projects through the characters, not just the power of television but their scepticism about the relationship between what they are watching and the real world. We know that everything that is seen on television screens arrives there only after a complex process of mediation involving many people and institutions and a great deal of technology and artifice. Even television news, which is expected to provide factual information, is really no different from other television genres. Its transparency and perceived factuality is a testament to the extent to which its conventions of representation have become naturalized. Indeed, understanding the semiotics of factuality is perhaps one of the most important literacy skills required by readers and viewers in today's world.

The visual element of news is perhaps, of all the semiotic codes, considered as the most straightforward and transparent. The relationship between words and pictures in news reports has been regarded as a relatively simple one. The pictures may be selective in what they show but without words they cannot tell the truth, nor for that matter can they lie. Factuality is not merely a question of truth or lies, but a more complex semiotic system, which provides for varying authority, certainty and appropriateness to be allocated to particular representations of the world (Graddol 1994).

For example, if we look at the following fragment of a news report:

The British maintain they cleaned the site up in 1957.

Graddol (1994) points out that the verb 'cleaned' has high modality. There is an implicit claim that there is no argument over this point. However, the evaluation of its factuality is not that of the speaker. Responsibility for the claim of factuality has been shifted to the 'British' through the verb 'maintain'. The woman actually speaking distances herself and us as viewers from the factual status of the 'cleaning up'.

Obviously factuality not only depends on high modality but also on the genre of the text. Television news is a high status television genre, perhaps the most privileged and prestigious media genre. It compares favourably against low status genres like soap operas and game shows. People tend to trust television news more than other sources because of the apparent lack of influence of 'partisan ownership', and because of the perceived veracity of the pictures (Goodwin 1990). Television news has a genre of its own because it represents a particular way of collecting and establishing facts which are different from the way scientific facts might be established.

The news on television seems to be divided into two primary phases. The first phase is the lead, which acts as an opening 'nucleus' containing the text's core informational meanings. The second phase comprises satellites or lead development which act not to introduce new topics but to qualify, elaborate, contextualize and evaluate the topics already present in the opening lead or nucleus.

The generic structure of television news reports can be represented as follows:

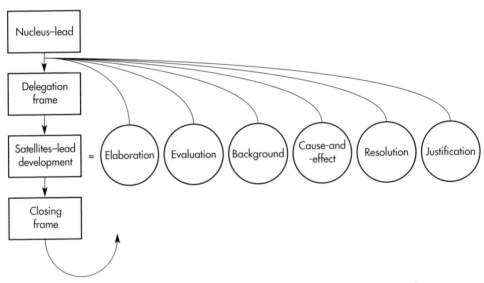

Figure 10.1 Generic structure of television news (Ao Ran 2002, adapted from Scollon 1998)

Besides the phases of the nucleus and satellites, Scollon (1998) identifies two further stages in the generic structure: the delegation frame and the closing frame.

The following data is from Ao Ran's (2002) study.

The nucleus or lead

The lead is the most distinctive feature of news discourse and acts as a summary of the featured story. For example:

> United States Middle East envoy Dennis Ross is expected to meet Palestinian president Yasser Arafat to resume mediation efforts.
> [Michael Holmes, World News]

The first sentence in the lead often starts with attributing the news source:

> Israel says, it agrees to cooperate with a US-led international investigation into the 9-week old conflict with the Palestinians.
> [Michael Holmes, World News]

Finally, the lead may also incorporate an evaluation category:

> To some people, the United States presidential election may be confusing. For others, it's democracy in action.
> [Anand Naidoo, World News]

As Bell (1991) points out, the lead has a dual function. It must begin to tell a story as well as summarizing it. However, as the news report develops, the news anchor or presenter in most cases passes the floor to the reporter.

Delegation frame

In most television news broadcasts, the reporter is introduced by the news anchor. The delegation frame according to Scollon (1998) is the statement which says to whom the following responsibility for authorship is delegated. This delegation is further constrained topically by the lead statement of the presenter. A typical example of this would be the following:

> CNN's Rebecca MacKinnon reports on what's at stake for North Korea's neighbour, China.

Various limiting words such as 'on' or 'about', appear as 'restriction devices':

> CNN's John King is travelling with the president.

> He now joins us to talk about the issues that divide the two countries. John?

The fact that the news anchor tells the audience that the correspondent 'is travelling with the president' who is the main participant in the news report, implies what is going to be reported live and is therefore a reliable fact. Another important function of the delegation frame is to attribute the source of news to the correspondent. In doing so, the responsibility is passed over from the news anchor to the correspondent.

The closing frame

Again according to Scollon (1998) this is where the correspondent signals that he/she is returning the floor and its accompanying responsibility to the news anchor.

A closing frame or signoff usually contains three elements:

- the reporter's name
- the reporter's location
- the reporter's news organization.

For example:

> Lindsey Hilsum, Channel 4 News, Harare.

The closing frame may also take the form of the news anchor retaking the floor:

> OK. Thank you, Matthew.
> Matthew Bigg of Reuter Television, talking to us from Abidjan.

We have seen how through a lead, delegation and closing frames the stages of a generic structure are established. By moving through these frames, the news anchor, passes the floor to the correspondent and brings out what are termed the satellite structures of the news.

The satellite structures

Scollon's use of the term satellite is meant to indicate a series of structures which orbit the lead nucleus. In other words the function of the satellite is to add details to the story, to repeat, or recycle information contained in the lead.

The following is an example of an extract from a television news broadcast.

Structural elements	Television news text
[Nucleus–lead]	ANAND NAIDOO, WORLD NEWS 1. Despite a state of emergency, opposition demonstrators are back on the streets in Ivory Coast's commercial capital Abidjan. 2. They're protesting a court decision banning one of the country's most popular politicians from parliamentary elections.
[Delegation frame] – passing the floor to the correspondent	3. For details, we're joined now by Matthew Bigg of Reuters Television. 4. Matthew, what can you see on the streets today?
Specification 1: Elaboration – reconstructing the event	MATTHEW BIGG, REUTERS TELEVISION: 5. Well, Anand, just after curfew was lifted this morning, 6. we went out 7. and took a tour around, 8. and the situation is quite different from yesterday.
Specification 2: Elaboration – contextualizing the event	9. Yesterday, the supporters of the opposition leader Alassane Ouattara took to the streets 10. and really shut down the whole of the city. 11. In some parts of town, there were up to 10,000, maybe more protesters, 12. Completely blocking off roads 13. and making sure no one got to work, nothing opened.
Specification 3: Elaboration – reconstructing the event	14. Today, the situation is much more mixed. 15. In some areas of the town, in some districts, there are road blocks with burning tyres and clashes. 16. Yet in other parts of the city, the security forces have taken back control. 17. We saw security forces forcing some of the young militants, opposition militants, to clear the roadblocks and the burning barricades that they made so that people could get to work.

Structural elements	Television news text
	18. And what you see is that a lot of people are trying to get to work.
	19. Some markets stores are opening.
	20. And in other places, things are very much still closed down.
Specification 4: Evaluation – commenting on the event	21. So it's a mixed picture.
Specification 5: Background – reconstructing the event	NAIDOO: 22. Matthew, give us a bit of background as to what triggered off this violence in the first place. BIGG: 23. Right. Well, Ivory Coast is obviously traditionally seen as a very stable and prosperous country within West Africa, a kind of a shining light. 24. This year, it's had a very difficult year, first of all, with a coup d'état, and then a popular uprising to kick out the military leader who tried to steal the elections. 25. which ended with elections in October.
Specification 6: Cause-and-effect – the cause of the riot	26. We now have President Laurent Gbagbo, 27. who won those elections. 28. But the main opposition leader was excluded from presidential elections on grounds of nationality. 29. An he has now been excluded from parliamentary elections due to take place on Sunday. 30. And it's that, [that his protesters are fighting for].
Specification 7: Resolution – stating the result of the event	NAIDOO: 31. And where is all this leading to? 32. Is there someone there with some kind of a plan to diffuse these tensions? BIGG: 33. Well, it's the position of the president that the protests should stop.

Structural elements	Television news text
	34. He last night declared a state of emergency for a week
	35. and imposed a curfew.
Specification 8: Evaluation – appraising the ease of the tension	36. But I think
	37. despite the sort of increased security measures that have been taken, at some point there is going to have to be a political settlement of some kind.
	38. if the tensions that have been generated in this once-stable country are to be calmed down.
[Closing frame] – retaking the floor	NAIDOO:
	39. OK. Thank you, Matthew.
	40. Matthew Bigg of Reuters Television, talking to us from Abidjan.

(Ao Ran 2002: 101–2)

This is a report describing a demonstration protesting because of a court decision banning one of the country's most popular politicians from parliamentary elections. The lead consists of two sentences, the first summarizing the news events 'demonstrators are back', the second elaborating on the purpose of the demonstration – 'protesting a court decision . . .'

The second phase of the television news report acts to specify the events presented in the lead through elaboration, background, evaluation, cause and effect, and resolution. That is to say, the primary role of the second phase is not to develop new stories but to refer back to the lead through a series of specifications.

Elaboration

This stage in the genre is often used to reconstruct the event in greater detail or to exemplify information already presented in the lead.

Evaluation

This is the means by which the significance of a news report is established. From the examples cited above the evaluation may be the correspondent's observations on the event 'So it's a mixed picture'. Or it may be in the form of expressing expectations on how the situation could develop next, such as 'there is going to have to be'. The correspondent may also use some expert external source to appraise the elements introduced in the lead. The source used for evaluation is often realized by direct quotations from the expert, for example:

> Alexi Malashenko, Political Analyst
>
> Afghanistan is a very convenient place and in a very convenient time to show the Russian authority, the Russian pretension to be a power in the region.

Interpersonal mental processes are also used, such as 'I think', 'I believe', 'I suppose', as explicit or subject evaluations.

Background

Background covers any number of events prior to the current event. They probably figured as news reports in their own right at an earlier stage of the on-going story. For example:

> Yesterday, the supporters of the opposition leader Alassane Ouattara took to the streets and really shut down the whole of the city . . .

The background is then a mini-story happening prior to the major events of today. What the reporter is doing is setting the scene in a temporal, spatial and social context.

Cause and effect

Cause and effect serves to tell the audience the reasons for the crisis presented in the lead. In the example that we have quote, the cause is the exclusion of the opposition leader from the elections. The cause and effect stage may also serve to predict the consequences resulting from the current news events, for example:

> Russia is threatening to do what the United States has done – attack alleged terrorist training camps in Afghanistan. And the message is much the same. Russia will do whatever it needs to do to protect its national interest.
>
> (Jill Dougherty, CNN Correspondent)

Resolution

While cause and effect specifies reasons and consequences of a news event, the resolution stage shows the result of a problem or crisis presented in the lead. An example of this was the following:

> [Naidoo]
> And where is all this heading to?
> Is there someone there with some kind of plan to diffuse these tensions?
>
> [Bigg]
> Well it's the position of the President that the protests should stop.
> He last night declared a state of emergency for a week and imposed a curfew.

However, news reports at this point in the generic structure often do not present clear-cut resolutions. When they do, any result will often be in the Lead rather than in the satellite element of the story.

Justification

The term justification is used as a stage in the genre when one or more sentences are used to provide the evidence or reasoning to support the newsworthy claim presented in the lead. An example of this is found in the following extract:

> [Naidoo World News]
> Marina, why do you believe that Japan is trying to normalize relations at this stage? Is it just because North Korea has assured the Japanese that it will put a moratorium on these missile tests?
>
> [Kamimura]
> Well, it goes back to this three pronged approach that the United States, South Korea and Japan have agreed to take when it comes to dealing with North Korea. I mean, you must remember that for Japan, this is a real security threat . . .

The lead of this news report was, 'There's been a major development in relations between Japan and North Korea'.

> (Ao Ran 2002: 107)

Although we have identified six stages or moves in the satellite sequence, not all are utilized at any one time, neither do they have to come in the sequence indicated here. This is because the generic structure of television news reporting cannot be merely taken as a series of stages in terms of language, but it is rather a system of social interaction, which is realized through language. As Fiske (1987) and Graddol (1994) have pointed out, we must keep in mind that television news genre is very vulnerable, in the sense that it has difficulty in maintaining its generic distinctiveness from other television genres such as documentaries or current affairs programmes. The authority, quality of sources and interpretations which television news offers are potentially contestable especially as the audience is heterogeneous. In order to accomplish factuality, television news must work hard to maintain the distinctiveness of the genre, and must use all the resources at its disposal for achieving high modality in its presentations. In other words, what is stated as a fact must appear as a fact.

This means that modality operates in visual representations as well as verbal ones. Hodge and Kress (1988) use the term 'modality cues' in relation to visual texts. In television advertising such devices as soft focus and colour saturation are routinely used to indicate forms of visual idealization and fantasy, but in such landscapes the image of the advertised product will be shown as detailed and well focused.

One problem in identifying visual modality is that the cues are not universal and vary with the genre. What expresses high modality in one genre may express low modality in another. Kress and van Leeuwen (1990) discuss how high visual modality in scientific genres is expressed through description of an 'objective world' regardless of the experience of the human agent. Since science is concerned with universal truths, context is irrelevant to descriptions. Photography tends to be black and white, which connotes high definition (high modality). There seems to be an underlying assumption that it requires miraculous technology to make scientific truth visible to the naked eye.

The modality conventions, which operate in television news are not those of science, though news reports may draw on the resources of science genres. High modality in television news is more typically achieved by showing the context in which the event occurs. Indeed that is sometimes all that news images do show. Television news also needs to report a variety of perspectives and points of view to evaluate these. The world, which it describes, is the transient world of today and what is news tonight is not news tomorrow. Above all, television news needs to communicate immediacy, geographical and temporal location. It must also persuade viewers of the authority and credibility of the world, which it portrays. The key to understanding how television news accomplishes factuality lies in recognising the tension between objectivity and subjectivity. It goes some way to explaining the complex and eclectic nature of the visual modality system, which television news employs.

The following example gives some idea of what is involved in the recreation of the world in fictional form in order to represent it realistically. These are reflections of the academic consultant for a television programme, which followed the journalist Victoria Makins while she researched and wrote a story, which appeared in the *Times Educational Supplement* (TES).

> One might conclude that, in order for television to provide viewers with a reasonably accurate impression of what 'normality' is like, it has to create conditions of considerable abnormality for the participants in order to achieve its effect . . . A number of 're-creations' of events occurred (during the filming at the TES) to represent different phases of a process that in reality had occurred over several weeks: e.g. chats between Makins and the feature editor about the progress of the story and the film of Makins making the initial phone-call to the head of Peers (school), which had actually taken place several weeks earlier (shots of the head 'answering' this call had already been taken during the visit to Peers!). To film all these things as they actually happened would have been too expensive (involving taking our film crews on many more days), and very unpredictable (because real life is like that); and, strangely perhaps, the chances of the television process disrupting the normality it sets out to capture are sometimes more severe if it attempts to film things as they really happen than if participants are asked to re-live the process for the benefit of the camera.
>
> (Boyd-Barrett 1987: 23 quoted in Graddol 1994)

Of course, it is standard practice to edit available shots in order to create a coherent story from what might be seen as a random actuality sequences story. Graddol describes an incident during the coverage of the Gulf War, when professional news footage from within the war zone was limited and amateur footage from camcorders was occasionally shown on television news. Such amateur tapes often contain a time stamp in the corner of the screen. One sequence showed a shot of a building, a close up of a missile explosion, and a third shot of the building in flames. The pictures flowed naturally . . . images of a fast moving piece of actuality. The time stamps showed that the close-up of the explosion had been filmed earlier than either of the other shots (and presumably occurred in a different location) while the two shots of the building were taken on different days. When edited together, they told a story of cause and effect, of before and after.

The editing conventions required to produce, what appears to be, factuality provides a dilemma for television and television news in particular. In the case of the Gulf War, material could be re-ordered to satisfy the conventions of realism, but in the majority of cases the news camera arrives at a scene only in time to show effects and consequences rather than causes. Indeed, showing causes can give rise to suspicion that there has been some fictionalization going on. In other words, that all the truth is not being revealed, which in fact, might be the case.

In responding to television news we respond to different interrelations between different modes of representations: visual (pictorial, written), and oral. Comprehension is influenced by inferences, which readers make between modes to arrive at an interpretation of what is going on. Inferences depend on culture-specific knowledge, which is highly conventionalized and activated by viewers in a largely automatic and intuitive way. We have already touched upon this in the previous chapter in relation to history texts.

So how can we approach the interplay of these factors as viewers respond simultaneously as they watch an item on television news? One way as suggested by Meinhof (1994) is to relate the pictures and the texts in terms of 'actors', 'events' and 'outcomes'.

She identifies three major procedures used in television news.

- Overlap: the film footage and the text share the same action component. For example overlap is typical for studio announcements, for the opening of news stories. Headlines next to the newsreader act as advance notifiers for viewers

- Displacement: film footage and text represent different action components of the same event. For example the film reports the causes and the film shows the effects of an event. There are obvious cases such as disasters, where the filming must fellow the event itself. The text will announce that an earthquake has happened. The pictures will show the effect of the disaster. However, as Meinhof (1994: 216–17) points out displacement may not be the inevitable result of having to film after the event. In the English news reports about the summer 1988 strike by Spanish air traffic controllers, the text talked about the strikers and the strike; the pictures showed passengers stranded at Gatwick airport. In terms of balance, between cause and effect, there was an over-representation of the effect, and an under-representation of actors, their grievances, and their reasons for striking.

- Dichotomy: film footage and text represent action components of different events. An example of this would be where the film shows unrelated images filmed on the location of the event. Meinhof gives as an illustration of this news reports of the withdrawal of Soviet troops from Afghanistan in January 1989. The text on the German satellite news programme *Blick* described the situation in Kabul as under the threat of collapse adding comments about an acute food shortage there. The pictures, however, showed an unrelated street scene from Kabul.

How do viewers respond to what Meinhof terms 'doubly-encoded presentations', where the action component of the text and the action component of the pictures are divergent? In the end the viewers must be able to combine the different action components to a single representation of the news item. But in order to so this they must be aware of what is happening. If the viewer (in this case) cannot rise to the necessary level of consciousness then the text and picture will project a 'preferred' reading, that of the producers. The 'reading' would then have a monolithic message. Obviously there has to be some combination of text and message in the conveying for example of television news. But the question to ask is do we see the pictures that we are told to see, or do the pictures tell us the real story by giving us a feeling of immediacy, influencing our attitudes and adding those to a seemingly neutral text (as in the example of the air traffic controllers)? Probably the answer lies in the possibilities for different responses from differences among the viewers themselves, and therefore a dependence on a number of factors. Among these factors we could list, background knowledge, a willingness to make inferences between the text and the pictures or even the level of involvement one might have with the news item. Viewers have many options to respond to in receiving information from television news. This could include commenting, disagreeing, not paying attention or finally switching off.

Another dimension of the multi-semiotic process of television is what might be called the 'ethnography of communication', that is to say considering the significance of television, as well as other forms of mass communication in the day-to-day lives and routines of the 'audience'. Hobson's (1982) study of the audience for the British television soap opera, *Crossroads*, looked at gender-differentiated readings and the domestic contexts of consumption. Describing one of the domestic viewing situations, Hobson wrote:

> The woman with whom I had gone to watch the programme was serving the evening meal, feeding her five- and three-year-old daughters and attempting to watch the programme on the black and white television situated on top of the freezer opposite the kitchen table.
>
> (1982: 112)

As she made clear, a viewing context of this sort is a far cry from the darkened room in which an academic might conduct a textual analysis. Watching television is not a separate, solitary activity; rather it is woven into the routine activities of the household. The programme, *The Royle Family* referred to earlier, actually exploits precisely this aspect of television watching as a dominant feature of life in a working-class household. Such rituals of television viewing for family relations become the power relations. Cubitt (1984: 46) as quoted in Moores (1994) called these rituals, 'the politics of the living-room'. Morley (1986) looking at the gender relations within the household structure saw television viewing as form of cultural behaviour. What was clearly shown was that domestic space itself had very different meanings for men and for women. For men, it was primarily a site of leisure, defined in relation to work time, which is spent outside the home. For women, such a separation is not always evident. While men, interviewed by Morley expressed a preference for watching quietly and attentively, the women described their viewing as a fundamentally social activity, involving ongoing conversation, and at least the performance of one other domestic activity such as ironing. Obviously we need to re-frame any studies of multiliteracies within a much broader field of analysis than has hitherto fore been the case, the structure of our day-to-day lives.

Up to now we have been focusing on the role of television as a multi-semiotic form of communication and in particular television news and its perceived factuality. We will now turn our attention to another multimodal form, that of the popular magazine.

10.2 Magazines

Kress and van Leeuwen (1990) in their approach to social semiotics suggest that communication firstly, requires the participants to make their messages maximally understandable in a particular context. Secondly, that representation requires the encoders of the semiotic signalling to choose forms, which they see as the most appropriate and plausible in the given context. So for example, if we apply this to the publication of a popular magazine, it means that the producers of the magazine will choose forms of expression that appear to be transparent to their readers. How transparent an article or message might be will depend upon the reader's background or world knowledge of various situations and issues. Also the interest of the producers of the magazine and the resulting theme of the article, picture or story will lead them to choose layouts, designs and points of view to be represented in order to realize the intended message for the reader (be this overt or covert).

Both language and visual communication express meanings belonging to and structured by cultures in society that results in degrees of congruence between the two. As we have already discussed, the distinction between subjective and objective meanings play an important role in cultures and such a distinction can be applied to both linguistic and visual coding. In order to elaborate on what this means we have chosen an international magazine for men *FHM* (For Him Magazine), which has various versions including one for Singapore. *FHM Singapore* is published monthly and is about 130–40 pages in length. There is always a cover girl although the main feature announced in bold print on the cover may have nothing to do with the female figure depicted on the cover.

The following table summarizes one year of issues of the magazine.

Month/year	*Cover girl*	*Title of the issue*
November 1998	Nadya	Watery graves
December 1998	Jennifer Lopez	Evel Knievel
January 1999	Yasmine Bleeth	Double agent
February 1999	Andrea De Cruz	Jobs from hell
March 1999	Anna Nichole Smith	World's worst destinations
April 1999	Denise Richards	Complete lunacy
May 1999	Mariah Carey	Vile food
June 1999	MTV Babes	Crazed collectors
July 1999	Bai Ling	LAPD
August 1999	Britney Spears	The murder cleaners
September 1999	Catherine Zeta Jones	Dying young
October 1999	Shania Twain	Terror in the sky

(Cordeiro 2000: 46)

In a multimodal text, the writing may carry out one set of meanings and images another. Covers are like previews as to what can be found beyond it. But covers are what sell magazines even before we as readers look through the contents or read the headlines on the covers. The glossy finish of the magazine, the background colour of the cover page and even the colours on the models on the cover page – her clothes, make-up and

skin tone – all provide for the reader a subtle but effective sensory experience. This is an experience that the reader wants to participate in and, the
publishers hope, will therefore buy the magazine.

The colours have a very strong influence on the reader. Warm, bold
colours such as red or orange are not only eye catching but encourage the
reader to infer passion. In the issues listed in the previous table from
FHM Singapore 9 are dominated by the colour red. When the background colour is not red, the colour still manifests itself in different
forms. For example, in Issue 5 the magazine logo *FHM* appears in bold
red accompanied by headlines in red. The following table indicates the
main colours used in each issue of the magazine.

Issue no.	*Background colour*	*Cover headlines*	*Sub headlines*	*FHM logo*
1.	White	Red	Black/Blue	Red
2.	Black	Orange	White	Orange
3.	Red	Yellow	White	White
4.	White	Red	Black/Blue	Red
5.	White	Red	Black/Red	Blue
6.	Blue	Orange	White/Orange	White
7.	Red	Yellow	White/Yellow	White
8.	Green	Orange/Red	White/Black/Orange	White
9.	Grey	Red	Black/Red	Red
10.	Light Blue	Red	Black/Red	Red
11.	Red	Yellow	White/Yellow	White
12.	Blue	Orange	White/Orange	Orange

(Cordeiro 2000: 49)

White is also used quite extensively especially as a background.
However, where white is used as a background, the women on the
covers wear black– black plastic or leather (Issue 4), black silk or satin
(Issue 1) and black netting and lace (Issue 5). Women modelling on a
white background also tend to have exaggerated poses, with their arms
behind their head and leaning hips that accentuate the natural curve of
the waist and hips (Issue 5).

Images involve two kinds of participants, 'represented participants' (the
people, the places and things depicted in images) and 'interactive participants' (the people who communicate with each other through images, the
producers and viewers of images). (Kress and Van Leeuwen 1990).

The knowledge of the producer and the knowledge of the viewer differ
in the crucial aspect of the former being more active in the sending as well

as the receiving of messages while the latter tends to be passive, allow the receiving of messages. For example the producers of FHM Singapore use this power relation as the more dominant participant in Issue 10 where the magazine's use of bold print acts in contrast to a pop star's innocent image.

The choice between the size of frame, whether it is a close-up, medium shot or long shot, offer another dimension in the interactive meaning of images. Image producers, in depicting their subjects for their messages in an image, must choose to depict them as approachable or distant and aloof. For example, at close personal distance, the distance in which people can touch each other, a magazine cover will frame and capture the head and shoulders of the represented subject.

Without exception, all subjects portrayed on the cover of *FHM Singapore* were taken with a medium shot such that the represented subjects were famed from the knees up or slightly above the knees. Most covers, with the exception of Issue 10 (Britney Spears sitting down with legs extended and crossed in front of her), have their represented subjects standing, with a frontal stance to the camera. 10 covers out of 12 portray their subjects as leaning their weight on one hip, so that the subjects subconsciously come across to the readers as more alluring. Thus the subjects are portrayed as though they were inviting the reader to get involved with them and therefore the magazine. Obviously the use of camera angles has an essential role to play in these poses.

All the represented subjects on the covers of the magazine are celebrities, either international or local. They epitomize the 'good life' or the life that most people would only dream of living. As such, these celebrities have to come across as larger than life characters and this can be done by the camera angles. The image producer's use of the full frontal, low horizontal angle serves several purposes. The full frontal angle allows for the image producer to portray the full figure of the subject and the medium shot frames the subject in a manner that is close to the readers. The subjects are portrayed in such a manner as allowing readers into their personal space, with an inviting attitude. However, the consistent use of the low horizontal angle implicitly states that the represented subjects are still celebrities, where most tend to look down into the camera and thus look down at the readers.

The language in *FHM Singapore*

Photographic presentation of celebrities together with the textual layout is further emphasized by the language used. Most celebrity women are written about in a manner that is far removed from the everyday reality of the reader. Some examples of how celebrity women are described include:

- Dream girl
- The powder keg of gorgeousness that FHM managed to bring to the desert metropolis.
- Louise Nurding, the most lusciously-curved nymphet ever . . .
- Meeting up with her, your eyes are at once trapped by the caramel skin, the blond-flecked hair and . . . the pneumatic figure doing all the right things to a swooping V-necktop.

Such an overwhelming use of adjectives places the represented subject at the passive end of a power relationship in which *FHM Singapore* views women through the eyes of men. While each celebrity woman is given her chance to speak her mind in the interview, the articles categorize and characterize each celebrity woman before the interview thus subverting even the idea that celebrity women have any material or mental agency.

On the other hand the language of the main feature articles in the sample years' issue of the magazine foregrounds violence (with its connotations of 'manliness'), which stand in contrast to the female images. These are listed in the following table:

Issue No	Title
1.	Death dive – cave diving is only for the foolhardy or the suicidal as Rob Paker found out.
2.	Hell on earth – one man against 300 psychotic rebels. Will Scully survived.
3.	Marked man – the incredible story of Raymond Gilmour's ten years as a double agent in the IRA.
4.	The elite – Duncan Falconer spills the beans on the Special Boat Service, a regiment which makes the SAS look soft.
5.	Death trap – you wouldn't believe the horrors on board Russia's geriatric space station Mir.
6.	The invisible man – imprisoned by the Viet Cong, a US soldier waited 14 years for freedom, only to find that his own government wanted him killed as a traitor.
7.	The evil monster of the Andes – serial killer Pedro Alonso López killed 350 girls in Ecuador. Now he's free.
8.	Road trips – through hell and high water, roads were made to be travelled upon.
9.	Don't call me Dibble – FHM goes on night patrol with the LAPD's elite gang-bursting unit.

10.   Murder cleaners– we follow the people who handle blood, sweat and bodily gore everyday.

11.   The high life – the story of surf legend Jeff Hankman and his search for drug money.

12.   Crash! – when highjackers seized flight ET961, they never expected it to run out of fuel.

(Cordeiro 2000: 56)

The titles and headlines alone give the general tone to the readership: 'death', 'hell', 'marked', 'kill', 'evil' . . . 'serial killer', 'murder', 'blood', 'gore' and 'seized'. The magazine helps to normalize that being involved with violence or experiencing violence vicariously through the magazine is a masculine trait.

Other articles in *FHM Singapore* reveal a certain ideology that projects male leisure as preferring the rougher side of nature. Road trips for example, are meant for men who should be unafraid to get dirty in both urban and rural landscapes. While the most salient places of interest in nature are land related such as mountains, deserts, canyons, rainforests and wildlife, the number of references to water sports as events of interest is even greater. White-water rafting, scuba diving surfing are presented as far more unpredictable sports than hiking or viewing wildlife from the safety of a safari jeep.

The other great pastime the producers of the magazine show interest in is clubbing, drinking and the nightlife in general.

On the more serious side of life, while women's magazines write about illness and prevention of illness, the descriptions in *FHM Singapore* on such topics are brutally honest but bordering on the gruesome. Graphic pictures of internal organs that are in an advanced stage of a disease such as lung cancer, or brain tumour often carry shock value. Death is a frequent topic in the magazine, through having unhealthy and sometimes illegal habits, too much drinking and smoking or taking drugs. So you have titles such as 'Gruesome illnesses' (Issue 1), 'Boozing' (Issue 7) and 'Dying young' (Issue no 11).

If we tried to summarize the general message that the producers are sending to the readers of a magazine such as *FHM Singapore*, we could list the following:

- Man as a fighter: violence was found in all the issues produced for the year 1998–9. What is being projected by various semiotic means is that maleness involves either directly or indirectly, getting involved in violence, aggression and fighting. The general message is that if the readers themselves do not actively and physically participate in violence, then vicarious participation counts as well.

- Sexual prowess: since covers are what first sell the magazine, the graphic representations on the cover are important. *FHM Singapore* sells on its image of being a sensual magazine for men. The editor when asked to describe the magazine said that it was 'funny, sexy and useful' (January 1998: 10). The use of salient colours such as 'red' shows that the main approach by the magazine is not going to be sub-liminal but direct. The marketing and attention grabbing strategies by using sexy cover girls in mostly full frontal horizontal shots encourages the readers into an imaginary interpersonal relationship with these celebrities as desirable women for the everyday man.

- Male insecurities: men are not infallible creatures and *FHM Singapore* tries to balance the desirable 'macho' image of men with their insecurities, thus the physical and mental illnesses coupled with unhealthy lifestyles.

10.3 Summary

Many other issues could be discussed and many other forms of multi-semiotic approaches to conveying 'information' could be analysed in this way. But what is important is the realization that multi-semiotic, or multi-modal means of communication are an essential part of what is means to be 'literate' in the modern world. We might argue that the rep-resentational functions of the communication system have changed over the past 30 odd years and that these changes have had an effect on the language used. Our 'literacy practices' now take place in a wider social, economic and cultural environment; consequently, we have to set our frame of thinking and of working more widely than before (Kress 1999). The world around us is changing the environment of representation and communication. If we take the example of the television news, which we have used as an illustration of the need to maintain a perspective of objectivity and relativity in our interpretation of how factuality is repre-sented, 30 years ago the television news consisted of an image of a 'newsreader' reading written scripts of the news. Today, there are no longer 'newsreaders', but 'news presenters'. The television news is largely visual with spoken language as a commentary and framing rather than as the central means of communication.

The vast changes in the technologies of communication have produced a communication landscape of a new kind. Indeed the effects of the new technologies are still developing. The move from 'page' to 'screen' is a move from the dominance of writing to the dominance of the image. Once direct voice to screen interaction has become a reality the present relations of language-as-speech to language-as-writing will change present conceptions of writing entirely. The very term literacy is a term that has grown out of the older social and cultural arrangements; its increasingly uneasy fit with newer situations is reflected in the fact that it is often pluralized, as in the title of this chapter:'multiliteracies' and the extension of the term to all domains of representation: visual, media, computer, mathematical, business and so on.The communicational demands of the societies into which children now at school will be moving extend beyond the demands of competence in speech and writing. Thinking of literacy in one mode, be it language or be it image cannot provide an adequate account of the extual objects as a whole. If we have a broader concept of literary as communication with a multimodal reality, then we have the means to account for the situation as it actually is. We are also, perhaps beginning to understand that we use distinct modes of representation and communication, with different media of dissemination. The new communicational landscape, of multimodality in multimedia environment means that we have to re-think our in-school and out-of school practices and treat 'literacies' not as a single mode but as multi-mode with the corollary that this means learning procedures to adapt to new situations in the larger frame of today's global society.

Points to ponder

Record a television news broadcast and apply the generic structure described on p.230 (Satellite structures) and see if you can find a similar outline structure.

- How standardized are television news broadcasts?

    Alternatively, you could take several copies of a popular magazine such as the one used in this chapter and examine the linguistic and visual juxtapositionings found in the texts. You could, for example, use similar tabular formats as this helps to summarize the information.

- What is your overall impression of the use of multimodality in these texts?
- What do readers have to learn to be able to understand the text in this way?

10.4 Further reading

Cook, G. 1992: *The discourse of advertising*. London: Routledge.

Fowler, R. 1991: *Language in the news*. London: Routledge.

Graddol, D. and Boyd-Barrett, O. (eds.) 1994: *Media texts: authors and readers*. Clevedon: Multilingual Matters and Open University.

O'Brien, T. (ed.) 1999: *Language and literacies* (BAAL). Clevedon: Multilingual Matters.

11 Learning language(s): creating a linguistic biography

The aim of this our final chapter is to outline a conceptual framework for understanding the processes of learning language(s) described in the earlier chapters as the creation of a person's 'linguistic biography' that is unique to each person and which is dynamic and hence changes over time. However, this is not to suggest that learning language is independent of the social and cultural contexts in which people live. Our model of learning language(s) recognizes the primacy of the social. A number of social contexts and contextual influences will be described to our view of how people learn language(s). It will be suggested that the variety and range of these contacts influence and in part, account for the dynamic nature of an individual's linguistic development and evolving repertoire. The chapter will describe these influential factors as a nested hierarchy of five levels of contextual influence.

The ideas on which this chapter is based emerged, very much like language itself, slowly and over a period of time. Looking around at one's friend and family members we are forced to realize that we are living and working with people who were both very like and very unlike ourselves. This sets us thinking about two things: the role that language played in creating us, our lives and our biographies and the extent to which people are autonomous in making choices about the languages they learn and perhaps, the lives they live. As linguists we may ask the question, 'Would I be me in spite of my linguistic repertoire, or does my language make me who I am?' Tollefson (1990: 1) begins his book *Planning Language, Planning Inequality* with a reflection:

> Recently, I had an interesting conversation with my friend Greg, a 37-year-old white monolingual speaker of standard American English, who has an MA degree in music education and is employed as a music teacher in an American high school. He is comfortable economically, owns a nice home in a middle-class section of town within walking distance of a beautiful lake, drives a new van, and spends summers cruising the coastal islands on his 28-foot sail boat.

In this conversation Tollefson speculates about how Greg's life would be different if Greg was a native speaker of Vietnamese rather than English and concludes not surprisingly, that Greg's life would indeed be different. Our point is a little different. We suggest that Greg's life would be different if he spoke any language other than English and further any variety other than standard American. Tollefson's book 'explores how the mechanism of language policy arbitrarily gives importance to language in the organization of human societies'. The claim in this chapter goes beyond this to suggest that there are a number of factor that influence a person's linguistic repertoire and that the language of everyday interactions, whether the direct consequence of language planning policy or not, will exert influence on interpersonal interactions, as well as on the organization of social groups and the communities they form. We shall demonstrate some factors that influence everyday interactions and how these influence individual speakers.

Perhaps surprisingly it was Noam Chomsky who provided further inspiration for the idea of language development as the creation of a linguistic biography. In an interview reported in the *Times Higher Education Supplement* (9 April 1999) Noam Chomsky said that his life had been one of multiple personalities. He used the term to explain his involvement in a seemingly diverse and disparate range of life activities that include being a Professor of Linguistics at MIT, being a political activist, a writer on human rights issues, as well as a world-renowned intellectual, to name some of these personae. It is perhaps surprising for Chomsky to respond in this way because as a linguist, he has always advocated a theory of learning language(s) that is founded in the belief that people are born with an innate predisposition, that he terms, a language acquisition device or LAD, a hard-wired, organic pre-disposition to acquiring language that is a universal human feature. So it is significant that he, when reflecting on his own life, uses the expression, 'multiple personalities' to describe himself since this is a term very close to the one used by another linguist, Firth (sometimes referred to as the founder of British systemic linguistics), whose own view of language development stands very much in contrast to that of Chomsky's. In his book *Tongues of Men* (Firth 1937/64) Firth outlined a socially orientated description of language development. Firth suggested that as we go through life we develop, with language and through our interactions with others, a bundle of personae. So it seems that although as linguists these great figures of our age may disagree, as ordinary people they share a common view of human life as multifaceted, wherein each person learns to play a variety of roles, some ascribed and some elected; some complementary and some so diverse that they may even seem to be contradictory. The study of language development is concerned with understanding how people develop their own unique bundle of personae. The view of language learning explored here seeks to understand the relation between the life lived and the role of language in creating that life and those life experiences. It is an exploration of language as lifelong learning that goes beyond Hasan's (1996: 1): 'idea that there is a continuity from the living of life on the one hand right down to the morpheme on the other'. The description of language learning explored here is a quest to demonstrate the continuity between the individual and above all, their linguistic repertoire.

In this book our concern has been to extend existing descriptions of language development in an attempt to reflect, a little more accurately on the lives of everyday language users and to describe how learning language represents learning for them. These are the ordinary people of all ages who need and use language(s) as part of their daily routines and life experiences. This chapter will outline a number of sources that together combine to provide sufficient foundation for viewing language development as the creation of a bundle of personae or multiple personalities. It will be argued that learning language(s) is both simultaneously a common human experience with sufficient common ground that allows for individuals to communicate reasonably successfully with each other and unique and individuated. Above all, our description takes into account the varieties of English now being learnt in communities around the world. This is significant because 'the number of people who speak English other than as a first language far outweighs the number of first language speakers. English is affected by global change. Graddol (1997) in his report *The Future of English?* records the major world languages in millions of first language speakers of these languages. This is reported in Table 11.1 below.

Table 11.1 Major world languages and the number of first language speakers

Major world languages	Speakers-in millions
Chinese	1,113
English	372
Hindi/Urdu	316
Spanish	304
Arabic	201

The number of people who speak these languages as their first language continues to change as these figures demonstrate. This suggests a changing international linguistic environment.

Giddens (1990, 1991) uses the phrase the 'reflexive project of the self' to explain the self, one's personal and social identity, and how this is created through processes of ongoing dialogue that individuals sustain with themselves in relation to their changing life experiences. In this sense the self is not stable. It is an evolving, dynamic, created through engagement in processes. Giddens suggests that the reflexive project of the self, consists in the sustaining of coherent, yet continuously revised, biographical narratives. This socially situated self is central to our view of learning language.

Our description of language learning begins with a focus on the individual, the locus of language. There is ample evidence to support the view that each person's life is unique. Bookshops are full of volumes of autobiographical accounts of varying degrees of interest. Hence the notion of each person having a life story or biography is a well-established social and intellectual concept. But can this individual uniqueness extend to the language(s) a person knows, a person's linguistic repertoire? The next section will examine aspects of the linguistic repertoire and describe the ways in which it can be regarded as developing unique qualities and characteristics.

11.1 Aspects of a person's linguistic repertoire

Let us begin with the qualities of the human voice. We are familiar with the scenario of being able to recognize the ways people speak and can recognize regional accents even when we cannot name or identify each one. While some may be easier than others to recognize, the notion of particular groups having distinctive ways of speaking is not novel or revolutionary, although it may infer different social connotations particularly in Britain. Can this notion of diversity be extended to suggest that each individual person has their own unique way of speaking? Consider the following scenario: you go to the telephone, dial a number, do not connect with a person, only an answering machine. So you decide to leave a message that may begin something like this, 'Hi, (it's only me), can you call me?' For some people, in some parts of the world, this is an everyday event. We expect those who know us well to recognize our voice and frequently they do! Many will be able to recognize not only the voices of those people whom we know very well but also with those voices that we hear frequently, of popular singers, media stars, politicians and other famous personalities, for example. All of these everyday experiences suggest that individual voices are unique and hence easily recognizable as such. Recent advances in technology confirm this intuitive ability. Computers are now able to identify the specific aspects of a voice that create its uniqueness. These include timbre, vowel quality and other linguistic features that combine to create a voice quality that is unique for each person. The science of voice recognition is now so sophisticated that it is increasingly used for security screening. Banks, passport control and similar secure centres now use voice recognition technology for security screening purposes to identify specific individuals. So there is firm scientific evidence to support the view that there are aspects of an individual's voice that are unique. We are now so certain about this that voice recognition is as established as the fingerprint as a way of identifying individuals. Voice recognition is considered a reliable way to identify individuals. Hence, voice recognition, one part of our description of what it means to learn language(s) is established as a unique, individualistic characteristic sufficiently reliable to be used for security purposes and identification.

Just as we might expect close associates to recognize our voices we are also familiar with the scenario of answering the telephone but *not* being able to identify the person from the voice we hear. Sometimes, we even confuse the voice we hear with another very similar sounding voice. When this happens the speaker is mistakenly identified as another person, someone else. Within families it is sometimes difficult to distinguish the voices of siblings of a similar age. This convergence may be due to a number of factors. The age of the speaker is one consideration. Convergence of the linguistic repertoire at the stage of language development that Halliday terms the 'protolanguage' has been discussed in Chapter 2. Age is an individualistic feature. There are other group and contextual factors that may also be taken into consideration, each of which may influence the language a person chooses to use.

There is a growing literature on new varieties of English that are appearing around the world (Crystal 1999). Singaporean Colloquial English (SCE) is one of these world varieties of English. Linguistic features unique to Singaporean English have been identified at different levels of linguistic description: the syntax (Alsagoff 1998); the phonetic (Bao 1998); the lexical (Wee 1998); and phonological (Lim 1999) have all been established. Singapore is a multilingual society comprising Chinese, Malay, Indian as well as standard and colloquial varieties of English (see Chapter 8 for further description). Lim (1999) has identified distinctive patterns of the pitch movement alignment that characterizes Singaporean English as different in each of the three main ethnic groups. However, she has also identified distinctive patterns in the intonation contour, specifically in segmental and prosodic aspects, that are no longer as distinctive between the ethnic groups as they once were in the not too distant past. However, Singaporeans listening to each other are able to distinguish between the different groups with a reasonably high success rate. Lim's findings suggest that two seemingly contradictory factors are emerging. One is dialect convergence amongst Singaporean English speakers and the other is the development of Singaporean English in ways that relate to the linguistic and cultural heritage groups to which the speakers belong and identify the languages of these groups. These recent developments in the linguistic repertoires of Singaporean English speakers support the view presented here that diversity exists between speakers of the same varieties of language(s) and that these change over time, throughout the lifespan. Further studies of Singaporean English speakers may be able to identify changes in individual speaker's repertoire that change to accommodate, converge or diverge with speakers of the same and different ethnic groups.

While other studies of cultural specific groups demonstrate this trend, there are also other studies of varieties of English have been able to identify distinguishing linguistic features within smaller grouping such as the family. In the USA, William Labov's studies have identified phonemic realizations that link teenagers with their grandparents, while in the UK Kerswill (1996) has demonstrated dialectal convergence among children who moved to the newly established town, Milton Keynes, from different parts of the UK. This led to the emergence of a new variety of English, now established as Estuary English. These studies all support the view that a number of factors influence and precipitate change in a person's linguistic repertoire. Changing geographic location is perhaps the more obvious but coming into contact with people who speak different language, or the same language differently, can also influence.

11.2 Contexts and the creation of a linguistic biography

The dimension of context as central to learning and using language(s) gets support from systemic linguists. Their description of language as a socio-semiotic system of signs makes context a central concern. It is important to emphasize that this should not be understood as regarding language and context as separate. Halliday (1978a) describes language as the dynamic process that actually creates social situations. Hence it is inevitable that the different life experiences, the people we meet, the places we visit and live in, will all contribute to our personal linguistic biography making it distinct from others. In addition, the different social contexts that we participate in and which we help to create will also contribute to our personal, social and linguistic biography. A person's life comprises a range of very different experiences. However, the social psychologist Jerome Bruner suggests that these varied and different spheres of personal experience are not separate or compartmentalized for people. He suggests that they combine in a variety of ways. For example, let us consider the family as a social unit to illustrate this point.

Families invent practices for themselves and their members. These practices exist on a number of levels and can include daily routines like how meal times are observed and conducted, as well as less frequent events like annual cultural events as well as religious and other celebrations. Very soon these routines, for example, how the family celebrates Diwali or Christmas, birthdays and marriages, become established within the family group as traditions. These become embedded within the family's common life experiences as part of the shared, collective experience for the members of that family. When this occurs, the rituals are established, frequently practised and rarely questioned. They can then go unchanged and pass from generation to generation. It is in this way that cultures establish traditions that are simultaneously shared events, established in essentially similar ways but which are created and re-created in individualized ways. These practices are socially defined and can be referred to as cultural schema. They vary within and between societies and cultures and between family and other groups in the same society and culture. (These have been discussed in Chapter 8 and in the discussion of common knowledge.) Bruner argues that the rationale for this is based on what he terms 'the push for connectivity' the human drive to make connections with other people and other events to make sense of our experience. While individuals experience these events, traditions and rituals in a commonly shared way, they also experience them uniquely in an individual manner, as well. Hence the notion of an individual's life as a unique biography gains further support from social psychology. Bruner

(1990) believes that individuals construct 'more or less coherent autobiographies centred around a Self acting more or less purposefully in a social world'. Since language is the means by which these cultural practices are created, conducted, learnt and carried or transmitted it becomes easier to accept a description of language that allows individuals to communicate with each other while simultaneously developing a uniquely individualized way of doing so. The push for connectivity demands channels for connection. Language is central to social interaction. One way of understanding the social contexts created through language is within the ecological description of language and social behaviour as mutually influencing, or what Lemke (1995) has termed 'meteradounding'.

11.3 An ecological description of language development

A central aim in this book is to outline a description of language development that is central to human development. We have taken the view that language is a human resource that can be used for a range of individual and collective functions. These include both social and intellectual. More recently Wells (1999) in his book *Dialogic Enquiry* has drawn together the ideas of Halliday and Vygotsky to explore the idea of a language based theory of learning. He uses this combination to develop a sociocultural practice and theory of education. To extend and complement this view we now turn to another psychologist, Urie Bronfenbrenner (1977 and 1979) who outlines a theoretical description of the structure of human development as ecology, which he terms his ecological systems theory (EST). Bronfenbrenner (1979: 188) defines the ecology of human development as the scientific study of the progressive, mutual accommodation, throughout life, between an active, growing human being, and the changing properties of the immediate settings in which the developing person lives. He suggests that this process of development is affected by the relations between these settings and by the larger contexts in which the settings are embedded. He portrays these settings as an ecological environment which is conceived topologically as a nested hierarchy of structures, each contained one within the other. Bronfenbrenner's EST (1977: 514–15; and 1979: 226–30) views the child at the centre of four hierarchical levels of context: the microsystem, the mesosystem, the exosystem and the macrosystem. These constitute his ecological framework for human development. There are some ways in which these descriptions concur with the view of language development as a linguistic biography. The following section will discuss some of the main features of Bronfenbrenner's four levels of context that influence human development and link them to a systemic description of learning language(s).

Bronfenbrenner's first level of context is the microsystem which he defines as the complex pattern of activities, roles and interpersonal relations that a developing person experiences. These are generally within interpersonal face-to-face encounters that take place within specific settings that have particular physical and material features. These are sometimes termed domains and will be discussed in more detail later in this chapter. The participants engage in particular activities and assume particular roles. For example, these can include the role of daughter, parent, teacher, employee, and so on. The interactions last for particular periods of time. It is during these interactions that the developing child encounters other individuals, each of whom will have their own distinctive characteristics, temperament, personality, systems of belief and linguistic repertoire. The first microsystem that the young child encounters will almost certainly be with immediate, primary caregiver(s). In some contexts this may be within the family unit. However, within the family context the range of roles that the child can play will be limited to family membership and kinship relations. These assume greater significance in some cultural and language systems than in others. For example, some languages such as, French and German signal familiarity between interlocutors structurally. In French the *tu* form is used to mark familiarity while *vous*, signals formality. German and other languages have similar markers but they are not always marked by grammatical case. In Chinese, for example, forms of address are important in marking respect, relationships and seniority. Whatever the social and linguistic rules are, the child will quickly learn the cultural and linguistic norms appropriate in the microsystem in which they are raised. Whatever the norms of the respective society, the child will be introduced to these roles, language and relationships within the first microsystem settings. The child will learn how to behave as a child, how to play the role of a child. The child may also learn other roles too, like being a sibling, as well as other kinship connections, being a cousin, niece, nephew, grandchild, and so on, perhaps sibling. The particular settings in which these encounters are constructed will be in the child's own home and the homes of close family members. The physical and materials construction, including the objects and things within the home, the organization of space within the home and the allocation of roles there will all be defined and determined by the wider contexts in which they are nested or embedded. The microsystem is the primary socializing influence and the environment in which the child begins to learn to be communicatively competent.

The second level of the Bronfenbrenner hierarchy is the mesosystem, made up from a system of microsystems. It comprises the linkages and processes, or interrelations between two or more major settings or domains containing the developing person. For example, early on it would be the relations between the home and external settings, such as the neighbourhood, the kindergarten, nursery school or playgroup. Later it would be between the home and the school, the setting of formal education. Later still, as the individual grows older and hence more independent of the immediate family unit, they will participate in a wider range of micro settings. The links and interrelationships between the settings of the microsystems that combine to form the mesosystem become more complex. This is due in part to the increase in the range of microsystems in which the child participates but also because of the wider variety of roles which the child assumes in these different micro settings.

The third level of the Bronfenbrenner hierarchy is the exosystem. This is an extension of the mesosystem embracing other specific social structures. These include both formal and informal structures but not ones in which the child would ordinarily participate directly. However, since the settings of the mesosystem are contained within the exosystem they are influenced by it. The exosystem can therefore influence, delimit, or even determine what happens within the mesosystem settings. The exosystem can be regarded as an indirect influence on the child, her behaviour and language. These exosystem structures include the major institutions of a society. They include deliberately structured as well as spontaneously evolving connections. At the level of the exosystem we find influences such as the local community and the mass media, the radio, television, newsprint, as well as agencies of government (local, state and national), the distribution of goods and services, communication and transport facilities, and informal and formal social network patterns as well as the world of work, workplaces and employment opportunities and educational settings from pre-school through to postgraduate. These all contribute to the wider linguistic environment in which the child lives. Exposure to these institutions may not be direct through first hand experience but their very existence contributes to the wider organization of society and hence exerts influence.

A fourth and final level of the hierarchy is the Bronfenbrenner macrosystem. This refers to the overarching institutional patterns of the culture or sub-culture of a society. It includes influences such as the economic, social, educational, legal, and political systems, of which micro, meso, and exosystems are the concrete manifestations. Macrosystems are conceived and examined not only in structural terms but as carriers of information and ideology that, both explicitly and implicitly, endow meaning and motivation to particular agencies, social networks, roles, relationships, activities, and their interrelations. What place or priority children and those responsible for their care have within such macrosystems is of special importance in determining how a child and the caretakers are treated and how they can and do interact with each other. Patterns of social interchange, language and social behaviours, are embedded within the macrosystem and also, within each of these three embedded levels of the micro, meso and exo systems.

All four levels of context influence the child's experiences and subsequent development. Bronfenbrenner acknowledges that his conception of the environmental factors that influence an individual's learning (as foregrounded) draws heavily upon the 'topological territories' outlined by Lewin (1935). Lewin's ideas connect Bronfenbrenner's EST directly with the conceptualization of language as a socio-semiotic as described by the systemic linguists including Christie, Halliday and others. Therefore there are a number of ways in which an ecological paradigm is appropriate for describing the individual's language development and learning. It is important to emphasize that language learning as described, is a dynamic phenomenon. Hence it is not only applicable to child language learners. It remains pertinent throughout life as individuals continue to enhance and develop their individual linguistic repertoires with new forms of language, new ways of speaking that they learn in order to fulfil a wider range of personal and social functions and participate in an increasing range of life settings and activities.

There are two key aspects of an ecological paradigm of learning and development that deserve highlighting. The first is the emphasis it places on the nature of learning as a dynamic phenomenon. The second is the view of human development as influenced by but not solely determined upon, external influences of the immediate setting and the wider societal structure(s). This view of the individual, influenced by the social structures of the society in which they are raised, and in which they live and work is described in the related fields of anthropology and sociology, as well as linguistics. The sociologist Anthony Giddens (1987) describes these links and interrelations between the individual and the societies in which we live as *structuration*. Hence there is support from different branches of social sciences, including sociology and social psychology, for the notion of learning as a dynamic process, influenced by contexts, situations and the other people with whom the individual comes into contact.

Contexts or spheres of influence are not so easy to identity and define when they are abstract concepts not linked to particular settings or transactions. Tollefson (1996: 42) is critical of Krashen's major theory of second language acquisition because it does not include historical or structural factors. The ecological model of language development proposed here aims to take Tollefson's comments into account. The nature of an ecological model is its ability to respond to changing circumstances. The turn of the twenty-first century heralds a new layer of societal influence. The next section will extend Bronfenbrenner's EST to include a fifth level in the hierarchy, the stratum of global influence or supra-nation state context.

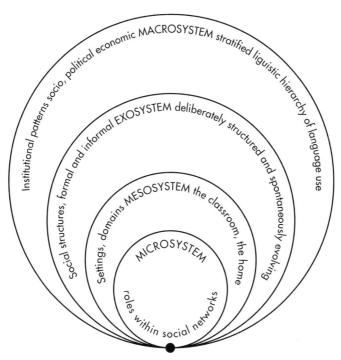

Figure 11.1 The individual – the focus of language within a context of embedded hierarchies

11.4 Context(s) and language development

Briggs (1996: 4) suggests that recent social models (of talk) have gravitated towards dynamic, and practice-based approaches that link institutional, national and transitional cultural forms to the texture of everyday life. Language is similarly now viewed less as an abstract structure that is internalized identically by every speaker (as in the views held by Saussure (1916/1959) and Chomsky (1965) than as consisting of socially and politically situated practices that are differently distributed on the basis of gender, class, race, ethnicity and other phenomena. At this point it seems appropriate to link these central ideas with those of SFL description of language learning and language development. The key characteristic, central to contexts of influence and the definition of the ecology of human development is the influence of context(s). Context is also a central concern to the description of language development as supported by

SF linguists, beginning with Malinowski (1923/66) and continued by others including Firth (1957), Halliday (1978) and Harris (1952). They all share Malinowski's (1923/66: 310–11) view that 'a statement spoken in real life is never detached from the situation in which it was uttered . . . the utterance has no meaning except in the context of situation'. Context of situation includes these links and interrelations within and across the hierarchy of social organization described here. It is what Giddens terms 'structuration' and Figures 11.1 and 11.2 identify levels of contexts that influence speaker(s) and utterance(s) both directly and indirectly.

Each level within the hierarchy is described as a complex pattern of activities. Roles and interpersonal relations are experienced by an individual in a variety of settings, each of which can be characterized by specific physical and material features. This corresponds to what systemic linguists have termed the generic structure of social situations. A number of situations has been described in detail using systemic semiotic frameworks. These describe the structure of social interactions in very particular and highly specific contexts such as doctor–patient interviews, bilingual courtroom discourse (Berk-Seligson 1990), pupil–teacher interactions in classrooms (Sinclair and Coulthard 1975) and sales service encounters (Ventola 1987). These linguistic descriptions of generic structure have also been extended to written texts. These include an account of the structure of nursery rhymes (Hasan 1984) and stylistic analyses of fiction (Hoey and Winter 1982) and non-fiction texts (Hoey 1983). Semiotic descriptions have also included aspects of visual images (Kress and van Leeuwen 1996 and O'Toole 1999). All of these descriptions take account of the interdependence of four elements in their analyses: the participants, the discourse, the social setting and the wider cultural context. Indeed, the actual terms used by Bronfenbrenner to describe his ideas concur with those used by linguists working both before and after the publication of his ecological systems theory (EST).

There are other ways in which the ecological description of learning language(s) concurs with systemic descriptions of language use. The framework stresses the interrelationship between the major settings that an individual experiences in life. Individuals participate in an increasing number of settings, creating a ever widening range of social contexts and contacts. Although the major setting for the young child will probably be the domestic, home setting, from a very early age, children encounter new settings. These may include moving to other home settings, experiencing the home settings of other people and even moving beyond domestic to other settings including those of semi and informal education, like the kindergarten and nursery school. These settings are analogous with what linguists Fishman, Cooper and Ma (1971) refer to as 'domains'. Their working definition of a domain is an abstraction which refers to a sphere of activity that represents a combination of specific times, settings and role relationships. They identify five specifics domains of family, friendship, the workplace, religion and education. While Fishman, Cooper and Ma's term domain is essentially an abstract concept, domains are frequently associated with specialist institutions. This is particularly the case with the workplace, religion and education. Domains are nested within each level of the contextual influence. The implicit and explicit value system operating at the exosystem level are similar to the factors that influence language learning, use and choice. These factors have been described by linguists as influential. They include factors such as language planning and education policy, employment policy, access to education, the language of society, the legal system and formal education and can extend positive and detrimental influences on an individual's personal linguistic repertoire (and hence biography) cf. Tollefson (1996); Pennycook (1994) and Phillipson (1996).

Finally, Levels 4 and 5, the economic, social, educational, legal, and political contexts of influence, their inherent value systems and the ways in which these are conveyed to society at large also find parallels in linguistic descriptions. A series of monographs edited by Bernstein, entitled, *Primary socialization, language and education*, show how in a coherent social theory a central place is occupied by language and that language is the primary means of cultural transmission. This is a view supported by systemic linguists, for example, language as social behaviour, or socio-semiotic. Halliday (1978) describes language use within a cultural context, while Malinowski's (1923/66) description that combines context with situation in descriptions of language use, reinforces the notion of language as potential social behaviour. The potential aspect means that from within a given framework of communicative competence or appropriate linguistic and social behaviour, there are a number of options available to individual speakers. So for example, a mother, teacher or other adult attempting to regulate a child's behaviour, have a number of options available to them. They can choose from a range of socially acceptable strategies, including reasoning, pleading, threatening and they also have the option of non-verbal responses (cf. Cloran and Hasan 1996). Bernstein's (1971 and 1972/77) theory of language and social learning suggests that meaning is only realized when the individual (mother or other example, the teacher) selects from the semantic options available. Meaning is realized in social contexts when individuals select their behaviour. The chain of realizations extends from the highest level in the hierarchy of contextual influence, through and across all of the other levels to Level 2, the specific social setting and can influence the choices which individuals select in their (social and linguistic) behaviour. Societal conventions determine the meaning potential by determining the acceptable and appropriate range of behaviours available for selection but it is the individual who makes the choice and thereby realizes an act of meaning.

Societal and individual values operate to varying degrees. Hence an individual's behaviour is neither consistent nor totally predictable. They are however, influenced by macrosystems which transmit information and ideology, both explicitly and implicitly. They act as potential determinants of the ways in which children and caretakers are treated and how they interact with each other. Patterns of social interchange are embedded in each of these levels of the hierarchy. Appropriate behaviour is culturally determined and is context specific. Learning to be a pupil in different cultures may require different patterns of behaviour. Learning a new language means more than merely learning the rules of grammar, and so on. Learning a language means learning how to behave in a new cultural context and the setting and domains (or sub cultures) within the new community. This combines appropriate linguistic and social behaviour, what Hymes (1972) terms communicative competence. Learning language requires learning to be communicatively competent. It means learning all of the appropriate social and cultural behaviour, the appropriate speech community and society.

Having established conceptual similarities and common concerns between a description of the ecology of human development and social semiotic (systemic) linguistic descriptions of language use, these two will now be combined to present the notion of an individual's language development and use of language as a unique individualized linguistic biography.

11.5 Characteristics of a linguistic biography

The concept of language development as a linguistic biography is founded on the concept of language ecology which arrived to linguistics from the natural sciences and sociology. Haugen (1972: 325) defines the ecology of language as, 'the study of the interactions between any given language and its environment . . . the true environment of a language is the society that uses it as one of its codes. Language exists only in the minds of its users and it only functions in reality through these users to another'. More recently, Haarmann (1988: 4) proposed the following general framework:

INDIVIDUAL = GROUP = SOCIETY = STATE

There are of course a number of problems in associating individuals' language use with hierarchical societal structures that embrace the concepts of state and nationhood. There is always an historical context to be taken into account when trying to understand the choice of a national language. This is perhaps more obviously the case in some geographical areas than others. Consider the region known as the former British Raj, which since 1947 has become three independent nation states. These are from west to east Pakistan, India and Bangladesh, each with its own official state language, respectively, Urdu in Pakistan, Hindi in India and Bengali in Bangladesh. Or a quite different example, that of Singapore which in 1964 adopted English as the lingua franca as a means of nation building. By not favouring any of the indigenous languages it was hoped to unify Singaporeans in their diversity and to emphasize social cohesion and national identity. Malay remains the official, national language and is taught in schools. Chinese and Tamil, the two other local mother tongues are also taught in schools but English is the official language of education and all official interactions. Recent discussions about language policy in South Africa also serve to illustrate the ways in which such language policy changes impact directly on the repertoire of individual people.

Language is always created by, and is therefore linked with, an individual speaker (or groups of speakers). The individual speaker is the locus of language use and successful implementation of a national language policy rests upon the success individuals achieve in learning the languages prescribed. There is however a number of extraneous contextual factors which influence individual use of language.

The term 'ecolinguistic' has been chosen to describe our view of language development because it is sensitive to contextual factors. Further, inherent in the term is the notion of the interdependence of individual learners (and other speakers) to the social context(s) which they are creating through their choice and use of language. Ecolinguistics acknowledges the consequences of even small changes in language use for other aspects within the contextual setting. It particularly accommodates the affective aspects of individual language use and the ways in which these can be seen to be influential on the linguistic and even physical behaviour of other interlocutors present in the micro setting. In Singapore, although English is the official language, there is clear evidence of language change and language shift. Singapore variety of English is now established as one of the world varieties of English. Hence relatively small numbers of people can precipitate language change. In the case of Singapore, the population of 4 million has precipitated a change across the chain of the English language, a world language, by creating a new variety, Singapore English or Singlish as it is now known colloquially. Even the small changes and accommodations which take place between individuals in their interactions can have repercussions which resound across coexisting quarters.

11.6 Language development within an ecolinguistic framework

In Figure 11.1 the Level 5 represents the increase in supra-state structures that have assumed increasing global significance in recent years. They can be divided into two types. The first are those pan-national, supra-state bodies that frequently comprise membership and influence from a range of nations. These can include organizations with some jurisdiction like, the World Health Organization, the World Bank, fora for discussion and collective policy such as the Arab League, ASEAN, SEAMO, charitable organizations such as Oxfam, Unicef, as well as voluntary bodies such as Amnesty International or Greenpeace. This group of pan global influence includes political, as well as apolitical influences such as WTO, SEAMO, the UN and others. In the last decade or so a second group has emerged as influential at Level 5 context. This group represents the commercial interests of the global economy. These include global multinational companies such as Microsoft, Coca Cola, McDonalds as well as international corporate bodies that influence the global media and communications. This sub division of Level 5 contexts of influence may prove to be more influential and powerful than the other group at this level because they are more autonomous and represent the vested interest of commercial profit rather than collective interests. The ways in which multinational companies come into close contact with individuals' daily lives is being increasingly documented by linguists, sociologists, economists and others.

Level 3, the exosystem represents formal and informal social roles, like being a pupil, being a friend, and being a consumer. This level is deliberately structured and yet also dynamic. A person's orientation towards the relevant institutions or micro settings that from the exosystem correspond to what systemic linguists term, the 'field'. Halliday and Martin (1993) define field as 'what is actually taking place. It refers to what is happening, to the nature of the social action, what the participants are engaged in, including the notion of activity sequences oriented to some more global institutional purpose.

Level 2 or the mesosystem represents the settings or domains of interactions. These include the home, the classroom, the playground and other specific settings and social institutions that demand particular codes of language use, register or styles of speaking. Being able to behave appropriately in these contexts corresponds to being communicatively competent. Learning language(s) or varieties involves learning to be communicatively competent for an increasing range of settings, with a wider and wider circle of participants, for increasing range of social and linguistic functions.

Level 1 the 'microsystem' represents roles that speakers assume when interacting with other participants in their interactions. These can include brief interpersonal contacts, like service encounters, created to perform a very specific function, as well as more durable social contacts and ties. Even within the family a child may be required to assume a range of kinship roles. In some contexts, each role may require a different way of speaking. Addressing a male family member may demand a different pattern of speech and language form of address from addressing a female member of the family. Some language(s) and settings may require markers for age, relationships and/or gender. Naming systems vary too. The roles assumed within the microsystem settings and the relationships between people interacting there correspond to what systemic linguists term, the 'tenor'. Halliday and Martin (1993: 32–3) describe the tenor as the role structure, for example, who is taking part. It refers to the nature of the participants, their relative statuses within the interaction and the roles they play. These role-relationships include permanent and temporary relationships, the types of speech roles that the participants assume and the whole cluster of socially significant relationships in which they are involved. Halliday (1978a: 33) further suggests that this also included the 'degree of emotional charge' in the relationship between the participants.

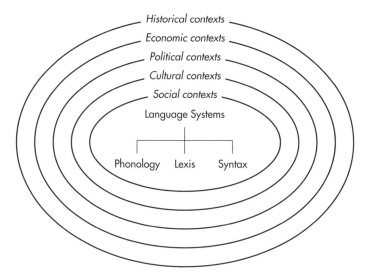

Figure 11.2 Nested hierarchies of the ecological contexts of language and other learning

A speaker's actual choice of language for interactions within these contexts of influences is what systemic linguists term the 'mode'. A number of systemic functional linguists (Hasan 19; Martin 1998) have written extensively about the relationship between language and context. They do not always agree over the detail. However, the central tenet of SFL is the way in which interpersonal meaning enacts social relations, ideational meaning and naturalized material reality, and the ways in which textual meanings organize interpersonal meanings into coherent and relevant text or semiotic reality. An SFL view of learning language(s) goes beyond communicative competence. Recent developments in SFL (Martin, 1998) propose modifications to the original Hallidayan model. Martin (and others) propose a holistic perspective on social purpose which involves a stratified model of context in which genre (social purpose) is realized through register, tenor, field and mode combined, In turn, social purpose is realized through language as interpersonal, ideational, and textual meaning. Learning language(s) requires learning this. Halliday and Martin (1993: 33) describe mode as the symbolic organization – the role language is playing, what the participants are expecting the language to do for them in the situation: the symbolic organization of the text, that status that it has, including the constitutive of what is going on and the potential for aural and visual feedback between interlocutors.

11.7 Summary

This chapter has outlined a concept of learning language(s) founded within an SFL description that concurs with other socially orientated descriptions of learning as dynamic, influenced by and instrumental in creating cultural, societal and interpersonal contexts. It is suggested that these contexts are interrelated and mutually influencing. The individual is the locus of the connections and is influenced, if not constrained by the contexts of influence. A nested framework of five hierarchical contexts of influence has been presented. It is suggested that learning language(s) is complex and is embedded within a nested hierarchy of contexts of influence that enable individuals to develop a uniquely personal linguistic biography, for themselves and that this is created in collaboration with others.

Activity

Within the concept of language learning as an ecological concept presented in this chapter can you identify specific contexts, interlocutors and other factors that have contributed to the creation of your own personal linguistic biography? Draw a diagram to identify these influences.

Looking ahead, as your life changes, can you envisage future domains of influence and new roles-relationships that you will learn linguistically? These may include being a parent or a grandparent, a spouse or partner, and so on.

11.8 Further reading

Briggs, C. (ed.) 1996: *Disorderly discourse: narrative, conflict and inequality.* Oxford: Oxford University Press.

References

Aldridge, M. 1991: How language grows up. *English Today* 25, 14–20.

Allwright, R.L. 1984: The importance of interaction in classroom language learning. *Applied Linguistics* 5, 2, 156–71.

Alsagoff, L. and Ho Chee Lick 1998: The grammar of Singapore English. In *English in new cultural contexts: reflections from Singapore*. Singapore: Oxford University Press and Singapore Institute of Management.

Anderson, J. 1992: *Coming home*. Singapore: Times Books International.

Ao Ran 2002: A genre-based analysis of TV news reports. Unpublished MA (applied linguistics) dissertation. RELC, National University of Singapore.

Aubrey, C., David, T., Godfrey, R. and Thompson, L. 2000: *Early childhood educational research: issues in methodology and ethics*. London and New York: Routledge Falmer.

Austin, J.L. 1962: *How to do things with words*. London: Oxford University Press.

Bailey, K. and Nunan, D. 1996: *Voices from the classroom: qualitative research in second language education*. Cambridge: Cambridge University Press.

Baker, C. 1993: *Foundations of bilingual education and bilingualism*. Clevedon: Multilingual Matters.

Bakhtin, M.M. 1981: *The dialogic imagination: four essays*. Austin: University of Texas Press.

Bamford, R. 1992: Process versus genre: anatomy of a false dichotomy. *Prospect* 8, 89–97.

Bao, Z. 1998: The sounds of Singapore English. In *English in new cultural contexts: reflections from Singapore*. Singapore: Oxford University Press and Singapore Institute of Management.

Bao, Z. and Wee, L. 1999: The passive in Singapore English. *World Englishes* 18, 1–11.

Barton, S. 1992: The contribution of a social view of literacy to promoting literacy among adults. Lancaster, Centre for Language in Social Life, Occasional Paper No.30, University of Lancaster Department of Linguistics.

Bates, E., Camaion, L. and Volterra, V. 1975: The acquisition of performatives prior to speech. *Merrell Palmer Quarterly* 21, 205–26.

Bateson, G. 1972: *Steps to an ecology of mind*. New York: Chandler.

Baynham, M. 1995: *Literacy practices: investigating literacy in social contexts*. London: Longman.

Bazerman, C. 1988: *Shaping written knowledge*. Madison, WI: University of Wisconsin Press.

Bazerman, C. 1994: Systems of genres and the enactment of social intentions. In Freedman, A. and Medway, P. (eds), *Genre and the new rhetoric*. London: Taylor and Francis.

Belcher, D. and Conner, U. (eds) 2001: *Reflections on multiliterate lives*. Clevedon: Multilingual Matters.

Bell, A. 1991: The language of news media. Oxford: Basil Blackwell.

Bell, N., Grossen, M., and Perret-Clermont, A-N. 1985: Sociocognitive conflict and intellectual growth. In M.W. Berkowitz (ed.), *Peer conflict and psychological growth*. (New Directions in Child Development No.29. San Francisco: Jossey-Bass.

Bereiter, C. and Scardamalia, M. 1987: *The psychology of written composition*. Hillsdale, NJ: Erlbaum Associates.

Bernstein, B. (ed.) 1971: *Class, codes and control 1*. London: Routledge.

Bernstein, B. (ed.) 1972/77: *Class, codes and control 3*. London: Routledge.

Bernstein, B. 1975: *Class, codes and control, Vol. 3*. London: Routledge and Kegan Paul.

Bernstein, B. 1987: Elaborated and restricted codes: an overview 1958–85. In Ammon, U., Dittmar, N. and Mattheire, K.J. (eds), *Sociolinguistics: an international handbook of the science of society, Vol. 1*. Berlin: De Gruyter.

Bernstein, B. 1990: *The structuring of pedagogic discourse: class, codes and control IV*. London: Routledge.

Bernstein, B. 1996: *Pedagogy symbolic control and identity*. London: Taylor and Francis.

Berry, M. 1975: *An introduction to systemic linguistics 1: structures and systems*. London: Batsford.

Bhatia, V.K. 1993: *Analysing genre: language to use in professional settings*. London: Longman.

Bialystok, E. 1978: A theoretical model of second language learning. *Language Learning* 29, 69–84.

Bloom, L. 1970: Language development: form and function in emerging grammars. In *MIT Research Monographs No.59*. Cambridge, MA: MIT Press.

Bloom L. 1991: *Language development from two to three*. New York: Cambridge University Press.

Bloom, L. 1993: *The transition from infancy to language: acquiring the power of expression*. Cambridge: Cambridge University Press.

Bodrova, E. and Leong, D.J. 1996: *Tools of the mind: the Vygotskian approach in early childhood education*. Englewood Cliffs, NJ: Prentice Hall.

Bourne, J. 1992: Inside a primary classroom: a teacher, children and theories at work. Unpublished PhD thesis, University of Southampton.

Braine, M. 1963: The ontogeny of English phrase structure: the first phase. *Language* 39, 1–13.

Britton, J. 1982: *Prospect and retrospect: selected essays of James Britton (ed. G. Pradl)*. London: Heinemann.

Britton, J. Burgess, T., Martin, M., McLeod, A. and Rosen, H. 1975: *The development of writing abilities (11–16)*. London: Macmillan Educational.

Bronfenbrenner, U. 1977: Towards an experimental ecology of human development. *American Psychologist* 32, 513–31.

Bronfenbrenner, U. 1979: *The ecology of human development*. Cambridge, MA: Harvard University Press.

Brown, R. 1973: *A first language*. London: George Allen and Unwin.

Brumfit, C. 1984: *Communicative methodology in language teaching*. Cambridge: Cambridge University Press.

Brumfit, C. and Mitchell, R. (eds) 1990: *Research in the language classroom*. ELT Documents 133: Modern English Publications.

Bruner, J. 1978: Learning how to do things with words. In Bruner, J., and Garton, A. (eds), *Human growth and development*. Oxford: Oxford University Press.

Bruner, J. 1981: The pragmatics of acquisition. In Deutsch, W. (ed.), *The child's construction of language*. London: Academic Press.

Bruner, J. 1986: *Actual minds, possible worlds*. Cambridge, MA: Harvard University Press.

Bruner, J. 1990: The narrative construction of 'reality'. Closing address to the Fourth European Conference on Developmental Psychology, Stirling, Scotland.

Cameron, D. 1995: *Verbal hygiene*. London: Routledge.

Cameron, D. 1998: *The feminist critique of language*, second edn. London: Routledge.

Cameron, D. 2000: *Good to talk? Living and working in a communication culture*.

Cameron, D. 2001: *Working with spoken discourse*. London: Sage.

Carter, R. 1996: Politics and knowledge about language: the LINC project. In Hasan, R. and Williams, G. (eds), *Literacy in society*. London: Longman.

Carter, R. and Nash, W. 1990: *Seeing through language*. Oxford: Blackwell.

Chomsky, N. 1957: *Syntactic structures*. The Hague: Mouton.

Chomsky, N. 1968: *Language and mind*. New York: Harcourt.

Christian-Smith, L.K. 1989: Power, knowledge and curriculum: constructing femininity in adolescent romance novels. In de Castell, S., Luke, A. and Luke, C. (eds), *Language authority and criticism*. London: Falmer Press.

Christian-Smith, L.K. 1990: *Becoming a woman through romance*. London: Routledge.

Christie, F. 1984: *Language studies, children writing*. Study Guide (ECT 418). Geelong, Victoria: Deakin University Press.

Christie, F. 1989: Language development in education. In Hasan, R. and Martin, J.R. (eds), *Language development, learning language, learning culture*. Norwood, NJ: Ablex.

Christie, F. 1995: Pedagogic discourse in the primary school. *Linguistics and Education* 3, 7, 221–42.

Christie, F. (ed.) 1999: *Pedagogy and the shaping of consciousness*. London: Cassell.

Christie, F. and Martin, J.R. (eds) 1997: *Genre and institutions: social processes in the workplace and school*. London: Cassell.

Christie, F. and Mission, R. (eds) 1998: *Literacy and schooling*. London: Routledge.

Clark, E.V. 1991: Acquisitional principles in lexical development. In Gelman, S.A. and Byrnes, J.P. (eds), *Perspectives on language and thought: interrelations in development*. Cambridge: Cambridge University Press.

Clark, E.V. 1993: *The lexicon in acquisition*. Cambridge: Cambridge University Press.

Clark, M.M. 1976: *Young fluent readers*. London: Heinemann.

Clark, R. 1992: Principles and practice of CLA in the classroom. In Fairclough, N. (ed.) *Critical language awareness*. London: Longman.

Clark, R., Fairclough, N., Ivanic, R., McLeod, J. Thomas, J. and Hearn, P. 1990: *Language and power: British studies in applied linguistics 5*. London: BAAL.

Clay, M.M. 1991: *Becoming literate: the construction of inner control*. Portsmouth, NH: Heinemann.

Cloran, C. 1999: Instruction at home and school. In Christie, F. (ed.), *Pedagogy and the shaping of consciousness*. London: Cassell.

Cloran, C., Butt, D., and Williams, G. (eds) 1996: *Ways of saying: ways of meaning*. London: Cassell.

Coates, J. 1994: No gap, lots of overlap: turn-taking patterns in the talk of women friends. In Graddol, D., Maybin, J. and Stiere, B. (eds), *Researching language and literacy in social context*. Clevedon: Multilingual Matters and the Open University.

Coe, R.M. 1994: An arousing and fulfilment of desires: the rhetoric of genres in the process era and beyond. In Freedman, A. and Medway, P. (eds), *Genre and the new rhetoric*. London: Taylor and Francis.

Coffin, C. 1996: *Exploring literacy in school history*. Sydney: Metropolitan East Disadvantaged Program, New South Wales, Department of School Education.

Cole, M. and Means, B. 1981: *Comparative studies of how people think: an introduction*. Cambridge, MA: Harvard University Press.

Cole, M. and Scribner, S. 1973: Cognitive consequences of formal and informal education. *Science* 182, 553–9.

Collerson, J. 1994: *English grammar: a functional approach*. Newton, New South Wales: Primary English Teaching Association.

Cordeiro, C.M. 2000: Creating masculinity: a linguistic and visual semiotic perspective on the construction of masculinity in the FHM (For Him Magazine) Singapore. Unpublished MA dissertation, Department of English Language and Literature, National University, Singapore.

Cranny-Francis, A. and Palmer Gillard, P. 1990: Constituting and reconstituting desire: fiction, fantasy and femininity. In Christian-Smith, L.K. (ed.), *Texts of desire: essays on fiction, femininity and schooling*. London: Falmer Press.

Cruttenden, A. 1994: *Language in infancy and childhood*. Manchester: Manchester University Press.

Crystal, D. 1997: *The Cambridge encyclopedia of language*, third edn. Cambridge: Cambridge University Press.

D'Ailly, H.H. 1992: Asian mathematics superiority: a search for explanations. *Educational Psychologist* 27, 2, 243–61.

Davies, N. 1996: *Europe: a history*. Oxford: Oxford University Press.

Defleur, M.L. and Dennis, E.E. 1994: *Understanding mass communication*. Boston: Houghton Mifflin Company.

Department of English Language and Literature (DELL) Language Development Data 1985–98. National University of Singapore.

Derewianka, B. 1990: *Exploring how texts work*. Newton, New South Wales: Primary English Teaching Association.

Derewianka, B. 1995: Language development in the transition from childhood to adolescence: the role of grammatical metaphor. Unpublished PhD thesis, Department of English and Linguistics, Macquarie University.

Deuchar, M. and Quay, S. 2001: *Bilingual acquisition: theoretical implications of a case study*. Oxford: Oxford University Press.

Donaldson, M. 1978: *Children's minds*. London: Fontana.

Doughty, P., Pearce, J. and Thornton, G. 1971: *Language in use*. Schools Council Publication. London: Arnold.

Edwards, C., Gandini, L. and Forman, G. 1994: *Hundred languages of children: the Reggio Emilia approach to early childhood education*. Chicago: Teachers College Press.

Edwards, V. 1986: *Language in a black community*. Clevedon: Multilingual Matters.

Ellis, R. 1997: *SLA research and language teaching*. Oxford: Oxford University Press.

Fairclough, N. 1989: *Language and power*. London: Longman.

Fairclough, N. (ed.) 1992: *Critical language awareness*. London: Longman.

Ferguson, C.A. 1977: Baby talk as simplified register. In Snow, C.E., and Ferguson, C.A. (eds), *Talking to children: language input and acquisition*. Cambridge: Cambridge University Press.

Field, T.M. and Fox, N. (eds) 1985: *Social perception in infants*. Norwood, NJ: Ablex.

Fillmore, C. 1978: On fluency. In Fillmore, C., Kempler, D. and Wang, W. (eds), *Individual differences in language learning behaviour*. New York: Academic Press, 85–101.

Firth, J.R. 1957: *Papers in linguistics 1934–1951*. London: Oxford University Press.

Firth, J.R. 1968: Ethnographic analysis and language with reference to Malinowski's views. In F.R. Palmer (ed.), *Selected papers of J.R. Firth 1952–59*. London and Harlow: Longman Green and Co.

Fishman, J., Cooper, R.L. and Ma, R. 1971: *Bilingualism in the Barrio*. Bloomington: Indiana University Press.

Fiske, J. 1987: *Television culture*. London: Routledge.

Flavell, J. 1985: *The development of the psychology of Jean Piaget*. New York: Van Norstand.

Fletcher, P. 1998: *Child language acquisition*. London: Arnold.

Foley, J. 1994: Moving from 'common-sense knowledge' to 'educational knowledge'. In Gopinathan, S., Pakir, A., Ho Wah Kam and Saravanan, V. (eds), *Language society and education in Singapore*. Singapore: Times Academic Press.

Foley, J. 1998a: Code-switching and learning among young children in Singapore. *International Journal of the Sociology of Language* 130, 129–50.

Foley, J. 1998b: Other cultural values and the teenage market in the Asian context. Paper presented at the International Conference on International Perspectives on English Studies in Asia 8–10 January, Srinskharinwirot University, Bangkok, Thailand.

Foley, J., Kandiah, T., Bao, Z. Gupta, A.F., Alsagoff, L., Ho Chee Lick, Wee, L., Talib, L.S. and Bokhorst-Heng, W. 1998: *English in new cultural contexts: reflections from Singapore.* Singapore: Oxford University Press.

Foster, S.H. 1999: *The communicative competence of young children.* London: Longman.

Freedman, A. and Medway, P. (eds) 1994a: *Learning and teaching genre.* New Hampshire: Boyton/Cook Publishers Inc.

Freedman, A. and Medway, P. (eds) 1994b: *Genre and the new rhetoric.* London: Taylor and Francis.

Freire, P. 1972: *Pedagogy of the oppressed.* London: Penguin.

French, J. and French, P. 1984: Gender imbalances in the primary classroom: an interactional account. *Educational Research* 26, 2, 127–36.

Gallaway, C. and Richards, B.J. (eds) 1994: *Input and interaction in language acquisition.* Cambridge: Cambridge University Press.

Garton, A. and Pratt, C. 1989: *Learning to be literate: the development of spoken and written language.* Oxford: Blackwell.

Gee, J. 1990: *Social linguistics and literacies: ideologies in discourses.* London: Falmer Press.

Giddens, A. 1984: *The constitution of society: outline of the theory of structuralism.* Cambridge: Polity Press.

Ginsberg, H.P. and Opper, S. 1988: *Piaget's theory of intellectual development*, third edn. Englewood Cliffs, NJ: Prentice Hall.

Good, T. 1970: Which pupils do teachers call on? *Elementary School Journal*, 190–8.

Goodwin, A 1990: TV news: striking the right balance. In Goodwin, A. and Whannel, G. (eds), *Understanding television.* London: Routledge.

Goom, B. in press: A multimodal analysis of a children's history text. In J.A. Foley (ed.), *Functional perspectives on education and discourse.* London: Continuum.

Gopnik, A. and Meltzoff, A.N. 1986: Words, plans, things and locations: interactions between semantic and cognitive development in the one-word stage. In Kuczaj, S. and Barrett, M. (eds), *The development of word meaning: progress in cognitive development research.* New York: Springer.

Graddol, D. 1994: The visual accomplishment of factuality. In Graddol, D. and Boyd-Barrett, O. (eds), *Media texts: authors and readers.* Clevedon: Multilingual Matters and the Open University.

Graddol, D. 1997: *The future of English.* London: British Council.

Graves, D.H. 1983: *Writing: teachers and children at work.* Portsmouth, NH: Heinemann Educational.

Gumperz, J.J. and Hymes, D. (eds) 1972: *Directions in sociolinguistics: the ethnography of communication.* New York: Holt Rinehart and Winston.

Haarman, H. 1988: *Language in ethnicity.* Amsterdam: Mouton de Gruyter.

Halliday, M. 1973a: Foreword. In Mackay, D., Thompson, B. and Schaub, B. *Breakthrough to literacy: teachers' resource book.* London: Longman/Glendale, CA: Bowmar.

Halliday, M. 1973b: *Explorations and functions of language,* London: Edward Arnold.

Halliday, M. 1975: *Learning how to mean: explorations in the development of language.* London: Edward Arnold.

Halliday, M. 1978a: *Language as a social semiotic: the social interpretation of language and meaning.* London: Arnold.

Halliday, M. 1978b: Meaning and construction of reality in early childhood. In Pick, H.L. and Saltzman (eds), *Modes of perceiving and processing of information.* Hillsdale, NJ: Erlbaum.

Halliday, M. 1979: One child's protolanguage. In Bullowa, M. (ed.), *Before speech: the beginning of interpersonal communication.* Cambridge: Cambridge University Press.

Halliday, M. 1985: *Introduction to functional grammar.* London: Arnold.

Halliday, M. 1988a: Language and socialisation: home and school. In Gerot, L., Oldenburg, J. and Van Leeuwen, T. (eds), *Language and socialisation: home and school.* Proceedings from the Working Conference on Language in Education, Macquarie University November 1986, 1–12.

Halliday, M. 1988b: Language and enhancement of learning. Paper presented at the Language in Learning Symposium held at Brisbane College of Advanced Education, Brisbane.

Halliday, M. 1991: The notion of 'context' in language education. In Thao Le and McCausland, M. (eds), Language Education: Interaction and Development. Proceedings of the International Conference, Ho Chi Minh City, Vietnam 30 March to 1 April 1991, Launceston, University of Tasmania.

Halliday, M. 1992: How do you mean? In Davies, M. and Ravelli, L. (eds), *Recent advances in systematic linguistics: theory and practice.* London: Pinter.

Halliday, M. 1993: Towards a language-based theory of learning. *Linguistics and Education* 5: 93–116.

Halliday, M. 1996: Literacy and linguistics: a functional perspective. In Hasan, R. and Williams, G. (eds), *Literacy in society.* London: Longman.

Halliday, M. 1998a: Things and relations: regrammaticising experience as technical knowledge. In Martin, J.R. and Veel, R. (eds), *Reading science: critical and functional perspectives on discourse of science.* London: Routledge.

Halliday, M. 1998b: Language and knowledge: the 'unpacking of text'. In Allison, D., Wee, L., Bao, Z. and Abraham, S.A. (eds), *Text in education and society.* Singapore: Singapore University Press and World Scientific.

Halliday, M. 2001: Literacy and linguistics: relationships between spoken and written language. In Burns, A. and Coffin, C. (eds), *Analysing English in a global context.* London: Routledge.

Halliday, M. and Hasan, R. 1976: *Cohesion in English*. London: Longman.

Halliday, M. and Hasan, R. 1985: *Language, context and text: a social semiotic perspective*. Geelong, Victoria: Deakin University Press (republished by Oxford University Press, 1989).

Halliday, M. and Martin, J. 1993: *Writing science: literacy and discursive power*. London: Falmer Press.

Hamers, J.F. and Blanc, M.H.A. 2000: *Bilinguality and bilingualism*, second edn. Cambridge: Cambridge University Press.

Harris, Z. 1952: Discourse analysis. *Language* 28, 1, 1–30.

Hasan, R. 1983: *A semantic network or the analysis of messages in everyday talk between mothers and their children*. Mimeo, Macquarie University.

Hasan, R. 1984: The nursery tale as a genre. *Nottingham Linguistic Circular* 13, 71–102.

Hasan, R. 1986: The ontogenesis of ideology: an interpretation of mother child talk. In Threadgold, T., Grosz, E.A., Kress, G. and Halliday, M. (eds), *Language, semiotics, ideology*. Sydney: Sydney Association for Studies in Society and Culture, No.3.

Hasan, R. and Cloran, C. 1990: A sociolinguistic interpretation of everyday talk between mothers and children. In Halliday, M., Gibbons, J. and Nicholas, H. (eds), *Learning, keeping and using language*, Vol. I. Selected Papers from the 8th World Congress of Applied Linguistics, Amsterdam: Benjamins.

Hasan, R. and Perrett, G. 1994: Learning to function with the other tongue: a systemic functional perspective on second language teaching. In Odin, T. (ed.), *Perspectives on pedagogical grammars*. New York: Cambridge University Press.

Haugen, E. 1972: *The ecology of language (essays)*. Stanford, CA: Stanford University Press.

Heath, S.B. 1983: *Ways with words*. Cambridge: Cambridge University Press.

Hobson, D. 1982: *Crossroads: the drama of a soap opera*. London: Methuen.

Hodge, R. and Kress, G. 1988: *Social semiotics*. Cambridge: Polity.

Hoey, M.P. 1983: *On the surface of discourse*. London: Allen and Unwin.

Hoey, M.P. and Winter, E.O. 1982: Believe me for mine honour: a stylistic analysis of the speeches of Brutus and Mark Anthony at Caesar's funeral in Julius Caesar, Act III, Scene 2, from the point of view of discourse construction. *Language and Style* 14, 4.

Hoffman, C. *An introduction to bilingualism*. London: Longman.

Holdaway, D. 1979: *Foundations of literacy*. Gosford, New South Wales: Ashton Scholastic.

Hollindale, P. 1992: Ideology and the children's book. In Hunt, P. (ed.), *Literature for children: contemporary criticism*. London: Routledge.

Holmes, J. 1992: *An introduction to sociolinguistics*. London: Longman.

Honey, J. 1997: *Language and power: the story of standard English and its enemies*. London: Pentagram.

Hopkins, A. and Dudley-Evans, T. 1988: A genre-based investigation of the discussion sections in articles and dissertations. *English for Specific Purposes* 7, 693–722.

Hymes, D. 1967: Models of interaction of language and social setting. *Journal of Social Issues* 33, 2, 8–28.

Hymes, D. 1968: The ethnography of speaking. In Fishman, J.A. (ed.), *Readings in the Sociology of Language*. The Hague: Mouton.

Hymes, D. 1972a: Competence and performance in linguistic theory. In Huxley, R. and Ingrams, E. (eds), *Language acquisition: models and methods*. New York: Academic Press.

Hymes, D. 1972b: On communicative competence. In Pride, J.B. and Holmes, J. (eds), *Sociolinguistics*. Harmondsworth: Penguin.

Hymes, D. 1980: Speech and language: on the origins of inequality among speakers. In Hymes, D. (ed.) *Language in education: ethnolinguistic essays*. Washington, DC: Center for Applied Linguistics.

Ianco-Worrel, A.D. 1972: Bilingualism and cognitive development. *Child Development* 43.

Ingram, D. 1989: *First language acquisition: method, description and explanation*. Cambridge: Cambridge University Press.

Ingram, D. 1990: *The teaching of languages and cultures in Queensland: towards a language in education policy for Queensland schools*. Queensland Education Department, Centre for Applied Linguistics and Language, Griffiths University, Australia.

Ingulsrud, J. and Allen, K. 1999: *Learning to read in China: sociolinguistic perspectives of the acquisition of literacy*. Lampeter, Wales: the Edwin Mellon Press.

Inhelder, B. and Piaget, J. 1958: *The growth of logical thinking from childhood to adolescence*. New York: Basic Books.

James, C.L.R. 1938: *The black Jacobins: Toussaint l'Overture and the San Domingo revolution*, second edn. New York: Vintage 1963.

Kachru, B.B. 1985: Standards, codification and sociolinguistic realism: the English language in the outer circle. In Quirk, R. and Widdowson, H.G. (eds), *English in the world: teaching and learning in language and literatures*. Cambridge: Cambridge University Press for British Council.

Kerswill, P. 1996: Children, adolescents and language change. *Language variation and change* 8, 2, 177–202.

Khoo, T. 1987: Children play: an exploratory study. Academic Exercise, Department of English Language and Literature, National University of Singapore.

Klein, M 1963: *Our adult world and its roots in infancy, and other essays*. London: Macmillan Medical.

Ko Peng Sim and Ho Wah Kam (eds) 1992: *Growing up in Singapore: the pre-school years*. Singapore: Longman.

Kress, G. 1988: Textual matters: the social effectiveness of style. In Birch, D. and O'Toole, M. (eds), *Functions of style*. London: Francis Pinter.

Kress, G. 1989: *Linguistic processes in sociocultural practice*. Oxford: Oxford University Press.

Kress, G. 1999: Issues for a working agenda in literacy. In O'Brien, T. (ed.), *Language and literacies*. Clevedon: Multilingual Matters for the British Association of Applied Linguistics.

Kress, G. and Threadgold, T. 1988: Towards a social theory of genre. *Southern Review* 21, 215–43.

Kress, G. and Van Leeuwen, T. 1990: *Reading images*. Geelong, Victoria: Deakin University Press (re-published, 1996: Oxford University Press).

Kress, G., Gunther, R. and Leeuwen, T. 1996: *Reading images: the grammar of visual design*. London: Routledge.

Labov, W. and Waletzky, H. 1967: Narrative analysis: oral versions of personal experience. In Helm, J. (ed.), *Essays on the verbal and visual arts*. Seattle: University of Washington Press.

Language Awareness 1992: Editorial: 'What is dat?' 1, 1.

Lazar, M.M. 1999: Family life advertisements and the narrative of heterosexual sociality. In Chew, P.G.L. and Kramer-Dahl, A. (eds), *Reading culture: textual practices in Singapore*. Singapore: Times Academic Press.

Lee, F. 1992: Do our children's behaviours reflect their parents and homes? In Ko Peng Sim and Ho Wha Kam (eds), *Growing up in Singapore: the preschool years*. Singapore: Longman.

Legarett, D. 1977: Language choice in bilingual classrooms. *TESOL Quarterly* 11, 9–16.

Lemke, J.L. 1990: *Talking science: language, learning, and values*. Norwood, NJ: Ablex.

Lemke, J.L. 1993: Discourse, dynamics and social change. *Cultural Dynamics* 6, 1–2, 243–75.

Lemke, J.L. 1995: *Textual politics*. London: Taylor and Francis.

Leopold, W.F. 1949: *Speech development of a bilingual child. a linguistic record*. Evanston, IL: Northwestern University Press.

Lewin, K. 1935: *A dynamic theory of personality*. New York: McGraw-Hill.

Lock, A. 1984: The emergence of language: on being picked up. In Lock, A. and Fisher, E. (eds), *Language development*. London: Croom Helm in association with the Open University.

Long, M. and Porter, P. 1985: Group work, interlanguage talk, and second language acquisition. *TESOL Quarterly* 19, 201–28.

Luke, A. 1992: The body literate: discourse and inscription in early childhood. *Linguistics and Education* 4, 1, 107–29.

Luria, A.R. 1976: *Cognitive development: its cultural and social foundations*. Cambridge, MA: Harvard University Press.

Luria, A.R. 1978: The making of mind: a personal account of Soviet psychology. In Cole, M. and Cole, S. (eds), Cambridge, MA: Harvard University Press.

Luria, A.R. 1979: *The making of mind: a personal account of Soviet psychology*. New York, Cambridge, MA: Harvard University Press.

Mackay, D., Thompson, B. and Schaub, P. 1970: *Breakthrough to literacy*, London: Longman.

Mackay, D., Schaub, B. and Thompson, B. 1988: The breakthrough connection. In Hasan, R. and Martin, J. (eds), *Language development: learning language, learning culture*. Norwood, NJ: Ablex.

Macken-Horarik, M. 1998: Exploring the requirements of critical school literacy: a view from two classrooms. In Christie, F. and Mission, R. (eds), *Literacy and schooling*. London: Routledge.

Mahler, M. 1963: Thoughts about development and individuation. *Psychoanalytic development of the child* 18, 307–23.

Maley, A. 1996: Teaching the unteachable: writing. In Abraham, S. and Hsui, V. (eds), *The English language in Singapore: current perspectives on the teaching of writing*. Singapore: Association for Applied Linguistics, Singapore Humanities Press.

Malinowski, B. 1923/66: The problems of meaning in primitive languages, supplement 1. In Ogden, C. and Richards, I. (eds), *The meaning of meaning*. London: Routledge and Kegan Paul, 296–336.

Markman, E. 1989: *Categorisation and naming in children: problems of induction*. Cambridge, MA: MIT Press.

Martin, J. 1984: *Language register and genre. Children writing: a reader*. Geelong, Australia: Deakin University Press.

Martin, J. 1992: *English text: system and structure*. Amsterdam: Benjamins.

Martin, J. 1993: Life as a noun: arresting the universe in science and humanities. In Halliday, M. and Martin, J. *Writing science*. London: Falmer Press.

Martin, J. 1997a: Analysing genre: functional principles and parameters. In Christie, F. and Martin, J. (eds), *Genres and institutions: social processes in the workplace and school*. London: Cassell.

Martin, J. 1997b: Beyond exchange: appraisal systems in English. In Hunston, S. and Thompson, J. (eds), *Evaluation in text*. Oxford: Oxford University Press.

Martin, J. and Rothery, J. 1980, 1981: Writing project rep. nos.1, 2 Working Papers in Linguistics, Linguistics Department, University of Sydney.

Martin, J. and Rothery, J. 1988: Classification and framing: double dealing in pedagogical discourse. Paper presented at Post World Reading Congress Symposium on Language and Learning. Mt Gravatt College, Brisbane.

Martin, J. and Veel, R. 1998: *Reading science: critical and functional perspectives on discourse of science*. London: Routledge.

McTear, M. 1985: *Children's conversation*. Oxford: Blackwell.

Mehan, H. 1979: *Learning lessons: social organisation in the classroom*. Cambridge, MA: Harvard University Press.

Meinhof, U. 1994: Double talk in news broadcasts. In Graddol, D. and Boyd-Barrett, O. (eds), *Media texts: authors and readers*. Clevedon: Multilingual Matters and Open University.

Mercer, N. 1985: *Communication in the classroom. Every child's language*. In-service pack for primary teachers (Course: P534) Book 1. Open University and Multilingual Matters.

Mercer, N. 1995: *The guided construction of knowledge*. Clevedon: Multilingual Matters.

Mercer, N. 1996: English as a classroom language. In Mercer, N. and Swann, J. (eds), *Learning English: development and diversity*. London: Routledge and Open University.

Mercer, N. 2000: *Words and minds*. London: Routledge.

Messer, D.J. 1994: *The development of communication: from social interaction to language*. Chichester: Wiley.

Miller, C. 1984: Genre as social action. *Quarterly Journal of Speech* 70, 151–67.

Miller, C. 1994: Rhetorical community: the cultural bias of genre. In Freedman, A. and Medway, P. (eds), *Genre and the new rhetoric*. London: Taylor and Francis.

Miller, W. and Ervin, S. 1964: The development of grammar in child language. In Bellugi, U. and Brown, R. (eds), *The acquisition of language*. Monographs of the Society for Research in Child Development.

Mills, S. 1995: *Feminist stylistics*. London: Routledge.

Moores, S. 1994: Texts, readers and contexts of reading: developments in the study of media audiences. In Graddol, D. and Boyd-Barrett, O. (eds), *Media texts: authors and readers*. Clevedon: Multilingual Matters and the Open University.

Morely, D. 1986: *Family television: cultural power and domestic leisure*. London: Comedia.

Nelson, K. 1991: The matter of time: interdependence between language and thought in development. In Gelman, A. and Byrnes, J. (eds), *Perspectives on language and thought: interrelations in development*. Cambridge: Cambridge University Press.

Nichol, J.L. (ed.) 2001: *One mind, two languages: bilingual processing*. Malden, MA: Blackwell.

Ninio, A. and Snow, C.E. 1996: *Pragmatic development*. Boulder, CO: Westview.

Norwita Bte, M. Ariff 1987: The communicative competence of a bilingual child. Academic Exercise, Department of English Language and Literature, National University of Singapore.

Nunan, D. 1989: *Designing tasks for the communicative classroom*. Cambridge: Cambridge University Press.

Ochs, E. and Schieffelin, B. 1983: *Acquiring conversational competence*. London: Routledge.

Oldenburg, J. 1987: From child tongue to mother tongue: a case study of language development in the first two and a half years. Unpublished PhD thesis, University of Sydney.

Oldenburg, J. 1990: Learning the language and learning through language in early childhood. In Halliday, M., Gibbons, J. and Nicholas, H. (eds), *Learning, keeping and using language*. Selected papers from the Eighth World Congress of Applied Linguistics. Amsterdam: Benjamins.

Oller, D. 1986: Metaphonology and infant vocalization. In Lindblom, B. and Zetterstrom, R. (eds), *Percursors of early speech*. Wenner-Gren International Symposium Series, Vol. 44. Basingstoke: Macmillan.

O'Toole, M. 1994: *Language of displayed art*. London: Leicester University Press.

Painter, C. 1984: *Into the mother tongue*. London: Pinter.

Painter, C. 1989: Learning language: a functional view of language development. In Hasan, R. and Martin, J.R. (eds), *Language development: learning language, learning culture*. Norwood, NJ: Ablex.

Painter, C. 1992: The development of language as a resource for thinking: a linguistic view of learning. Paper presented at the 19th International Systemic Functional Congress, Macquarie University, Sydney, Australia.

Painter, C. 1996: The development of language as a resource for thinking: a linguistic view of learning. In Hasan, R. and Williams, G. (eds), *Literacy in society*. London: Longman.

Painter, C. 1999: *Learning through language in early childhood*. London: Cassell.

Paré, A. and Smart, G. 1994: Observing genres in action: towards a research methodology. In Freedman, A. and Medway, P. (eds), *Genre and the new rhetoric*. London: Taylor and Francis.

Pennycook, A. 1994: *English and the discourses of colonialism*. London: Routledge.

Phillipson, R. 1996: *Linguistic imperialism*. Oxford: Oxford University Press.

Phoon Lee Hiang 1998: Portrayal of women in local romance fiction. Unpublished MA dissertation, Department of English Language and Literature, National University of Singapore.

Piaget, J. 1962: *Play, dreams and imitation in childhood*. New York: Norton.

Pica, T. and Doughty, C. 1988: Variations in classroom interaction as a function of participation pattern and task. In Fine, J. (ed.), *Second language discourse: a textbook of current research*. Norwood, NJ: Ablex.

Pinker, S. 1994: *The language instinct*. New York: William Morrow and Co. Inc.

Plann, S. 1977: Acquiring a second language in an immersion situation. In Brown, H., Yorio, C. and Crymes, R. (eds), *On TESOL '77*. Washington, DC: TESOL.

Plum, G.A. and Cowling, A. 1987: Social constraints on grammatical variables: tense choice in English. In Steele, R. and Threadgold, T. (eds), *Language topics: essays in honour of Michael Halliday*, Vol. 2. Amsterdam: Benjamins.

Qiu, S. 1985: Early language development in Chinese children. Unpublished dissertation, Department of Linguistics, University of Sydney.

Ramirez, J. Yuen, S., Ramey, D. and Merino, B. 1986: First year report: longitudinal study of immersion programs for language minority children. Arlington, VA: SRA Technologies.

Rampton, B. 1995: *Crossing: language and ethnicity among adolescents*. Harlow: Longman.

Reid, J.F. 1974: *Breakthrough in Action: an independent evaluation of breakthrough to literacy*. London: Longman for the Schools Council.

Richards, J., Platt, J. and Weber, H. 1992: *Longmans dictionary of applied linguistics*. London: Longman.

Roberts, G.R. 1989: *Teaching children to read and write*. Oxford: Blackwell.

Rogoff, B. 1990: *Apprenticship in thinking*. New York: Oxford University Press.

Rogoff, B., Malkin, C. and Gilbride, K. 1984: Interaction with babies as guidance in development. *New directions for child's development*. 23, 31–44.

Romaine, S. 1984: *The language of children and adolescents*. Oxford: Basil Blackwell.

Romaine, S. 1989: *Bilingualism*. Oxford: Basil Blackwell.

Rothery, J. 1994: *Exploring literacy in school English*. Sydney: Metropolitan East Disadvantaged Schools Programme.

Saffiah Bte, M. 1984: The teaching of writing in primary six and the first year of secondary school. Academic Exercise Department of English Language and Literature, National University of Singapore.

Samboo, S.A. 1998: Child language acquisition: a case study of native English speakers in Singapore. Unpublished MA dissertation, Department of English Language and Literature, National University of Singapore.

Sampson, G. 1997: *Educating Eve*. London: Cassell.

Samraj, B. 1988: Picture talk as a curriculum genre. Unpublished MA dissertation, Department of English Language and Literature, National University of Singapore.

Saussure, F. 1974: *Course in general linguistics*. Suffolk: Fontana.

Saville-Troike, M. 1982: *The ethnography of communication*. Oxford: Basil Blackwell.

Saxena, M. 1994: Literacies among the Panjabis in Southall (Britain). In Maybin, J. (ed.), *Language and literacy in social practice*. Clevedon: Multilingual Matters and the Open University.

Schank, R. and Abelson, R. 1977: Scripts, plans, goals and understanding. Hillsdale, NJ: Lawrence Erlbaum.

Schegloff, E and Sacks, H. 1973: Opening up closings. *Semiotica* 7, 4, 289–327.

Schickendanz, J. 1982: The acquisition of written language in young children. In Spodek, B. (ed.), *Handbook of research in early childhood education*. New York: Free Press.

Schlesinger, I. 1977: The role of cognitive development and linguistic input in language acquisition. *Journal of Child Language* 4, 153–69.

Schryer. C. 1994: The labs vs. the clinics: sites of competing genres. In Freedman, A. and Medway, P. (eds), *Genre and the new rhetoric*. London: Taylor and Francis.

Scollon, R. 1979: A real early stage: an unzipped condensation of a dissertation on child language. In Ochs, E. and Schieffelin, B. (eds), *Developmental Pragmatics*. New York: Academic Press.

Scollon, R. 1998: *Mediated discourse as social interaction: a study of news discourse*. London: Longman.

Scribner, S and Cole, M. 1981: *The psychology of literacy*. Cambridge, MA: Harvard University Press.

Searle, J. 1969: *Speech acts*. Cambridge: Cambridge University Press.

Sinclair, J. and Coulthard, M. 1975: *Towards an analysis of discourse*. Oxford: Oxford University Press.

Slobin, J. 1978: A case study of early language awareness. In Sinclair, A, Jarvella, R. and Levelt, W. (eds), *A child's conception of language*. New York: Springer.

Sloutsky, V. 1991: Comparison of factor structure of intelligence among family-reared and orphanage-reared children. *Vestnik Moskovskogo Universiteta* 1, 34–41.

Smart, G. 1993: Genre as a community invention: a central bank's response to its executives' expectations as readers. In Spilka, R. (ed.), *Writing in the workplace: new research perspectives*. Carbondale, IL: Southern Illinois University.

Smith, Z. 2000: *White teeth*. London: Penguin.

Stanworth, M. 1981: *Gender and schooling: a study of sexual divisions in the classroom*. London: Women's Resource Centre.

Stark, R.E. 1986: Pre-speech segmental feature development. In Fletcher, P. and Garman, M. (eds), *Language acquisition: studies in first language development*. Cambridge: Cambridge University Press.

Street, B.V. 1994: Cross-cultural perspectives on literacy. In Maybin, J. (ed.), *Language and literacy in social practice*. Clevedon: Multilingual Matters and the Open University.

Swales, J. 1986: A genre-based approach to language across the curriculum. In Tickoo, M.L. (ed.), *Language across the curriculum*. Singapore: SEAMEO Regional Language Centre.

Swales, J. 1990a: *Genre analysis: English in academic and research settings*. Cambridge: Cambridge University Press.

Swales, J. 1990b: Non-native speaker graduate engineering students and their introductions: global coherence and local management. In Connor, U. and Johns, A. (eds), *Coherence: research and pedagogical perspectives*. Washington, DC: TESOL.

Tan, S. 1998: Language development of a three-year old in English and Chinese in the Singapore context. Unpublished MA dissertation, Department of English Language and Literature, National University of Singapore.

Tannen, D. 1979: What's in a frame? In Freedle, R. (ed.), *New directions in discourse processing*, Vol. 2, 137–83, Norwood, NJ: Ablex.

Tannen, D. and Wallat, C. 1982: Interactive frames and structure schemes in interaction: examples from a paediatric examination. Paper presented at Seminar on Natural Language Comprehension, St Paul les Durances, France.

Teale, W. and Sulzby, E. (eds) 1986: *Emergent literacy: writing and reading*. Norwood, N.J: Ablex.

Thomas, L and Wareing, S. 1999: *Language, society and power*. London. Routledge.

Thompson, G. 1996: *Introducing functional grammar*. London: Arnold.

Thompson, L. 1995: Patterns of cross-cultural communication between monolingual teachers and bilingual pupils in a UK nursery school. Paper presented at the 22nd International Systemic Functional Congress. Beijing, Peking University July 1995.

Thompson, L. 1999: *Young bilingual learners in the nursery schools*. Clevedon: Multilingual Matters.

Thompson, S. 1994: Framework and contexts: a genre-based approach to analysing lecture introductions. *English for Specific Purposes* 13, 171–86.

Threadgold, T. 1986: Semiotics, ideology, language. In Threadgold, T., Grosz, E., Kress, G. and Halliday, M. (eds), *Language, Semiotics, Ideology*. Sydney: Sydney Association for Studies in Society and Culture, No.3.

Tollefson, J.W. 1990: *Planning language, planning inequality*. London: Longman.

Toolan, M.J. 1988: *Narrative: a critical linguistic introduction*. London: Routledge.

Trask, L. 1993: *A dictionary of grammatical terms in linguistics*. London: Routledge.

Trevarthen, C. 1974: Conversations with a two-month old. *New Scientist* 62, 230–4.

Trevarthen, C. 1979: Communication and cooperation in early infancy. A description of primary intersubjectivity. In Bullowa, M. (ed.), *Before speech: the beginning of human communication*. Cambridge: Cambridge University Press.

Trevarthen, C. 1980: The foundations of intersubjectivity development of interpersonal and cooperative understanding in infants. In Olson, D. (ed.), *The social foundations of language and thought: essays in honor of J.S. Bruner*. New York: W.W. Norton.

Trevarthen, C. 1983: Interpersonal abilities of infants as generators for the transmission of language and culture. In Oliverio, A. and Zapella, M. (eds), *The behaviour of human infants*. London and New York: Plenum.

Trevarthen, C. 1986a: Form, significance and psychological potential of hand gestures of infants. In Nespoulous, L., Perron, P. and Roch Lecours, A. (eds), *The biological foundations of gestures and semiotic aspects*. Cambridge, MA: MIT Press.

Trevarthen, C. 1986b: Development of intersubjective motor control in infants. In Wade, M. and Whiting, H. (eds), *Motor development in children*. The Hague: Martinus Nijhof.

Trevarthen, C. 1987: Sharing makes sense: intersubjectivity and the making of an infant's meaning. In Steele R. and Threadgold T. (eds), *Language Topics: essays in honour of Michael Halliday, Vol.1*. Amsterdam: Benjamins.

Trevarthen, C. and Hubley, P. 1978: Secondary intersubjectivity: confidence, confiding and acts of meaning in the first year. In Lock, A. (ed.), *Action, gesture and symbol*. London; Academic Press.

Trevarthen, C., Murray, L. and Hubley, P. 1981: Psychology of infants. In Davies, J. and Dobbing, J. (eds), *Scientific foundations of clinical paediatrics*, second edn. London: W. Heinemann Medical Books Ltd.

Veel, R. 1999: Language, knowledge and authority in school mathematics. In Christie, F. (ed.), *Pedagogy and the shaping of consciousness: linguistic and social processes*. London: Cassell.

Veel, R. and Coffin, C. Learning to think like an historian: the language of secondary school history. In Hasan, R. and Williams, G. (eds), *Literacy in society*. London: Longman.

Venger, L.A. 1988: The origin and development of cognitive abilities in preschool children. *International Journal of Behavioural Development* 11, 2, 147–53.

Ventola, E. 1987: *The structure of social interaction*. London: Frances Pinter.

Vygotsky, L. 1962: *Thought and language*. Cambridge, MA: MIT Press.

Vygotsky, L. 1966: Development of higher mental functioning. In Leontiev, A.N. (ed.), *Psychological research in the USSR*. Moscow: Progress Publishers.

Vygotsky, L. 1978: *Mind in society: the development of higher psychological processes*. In Cole, M., John-Steiner, V., Scribner, S. and Souberman, E. (eds), Cambridge, MA: Harvard University Press.

Vygotsky, L. 1981: The development of higher forms of attention in childhood. In Wertsch, J. (ed.), *The concept of activity in Soviet psychology*. New York: Sharpe, 191–240.

Vygotsky, L. 1992: *The collected works of L.S. Vygotsky*, Vols 1–2. New York: Plenum Press.

Wareing, S. 1999: What is language and what does it do? In Thomas, L. and Wareing, S. (eds), *Language society and power*. London: Routledge.

Wee, L. 1998: The lexicon of Singapore English. In *English in new cultural contexts: reflections from Singapore*. Singapore: Oxford University Press and Singapore Institute of Management.

Wells, G. and Gutfreund, M. 1987: The development of conversation. In Steele, R. and Threadgold, T. (eds), *Language topics: essays in honour of Michael Halliday*, Vol. 1. Amsterdam: Benjamins.

Wells, G. 1984: Talking with children: the complementary roles of parents and teachers. In Donaldson, M., Greive, R. and Platt, C. (eds), *Early childhood development and education*. London: Blackwell.

Wells, G. 1999: Dialogic enquiry: towards a sociocultural practice and theory of education. Cambridge; Cambridge University Press.

Wertsch, J. 1984: *Culture, communication and cognition: Vygotskian perspectives*. Cambridge: Cambridge University Press.

Wertsch, J. 1985: *Vygotsky and the social formation of mind*. Cambridge, MA: Harvard University Press.

White, P. 2000: Media objectivity and the rhetoric of news story structure. In Ventola, E. (ed.), *Discourse and community: doing functional linguistics. Language in performance* 21. Tübingen: Gunter Narr Verlag.

Widdowson, H.G. 1983: *Learning purpose and language use*. Oxford: Oxford University Press.

Wignall, p. 1998: Technicality and abstraction in social science. In Martin, J.R. and Veel, R. (eds), *Reading science: critical and functional perspectives on discourse of science*. London: Routledge.

Willes, M. 1983: *Children into pupils: a study of language in early schooling*. London: Routledge and Kegan Paul.

Index

Abelson, R. 56
Académie Française 2
Acquiring Conversational Competence
  (Ochs and Schieffellin) 52–3
advertising, and sexism 224
Aldridge, M. 7
Allen, K. 13
Alsagoff, L. 253
Anderson, J. 219
anthropology 18
Ao Ran 228, 235, 237
appraisal, language of 210–11, 213
appropriateness
  and pragmatics 51
  situations, strata of embedded contexts
    of 45–6
  social contexts, emphasis on 49–50
artificial intelligence (AI), and script
    theory 55
Austin, J.L. 16, 17, 18
authentic texts 34–5

babbling 24
Baker, C. 102
Bakhtin, M.M. 206–7
Bamford, R. 177
Bao, Z. 253
Barton, S. 169
Bates, E. 90
Bateson, G. 54
Bazerman, C. 179, 180
Belcher, D. 106
Bell, A. 229
Bell, N. 166
Bereiter, C. 176–7
Bernstein, B. 53, 81, 110, 116, 145,
    146, 160, 167, 171, 214
Bhatia, V.K. 178
Bialystok, E. 163
bilingual and multilingual development
  caregivers, influences from 149–50
  code-mixing 128–9, 143
  code-switching 66, 99–101, 106, 130–3
  dual language systems, learning of 5, 8

mixing 106
mother tongue, range of meanings
    of 98–9
  societal and linguistic diversity 101–3
  see also cognitive development;
    multilingual environment
Blanc, M.H.A. 106
Bloom, L. 97, 123
Bodrova, E. 116
Bourne, J. 169, 170
Boyd-Barrett, O. 239
Braine, M. 25
Breakthrough to Literacy programme
    (UK) 177
British Contextualism 69
Britton, J. 176
Bronfenbrenner, U. 255–59
Brown, R. 8, 9, 25–6
Brumfit, C. 164, 166
Bruner, J. 61, 90, 128, 153, 254–5
Bullock Report (DES) 3, 18

Cameron, D. 17, 65, 170, 171
caregiver-child interaction 89, 149–50
Carter, R. 18, 211, 222
child language development
  abstract metafunctions, development
    of 95–6
  context, taking into account 72–3
  diary accounts of
    as bona fide approach to child
      study 22
    individualized nature of 22–3
    linguists' criticisms of 23
  environmental factors 27
  factors affecting 7–8
  individual nature of 7–8
  language and context, relationship
    between 96–7, 110
  lexico-grammatical level, transition
    to 76
  longitudinal studies of 25–6
  meaning potential, creation of through
    phonological contours 77–8, 81